Value-based Marketing Strategy

Pricing and Costs for Relationship Marketing

Santiago Lopez

Vernon Press

www.vernonpress.com

In the Americas:
Vernon Press
1000 N West Street,
Suite 1200, Wilmington,
Delaware 19801
United States

In the rest of the world
Vernon Press
C/Sancti Espiritu 17,
Malaga, 29006
Spain

Library of Congress Control Number: 2014942085

ISBN 978-1-62273-020-9

Preface

This book offers novel methods for developing Value-based marketing strategies aimed at increasing revenue and profits. Several new approaches are set forth for marketing and pricing decision-making:

- The concept of Value integrates marketing, finance, economics and accounting, in order to link Value-based pricing with relationship marketing.
- The law of supply and demand is restated with quantity as a function of Value instead of price; this makes it a more realistic and practical tool for understanding today´s highly competitive business environment.
- The confrontation and complementation concepts provide useful tools for guiding marketers into new segments, and price products accordingly. They play a key role for devising win-win strategies, not only with customers, but also with competitors.
- The Value Matrix is a practical tool for understanding the product´s positioning, analyzing its competition, setting strategy and pricing. It aims at achieving an optimal balance between customer loyalty and product mix profitability.
- The Value Life Cycle illustrates how Value acts as a force that constantly changes revenue, providing insight for developing strategies in each phase of the product´s life cycle.
- Analogies of marketing with physics illustrate how policy constraints create resistance to sales velocity, thereby determining the rate at which a firm advances towards its financial and marketing goals.
- The strategy for pricing business services applies Value to balance supply with demand; this leads to increased revenue.
- The marketing approach set forth unifies product portfolio and inventory management with Value-based pricing for maximizing income.

The reader learns quickly how to integrate key marketing, economics, finance, and accounting issues, in order to develop and implement strategies, set prices and use costs effectively. It provides practical explanations for major marketing concepts; how the forces of supply and demand interact with customer Value; how to develop effective competitive strategies; understand the relationship between benefits, quantities, prices and costs; manage inventory and product mix efficiently; apply the Value model to increase profitability, and solve major marketing problems.

Price is the only marketing variable directly linked to revenue and profits; it is a function of the product's benefits, the needs it satisfies, and the alternatives available to customers. The Value concept relates all the benefits offered by a product with its price and the effort required to obtain it. Global competition requires managing Value rather than individual products or brands, in order to succeed and be profitable; this fosters customer loyalty, and provides a solid basis for relationship marketing.

Improper pricing is probably the most common error in business; it is also the least understood marketing variable. This not only reduces revenue, but also affects profits, market share, and brand image; therefore, proper pricing is paramount.

Marketing is often seen as a business function primarily related to sales, but with only a transverse, or weak, relationship with the other functional areas of a company. However, for a firm that is truly customer-oriented this is not so; there are myriad decisions that pertain to non-marketing areas, yet they are driven by a marketing and Value framework; this point is illustrated with several business cases.

The reader may refer to the appendices, where the subjects are analyzed further and the mathematical foundations are laid out; numerous solved problems of pricing and costs are included.

This book aims at readers who wish to learn about strategy and pricing in a competitive environment. It is suggested for courses in:

- Pricing in marketing.
- Pricing and costs in MBA or marketing management programs.
- Marketing for students of economics, finance, accounting or law.
- Continued education in strategy, finance and marketing.
- Management for executives and other professionals.
- Business training.

Contents

Learning Objectives

- Understand the relationship between economic forces, marketing, finance and accounting.
- Learn how to increase sales velocity and profits using the Value model.
- Use the concept of contribution margin to solve sales and cost problems.
- Optimize inventory management and thereby increase profitability.
- Apply the Value Matrix to develop strategies and set prices.

Chapter 1

The Business Environment

1.1 Supply and demand

Economics studies how scarce resources can be efficiently allocated; marketing, on the other hand, deals with how to use resources profitably in order to satisfy customer needs. The basis for setting prices lies within the basic laws of economics; the types of markets in which buyers and sellers interact; and, understanding the marketing relationship of the firm with its customers and competitors.

In marketing, a large number of variables determines the demand for a product. Amongst these are the benefits it offers, its price, the competition, and market forces. Retailers are well aware that when a product is scarce, its price tends to rise, and conversely, if a product is in surplus, its price tends to fall. In order to understand this, let us review how the mechanism of supply and demand based on price operates.

The following graph illustrates the law of supply and demand.

Figure 1.1 Law of supply and demand

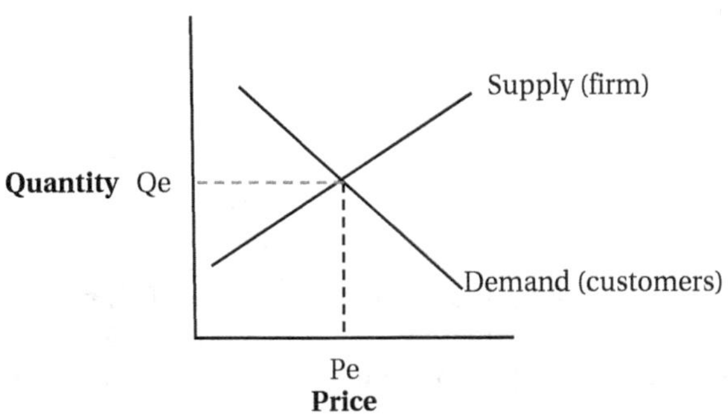

This orientation model does not provide a precise mathematical answer, but it facilitates understanding the underlying principles that govern markets. It can be a valuable tool for analyzing pricing decisions.

An alternative graphical presentation of the law of supply and demand plots price on the vertical axis and quantity on the horizontal axis; this conveys the idea that price depends on the quantity brought to market. However, from a marketing perspective, it is more realistic to consider the quantity demanded or supplied as a function of price and many other marketing variables.

The graph reflects the willingness of suppliers to sell more as prices rise, increasing the quantity supplied, as these may be indicators of potentially higher profits. Supply is directly proportional to price: the attraction of higher prices prompts firms to increase output; when prices are low, supply, or output, is also low.

In contrast to supply, the demand relationship is inversely proportional: the higher the price, the lower the demand. This schedule shows decreasing quantity demanded as prices rise. Given that customers have a limited purchasing capacity, it is reasonable to think that the quantity customers are willing to buy decreases when the selling price of a product increases; this is true as long as there is no change in the benefits offered, and without taking into account the reactions of competitors.

Figure 1.1 shows that there is a price Pe, in which the quantity Qe offered by the firm is equal to the quantity demanded by its customers. At a price lower than Pe, demand is greater than supply, this leads to shortage, and therefore prices are pressured upward.

From a marketing standpoint the quantity supplied, or demanded, depends largely upon the price of the product; therefore, price is plotted along the X-axis as the independent variable.

If the price is above Pe, supply is greater than demand; this would give rise to a surplus that would pressure the price down. Only at Pe are these opposing forces of supply and demand balanced; this is precisely the "equilibrium point"; that is, the "market price", Pe.

The market forces that act on an individual firm also act on the rest; for each customer and firm, there is a function that represents supply and demand. If we add (aggregate) all the functions of all firms and customers, we get a representation of the aggregate supply and demand; that is, the entire market.

When a good is scarce, demand is higher than supply, and its price tends to rise. As its price increases, the quantity demanded decreases, thereby rationing a scarce good; when it is abundant, the same mechanism operates by reducing its price and stimulating consumption; this mitigates surplus and waste; therefore, an efficient allocation of resources is achieved.

The pricing mechanism also sends valuable signals to the market: if a price is rising, it indicates that either demand is increasing, or supply is not enough; this encourages firms to increase output. If a price is falling, producers receive the signal to reduce output and this prevents overproduction.

When supply and demand are balanced, there are neither shortages nor surpluses; therefore, the price mechanism allocates resources efficiently. However, it must be able to operate without any interference. If this mechanism is interfered with, the market´s natural equilibrium is lost, inefficiencies are created, and this leads to surpluses or shortages.

Changes in price are represented as *movements* within the supply and demand curves; however, changes in non-price variables that affect supply and demand are represented as *shifts* in their respective curves; for example, an increase in overall income may shift upwards (or to the right) the demand curve for the so-called "normal goods"[1]; with higher income more is purchased.

In the case of "inferior goods"[2], such as public transportation, an increase in income may actually reduce its consumption, as people with higher income will resort to private transportation; this is represented as a downward (or left) shift of its demand curve.

---

[1] These are goods that people buy more when they have more income, for example clothing.

[2] Generally low grade or low quality items, such that with higher income people quickly substitute them.

The supply curve can also be shifted by changes in non-price variables; for example, a natural disaster would reduce supply at any price. In Figure 1.1 this would be reflected as a downward (right) shift of the supply curve; this leads to a price increase and less quantity offered in the market.

If, for any reason, production costs fall, then more can be produced; or, from another perspective, if costs fall, it is still profitable to produce more at any price, and suppliers are more willing and able to increase output. This shifts the supply curve upward (left), which results in larger quantities offered at lower prices.

1.2 Markets and the Economy

Perfect Competition

The term "perfect" perhaps may not be the most appropriate; but, in practical terms, this means that for each type of product, there are a very large number of buyers and sellers. Prices are mostly determined according to supply and demand.

The commodities market, with goods such as coal, salt, oil, sugar, copper, gold, etc., resembles a near "perfect" competition. This assumes all these goods are similar, without any major distinction amongst them, regardless of who produces them: salt is salt, coal is coal, etc.

A good example is a large farmers´ market, where there is much competition among sellers, but no one, individually, has an important influence on prices. This type of market illustrates how the forces of supply and demand gradually establish the price of each product.

If a retailer´s price is too high, buyers will most likely purchase from a competitor who may possibly offer lower prices. At the end of the day, he will end up with surplus inventory and he will be forced to reduce his price.

If the product is perishable, it is likely to spoil; therefore, it is imperative to sell it *quickly*. If it is not perishable, it still has to be sold in a relatively short time; otherwise, it might end up obstructing the sales of other products with better turnover[3], or perhaps even preferred by customers; this pressures the retailer to reduce his price.

On the other hand, if the price is too low with regard to its competition, it will be sold quickly, as customers will prefer it. The seller will soon realize that he could have sold a larger amount, or he could have sold the same amount at a higher price, and with less effort.

If a good is in shortage, it is likely to be in shortage for the whole market; therefore, securing additional quantities for sale becomes impractical, and probably cost more. The seller needs to make enough money to cover his costs and make a profit with fewer units sold; this pressures him to raise his price, but, it must not be too high, otherwise his competitors may outsell him and he will end up with a surplus.

This analysis suggests that a price cannot be too high, or too low. As mentioned previously, the price will eventually reach an equilibrium point; that is, the market price.

Given that this happens to all retailers simultaneously, they must all make the same pricing choices, so that in the end, there will be neither shortage, nor surplus; therefore, the market effect of aggregate supply and demand gradually stabilizes the market price, and all retailers eventually submit to it.

If the market forces can operate freely, and without interferences, goods are allocated efficiently and, in theory, without surpluses or shortages. Markets with interferences are forms of "imperfect competition", which, therefore, lead to inefficient resource allocation.

Under this scheme of perfect competition the final price achieved would be, theoretically, the lowest possible. No one would be willing to sell for less, and the winner in the end is the final consumer. Under this

---

[3] Turnover indicates the number of times an inventory is sold over a given period

market scheme, prices self-regulate themselves; this is why perfect competition is the ideal market model.

A perfectly competitive market includes the following requirements:

- *Homogeneous products.* The products are undistinguishable from each other.
- *Large number of buyers and sellers.* The number of sellers is so large, that no one individually can influence the price of the goods supplied.
- *Independence.* Sellers are free to make decisions.
- *Perfect information.* All participants possess market information.
- *Free entry and exit.* There are no barriers for entering or exiting the market.
- *No transaction costs.* Buyers and sellers do not incur in costs for buying or selling.

From a marketing standpoint, what is most significant about perfect competition is precisely that it is not “perfect”; in fact, the above requirements are rarely met.

Businesspersons wish to maximize their profitability in the *shortest time possible*; to achieve this, they must strive to retain their customers, and make sure they return for their next purchase.

What can they do? In marketing, it is called *differentiation*; this means that their products must, in some way, stand out from their competition.

The retailer must excel in the service he offers; serving customers promptly and in a friendly way. He will inquire about their needs, and do whatever is within his reach to satisfy them; moreover, he may even be able to offer them better benefits than his competitors. Satisfying their needs so that they are retained is known as developing customer loyalty.

If the retailer is sufficiently creative and imaginative, he will adapt his entire business around his customers´ needs; this includes its location and other elements such as product selection by quality and variety, training of employees, cleanliness, and product display ("merchandizing"). This is how he manages to differentiate himself from the competition, and his service becomes a powerful differentiator.

Notwithstanding differentiation and loyalty, the competitor plays a key role: he is not necessarily an adversary, he can be an important ally; his presence attracts customers. Moreover, if a product is out of stock, mutual cooperation is of great help. Retailers know that to maintain their inventory turnover, they need to balance competition with cooperation.

The graph (figure 1.1) represents the supply and demand functions of a firm. It sells a number of units Qe with a price Pe, so that *sales* (in money) would be Sales = Qe x Pe. These sales are shown in the graph as the area of the rectangle enclosed by the dotted lines and the axes of the graph. Qe is the maximum amount of units the company sells at a price Pe, their best price. These sales shown are therefore the maximum achievable by the firm.

The price Pe represents the quantity Qe the firm is willing to offer at that price and the quantity that customers are willing to purchase at that price.

Monopoly

In the broad spectrum of the market this is the extreme opposite of perfect competition; in fact, it is the best example of interference with the free forces of supply and demand.

A single seller dominates the market. He has no competition and has total freedom to set prices; there is no one else to buy from. The seller´s financial target generally establishes prices. Examples of these can be found in state-owned enterprises, or perhaps in public utility companies.

Does this mean that the seller, by virtue of its monopoly position, does not have to practice marketing? His goal, as in the previous case, is to maximize his profitability in the shortest possible time. He cannot set a price at whim because he must take into account his customers´ purchasing power, needs and preferences. In fact, he wants his customers to purchase with greater frequency.

He must therefore set a price, not too high, not too low; a price, which coupled to the customers´ purchasing frequency, should yield the best possible profit. However, this does not stop there: he will search for additional mechanisms to increase not only the purchasing frequency, but also the price, given his monopoly position.

Monopolies, despite their power, will also offer benefits to meet the needs of their customers and raise prices. They may even offer attractive financing in order to sell other goods; no one will hesitate to pay them, unless they can do without their product or service.

Monopolies can also play by the marketing rules that apply to a competitive market; their motivations and actions are very similar; the key difference lies in setting prices: they have a greater capacity to impose them.

However, something interesting happens here: not just any price is good for the monopoly. There is only one price that is most profitable; not too high and not too low. If it is too high, the quantity sold will not be enough to generate an acceptable profit; if it is too low, the quantity sold will not be sufficient to compensate for the small profit on each unit sold.

This possibility exists because monopolies, from a practical standpoint, also compete for the financial resources of their customers. There may come a point in which customers simply have no choice but to refrain from buying; simply because they may not have enough money, or because they may have other more pressing priorities; for example, food or clothing.

When monopolies set prices somewhat arbitrarily, they interfere with the natural forces of supply and demand. This does not allow the price adjusting mechanism to operate freely; therefore, inefficiencies are created in the process of resource allocation; this results in either surpluses (slow moving inventory), or shortages (not enough).

In a monopoly market the final price achieved would be, theoretically, the highest possible; the loser, of course, is the end consumer; this is why a monopoly is considered the opposite to perfect competition.

Monopsony

This market is controlled not by a single seller, but rather by a single buyer facing a large group of sellers (suppliers). A monopsony, just like a monopoly, is also an opposite of perfect competition; here the buying firm has an almost total bargaining power; it has the capacity to impose the prices and terms of purchase.

In general, the purchase prices are set according to its financial goals, but they must be attractive. If the firm operates rationally, it will strive to maximize its profitability; this leads to price and purchasing terms that will benefit it, and encourage its suppliers to offer a wide range of products and qualities. They set their purchasing prices in a fashion similar to the monopoly.

The monopsony suppliers must also strive to achieve their goals; they will seek to differentiate themselves and offer benefits that will allow them to stay one step ahead of their competitors. They will most likely focus on offering good quality and work with low operating costs in order to satisfy, one way or another, their powerful client; of course, provided they receive a fair price that justifies the effort and resources invested.

Oligopoly

In this type of market, a large number of buyers face a reduced number of sellers that, individually or collectively, have some degree of control over prices. Frequently there is a leader with great influence and his price is taken as the reference point. Oligopoly is an example of imperfect competition, as prices are not freely established by the forces of supply and demand.

Here we find, for example, large supermarket chains that, amongst very few, can control a large percentage of their markets. Also included in this category are large capital-intensive industries such as the automotive or aerospace industries.

Companies comprising an oligopoly have several advantages, which include:

- Limited competition.
- Possible cooperation with competitors.
- Some control of the market in terms of prices and distribution.
- Relatively high prices.
- Recognized brands.

- Possible horizontal[4] and vertical[5] integration.
- Economies of scale[6].

Notwithstanding these clear advantages, competition in these markets tends to be intense. It is very likely that such competition may not necessarily take place in pricing; this is because with a limited number of competitors price comparisons can be made very easily. They may even share many suppliers, so that their cost structures can be very similar.

Competing aggressively with prices is not a good strategy, as it can turn easily into a lose-lose game ("price war") that ultimately no one wins.

In oligopoly, competition takes place as follows:

- Offer superior benefits: service, warranty, comfort, location, distribution, variety, quality, payment facilities, etc.
- Reduce costs of goods and operating expenses; special negotiations with suppliers, outsourcing, partnerships, etc.
- Maintain a competitive and favorable benefit/cost relationship for customers.

Oligopsony

Oligopsony is to oligopoly as monopsony is to monopoly. In this case, the market is dominated by a very small group of buyers facing a large number of sellers. The purchasing firms have a high bargaining power and may impose prices and terms according to their financial goals. The firms that comprise an oligopoly may be commonly found in this group, and with the same pricing policies.

---

[4] The firm sells products in different markets, within the same industry, using alliances, acquisitions, or mergers with competitors.

[5] The firm has some degree of property and control over its supply and distribution chain.

[6] Unit costs tend to decrease as production increases.

Monopolistic Competition[7]

This is the most common type of market and is the best representation of imperfect competition; it consists of a large number of sellers and buyers without any clear market leader. In contrast to perfect competition, the forces of supply and demand do not set prices.

Here firms compete in terms of both benefits and prices, and buyers have many options of differentiated products. This is the best environment for the development marketing techniques: customers can compare and choose the best option among a large number of competing offers.

Characteristics of monopolistic competition:

- Highly dynamic markets due technological developments, global competition, changing habits and customer preferences, fashion, etc.
- Intense competition for securing new customers.
- Aggressive advertising and promotion strategies.
- Highly creative strategies for securing customer loyalty.
- Competition for raw materials, supplies and human resources.
- Intense competition in brands, benefits and prices.
- In general, the immediate competition tends to be confined to a limited area.
- There are few barriers for entering and exiting the market.
- Competitors have a certain degree of control over their prices.
- Products and services are differentiated mainly by the benefits and prices offered.
- Market information is readily available.

In these markets, firms compete to:

---

[7] Edward Chamberlin "*The Theory of Monopolistic Competition*".

- Increase market share.
- Position brands.
- Offer new products and services.
- Enter new markets, both local and global.
- Achieve competitive advantages in benefits, prices and costs.

Each competitor behaves in his own surrounding market as a "small" monopoly. This grants him a fair amount of freedom to establish prices, based mainly upon the benefits offered by his products and services. In the medium and long term, it is likely that their profits attract new competitors, and their status of "local" monopoly gradually erodes.

When this happens, their best strategic option is to concentrate in offering better benefits as competition gradually limits the freedom to set prices. Over the long run, the relationship between benefits and prices eventually maintains and determines profitability.

Success is based on a wide range of possibilities and opportunities available in each industry or business. Nonetheless, there is one thing they all have in common: customers wish to receive enough benefits to justify the price and effort they are willing to sacrifice, in order obtain the products that best meet their needs.

1.3 Market Forces

Inflation

The term refers to a general increase in prices in a given period of time (years, months, etc.). The end effect is that the purchasing power of citizens diminishes; the same amount of money gradually buys less each time. Inflation resembles taxes: it reduces citizens´ purchasing power. If household income does not keep pace with increasing prices, welfare gradually erodes.

Overall, this constant long-term price increase is strongly associated with the amount of money available in the economy, mainly in the form of bank accounts and cash (bills and coins). Money is created by the banking system in response to the needs of the economy, but excessive supply of money leads to inflation: more money chasing the same amount of goods; the growth in the money supply must not exceed economic growth.

Inflation is measured by the consumer price index, which indicates how much prices increase from year to year on a percentage basis. This is a good benchmark for adjusting the selling prices in a firm; it is very likely that all other costs will also increase by this amount; in effect, the higher costs are transferred to customers via higher prices.

There is a consensus that an excessive amount of money in circulation creates inflation in the long term. Let us perform a thought experiment: suppose that miraculously, from one day to the next, the wages of all workers could be doubled with money created by the central bank.

Thereupon, all workers, seeing their incomes doubled, go out and spend as quickly as possible. The local baker notices that all the bread is sold out within a few hours; more customers arrive; but, there is nothing left to sell; the same may happen with all the available goods and services.

Next day, every retailer realizes that he can probably sell the same amount, but, at a higher price. Since the amount of goods and services available remains unchanged, all prices begin to rise; as more money is created, higher inflation ensues.

Workers are soon surprised to find out that no one is better off; the only thing that really happened was that prices rose; but, besides that, nothing else. No matter how much more money they have, they cannot buy any more simply because there are no more goods available.

If this money-making process were to continue, the price increase expectations would create a collective panic that would, in effect, leave the economy out of control (hyperinflation). High rates of inflation also push up interest rates as lenders need to offset the loss of value of the currency; this increases interest expenses for firms, thereby reducing their purchasing capacity, their profits and the amount available for investment in capital goods such as property, plant, equipment and machinery.

Inflation has other consequences that also affect prices:

- People begin to fear holding money due to its high opportunity cost[8] as it loses value very rapidly; they prefer to exchange it for other currencies, precious metals, art, jewelry, property and other tangible goods that can hold their intrinsic value.
- As consumers and retailers fear prices increasing, they begin hoarding goods; this leads to a self-feeding vicious circle that creates further scarcity and still higher prices, thereby making the economy more difficult to control.
- The public avoids the banking system and reduces saving and investment.

Inflation has an important effect on pricing. If the firm purchases goods with rising costs, it must transfer to its customers the higher costs through increased prices in order to maintain its profits. However, at the end of the day, this may not be a marketing problem, since all competitors and customers are also subject to the same forces; what it is required, is great care on how to carry this out.

For retailers, however, inflation may even turn out to be somewhat of a blessing, as it provides them with an automatic mechanism for raising prices. Customers are already accustomed to this. In slow-moving products, or for those that need promotion, the technique can be simply to leave the price unchanged. The price of products with high turnover can be increased beyond the inflation rate. Some prices may be offset by others, and, in the end, they can average out to a target set by the firm´s financial goals.

If retailers carry this out gradually, and not with all products at the same time, customers will hardly notice the price adjustments. Businesspersons can therefore cope with inflation, and even use it to implement their pricing strategies successfully.

In the short term, however, there are also other forces that may have a significant effect on the price level; these may be due to the shortage of

---

[8] The cost of an alternate decision: for example, sleeping instead of working has a high opportunity cost; or the earnings foregone by making a less profitable investment represent an opportunity cost.

certain goods, or excessive demand due to cyclical or commercial reasons. The price level can fluctuate in either direction, depending upon the acting forces.

Rising prices are commonly associated with inflation, but falling prices (although rare) can also exist; this is termed deflation. A temporary or short-term slowdown in economic activity is referred to as a recession; a very severe and prolonged slowdown is a depression, such as the famous Wall Street crash of 1929. These cycles are characterized by high unemployment and stagnant or falling prices.

Inflation is a force that must be coped with: if the replacement cost of raw materials, and operating expenses increase, businesses must anticipate this and adjust their selling prices accordingly; delays in doing so may lead to lower profits.

Interest rates

Money, just like foreign currencies, or any other good, is traded regularly; it also obeys the law of supply and demand, and is supplied and demanded in the form of loans or credit. It too has a cost, known as the interest rate, which reflects how much has to be paid for the use of loaned funds. Financial institutions supply money in the form of credit to households and firms and charge interest for this service.

Money has a circular flow in the economy, as households and firms also deposit money in financial institutions; in effect, they are also lending them money, although at a lower rate. The difference, or spread, between these two rates (borrowing vs. lending) contributes significantly to the profits of financial institutions.

Central banks regularly lend money to commercial banks at a rate known as the discount rate; this has a ripple effect in the banking system, as it also affects the rates at which banks lend funds to their own customers. It also has a significant impact on investment and savings; high interest rates make credit more expensive, thereby restraining investment and consumption.

Central banks use interest rates as means of "stabilizing" the economy, as it affects the cost and availability of credit: low rates "expand" the economy (money is more readily available) and high rates "contract" it. Restricting credit and restraining growth in the money supply are often used as a means of controlling inflation.

Interest rates play a key role in pricing and on sales terms. Receivables, like inventory, have carrying costs related to the firm's financing costs (interest expenses); therefore, a 30-day outstanding credit has a cost. If the interest rate is, for example 1% per month, then a loan of $ 100 costs $ 1.00 every month. Similarly, if a product sells for $ 100, and customers regularly pay at 30 days, the firm may then adjust the sale price of its product to $ 101. Moreover, if the firm knows it can earn more than 1% on the money it uses, it may even extend customers a discount higher than 1% for payments in advance.

High interest rates increase the carrying cost of all assets, including inventory and receivables. Depending upon the debt structure of customers, their purchases and payments may respond in different ways to rising rates; this may lead to reconsidering credit policies as collections may become more difficult.

Interest expenses must be absorbed through revenue; therefore, pricing policies must consider them to achieve the firms´ financial goals.

Exchange rates

Money from different countries is traded worldwide, and just like any other good, the forces of supply and demand determine its price. The price paid in the currency of one country to buy that of another country is known as an exchange rate. It expresses the amount of local currency that must be paid for one unit of foreign currency.

For example, one euro may be purchased with 1.3 dollars. If the supply of euros exceeds their demand, the exchange rate tends to fall; conversely, if the demand for euros exceeds its supply, then its exchange rate rises. If the exchange rate for a given currency rises, it appreciates, or costs more; if it decreases, it depreciates *(devalues)*, or costs less.

The economies of almost all countries are interrelated through foreign trade. In a globalized economy, competitors, suppliers and customers exist anywhere in the world; they all import and/or export goods and services; their prices and costs depend on the relative value of their respective currencies.

The demand (buying) and supply (selling) of a currency depends upon:

International trade (imports and exports).

An importing firm needs to purchase the currency of the exporting firm's host country; this creates demand for that foreign currency.

When an exporting firm is paid with a foreign currency, it converts it into local currency by selling it; this supplies foreign currency to its domestic market.

A high level of exports creates a strong currency (it appreciates) for the exporting country, as importing countries need to purchase (demand) the exporting country´s currency.

Tourism.

Tourists travelling abroad need to purchase foreign cash to pay for goods and services overseas; this creates demand for that currency.

Incoming tourists from foreign countries sell their foreign money in the host country; this supplies foreign currency.

Foreign loans.

Payment of foreign loans requires purchasing the currency of the lending country; this creates demand for that currency.

When a loan in foreign currency is acquired, this currency is sold (or monetized) in the receiving country; this supplies foreign currency to its exchange markets.

Interest rates and inflation

If interest rates are comparatively high in a given country, investors will purchase (demand) its currency in order to be able to invest in its financial markets. In contrast, if they are comparatively low in a given country, its currency will be sold; this provides a supply of that currency.

As indicated previously, inflation can lead to high interest rates, but it can also trigger devaluations of the inflationary currency due to its loss of value.

During economic downturns inflationary pressures decrease, as demand for goods and services is lower; interest rates also tend to fall as the demand for credit also decreases.

Inflation has an important effect on exchange rates for two reasons: First, as a currency loses its value due to inflation, it depreciates; this is reflected on how much more money will be needed to purchase foreign currencies, or any other good for that matter. Second, the public avoids holding a currency that depreciates, therefore it is sold to purchase stronger currencies, or invest in other countries; this adds to the downward pressure on its price (devaluation).

Capital flows.

This is money flowing in and out between different countries for trade, investment, and credit. It includes mainly cash, stocks, bonds, loans, etc. This leads to supply as well as demand for different currencies.

Expectations.

These can lead to sales or purchases of foreign currencies, and they generally respond to government policies, interest rates, speculation, social, political and economic factors, etc.

All the previous factors create supply and demand forces that determine exchange rates rather swiftly, and, as in most business situations, there are both winners and losers. A devaluating currency benefits exporters, as they will collect more local currency when their foreign customers pay them; but it will harm importers, as they will spend more local currency to pay for foreign goods. Conversely, an appreciating currency harms exporters and benefits importers.

The value of foreign-denominated receivables and payables may also increase or decrease in terms of domestic currency, thereby giving rise to what is known as exchange gains or losses.

For example, suppose a firm operating in Latin America has an outstanding loan for USD $ 1,000. If its currency depreciates 10% against the dollar (or the dollar appreciates), the firm still owes the same USD $ 1,000, but in local currency it owes 10% more; this amount is recorded in its financial statements as an exchange loss. Similarly, if it has an outstanding customer receivable, then a 10% depreciation of its currency would mean that when it collects its receivable and exchanges it into local currency, it would have obtained 10% more; an exchange gain.

This indicates that since prices and costs are affected by exchange rates, then so are contribution margins, operating expenses and profits. As in the case of inflation (or deflation), these increases (or decreases) are transferred to customers through the products` selling prices.

Marketing plans therefore require considering, and if possible, anticipating how exchange rates are likely to move, and how they will affect revenue, prices and costs; this may have a significant impact on the firm´s cash flows and profits.

Unemployment

This term refers to the population that is out of work, and is calculated as a percentage that relates the number of unemployed with the number active in the labor force. The supply of people requiring work is greater than the demand for their services; there are not enough businesses to employ that many workers; the labor market is in disequilibrium.

Decreasing the supply of workers is not feasible, as it relates to the general population and their respective skills. On the other hand, demand relates to the number of firms requiring qualified workers; therefore, the goal is to increase the demand for their services by promoting business development and growth.

The real problem, however, lies in the multiple interferences and difficulties that exist for developing sufficient successful companies with the capacity to employ the supply of workers available.

Eliminating, or mitigating, such interferences is complex and politically difficult; this creates a shortage of workers in certain fields, and an oversupply in others.

Employment, unfortunately, is not exempt from the scope of the law of supply and demand; high unemployment reduces the purchasing power of the general population, and therefore business revenue is adversely affected; manufacturers and retailers cope with high unemployment with lower-priced goods.

Unemployment increases in economic downturns; during recessions, it is aggravated, and in a full-fledged depression, it becomes catastrophic. It is evidently a major problem as it is a waste of human resources, increases inequality (the gap between rich and poor), and can lead to social unrest and strife.

Under high unemployment, consumers can drastically alter their buying patterns, for example:

- More time is spent searching for goods with more favorable prices.
- Smaller quantities are purchased more frequently as consumers cannot afford stocking goods: weekly purchases turn into daily purchases.
- Consumers become willing to sacrifice benefits in exchange for lower prices.
- Promotions, discounts and bargains are highly desired.
- They eagerly seek opportunities in sweepstakes, contests, etc.
- The purchases of luxury items are reduced.
- Some product categories are substituted and others are eliminated altogether.
- Purchasing channels are changed; they no longer buy in the same stores.

In short, the market is transformed: businesses must direct their efforts to identify, locate and exploit new opportunities; different products and services are priced for customers with lower income; competition focuses more on prices, even though this may lead to reductions in benefits, quality, or service.

If packaging costs are significant, substitution becomes imperative; customers may even do without them. Bulk sales for any amount, large or small, are a good example: this can be seen in goods such as cooking oil, sugar, beans, rice, salt, etc.

The amount included per package may also vary: it is likely that low-income consumers may prefer products with less quantity at lower prices; they may even prefer lower quality, as long as this is reflected in the prices.

In cycles of prosperity the opposite occurs: package designs, with their respective prices, are geared towards more affluent customers.

This represents a major marketing challenge and pricing strategies must be adapted according to changing circumstances. What should be clear is that companies cannot remain static in a changing environment; it is critical to promptly identify and react to threats, opportunities and market trends.

1.4 Types of Buyers

Prices should consider the type of buyer, or customer, for whom the goods are intended. From a sales standpoint, it is very practical to classify consumers into three basic categories[9]:

Subsistence consumers

These consumers purchase low-priced products, even if that requires sacrificing benefits such as quality and warranty. Brand is a minor consideration, and they are keen at making all sorts of price comparisons amongst substitute or competing products.

The product´s low price must be clearly advertised, and shown on its package, which must look inexpensive. Examples of such packaging can be observed with staple foods such as rice, salt, sugar, etc.

Products aimed at this market segment are excellent candidates for bargains, coupons, sweepstakes and the like; they should have wide distribution through large chain stores, discount outlets, small corner stores and e-commerce.

These products have a relatively high price elasticity, and a low-cost structure; profits depend upon selling very large volumes.

Selective consumers

These buyers value product quality above all other considerations, even if it carries a relatively high price. Product prices are of a dynamic nature as they may be constantly changing while the product advances through its life cycle; they may also depend upon market opportunities.

Product packaging must carry good quality images and print; if possible, it should clearly indicate the multiple benefits offered by the

---

[9] "*El Mundo del Envase*", Editorial Gustavo Gili, S.A., Barcelona, 1995

product, and convey the message that the customer is certainly receiving his money's worth –or even more.

The packaging of technology products such as cell phones, computers, TVs, provides a good example etc.

In general, these are products with intermediate price elasticity.

Sybarite consumers

This category refers to consumers that mainly seek luxury, independently of the cost involved; for them price is not an obstacle; to the contrary, a high price enhances the pleasure of their purchasing experience, as it adds to their perception of wealth and status.

Products aimed at this market segment carry a high price tag; their profitability is based more on individual profit margin rather than sales volume.

Product packaging must reflect prestige and it should make the product look "expensive", such as is used with high-end perfumes and liquors.

The price need not be printed on the package, but it must be placed nearby to be clearly visible, and such that it conveys the image of a product few can afford. These customers will show-off the product in their social circles, so it must live up to its commitment in terms of quality and design.

Brand is very important as it may provide the status symbol required by the customer.

Salespeople must be well trained in dealing with these types of customers. Their complexion, attire, language, and script must be carefully chosen.

These are products with low price elasticity; therefore, there is great flexibility when they are being set or changed.

In the business-to-business markets ("B2B") buyers may be classified into four major categories[10]:

Price Buyers

In general, these tend to be oligopolies, or monopolies, in highly concentrated markets; they favor suppliers offering the lowest prices. Here we find, for example, government agencies and large corporations whose business is procured mainly through a bidding process. Price quotes must be very specific; with clearly specified payment terms. Success is determined by very competitive prices, which in turn requires operating with very low costs.

Relationship Buyers

Here we find well-established companies (30 years plus). They are, in a way, the opposite of the "price buyers"; their purchases focus on risk aversion and, if possible, they avoid buying from strangers. They favor experience, reliability, tradition, and, above all, the friendship with their established suppliers; they tend to be very reluctant to change suppliers and prefer "proven" solutions; prices and terms of sale need to be very competitive.

Experienced and highly skilled salespeople are required in order to overcome these barriers; in general, they should excel in public relations and be "well-connected".

Convenience Buyers

These buyers have little to study and perform product evaluations. their main priority is to make a quick and impulse purchase, while brand and quality are secondary. In general, sales for these consumers are fast, low-priced, for small quantities, and without much concern for customer needs.

In these types of goods, competition is significant; therefore, the product´s price must consider it. The seller's priority is to execute the sale as quickly as possible, without paying much attention to customer

---

[10] Thomas Nagle, Reed K. Holden, "*The Strategy and Tactics of Pricing*", Pearson, Prentice Hall, 2002. pp.. 112 - 114

satisfaction; this requires a salesperson that is sharp, fast and with a keen sense for negotiation.

Value Buyers

These are frequently "young" and dynamic companies, in highly competitive markets; their key to success is marketing well-differentiated products. In contrast to relationship buyers, alliances and loyalties are not predetermined; they recognize and justify prices based on benefits and quality. They do not necessarily want the most benefits, or the lowest price; they seek the best balance between benefits and price. This requires well-qualified salespeople that can professionally advise the customers.

1.5 Competition

The relationship between the firm and the client must be a win-win, but with competition it need not necessarily be a win-lose. Why? If we look around us, we notice that product and brand variety depend upon all the goods and services supplied by competing firms.

Therefore, the pricing policy need not be aimed at seeking to eliminate competition; on the contrary, "peaceful coexistence" or even "productive coexistence", may turn out to be better options; in fact, both competition and cooperation offer significant opportunities for manufacturers, retailers and customers.

The Value concept indicates that there are multiple combinations of benefits and price, which provide the same amount of purchase satisfaction. This means that there are myriad ways to participate, rather than compete in the same market segment, or product category; firms are in fact sharing markets.

If businesses can successfully complement one another, everyone wins. We can therefore conclude that the objective is not so much to compete, but rather to complement; offering the market many other options in both benefits and prices.

Let us look at some examples.

- In shopping malls, stores are frequently laid out according to competing product and service categories; but, they all have subtle differences; this adds variety and enhances the shopping experience.
- Food courts are replete with competitors, each offering his own specialty.
- Department stores offer many competing brands within the same product category and in the same location.
- Locations where many competitors converge to offer many products within the same category; this, far from being a problem, facilitates trade and attracts customers.
- Complementation offers many product and service opportunities, whereas confrontation is more specific, thereby limiting its scope.

Competition has several advantages:

- Localized competition attracts customers.
- It provides market synergy as a group of competitors is more effective at luring customers than each competitor acting single handedly or in isolation.
- Promotes innovation with new products and services.
- Presents opportunities for business alliances that may offer added value to customers.
- A wider variety of choices is made available to customers.
- Eliminates companies that fail to complement the market.
- Stimulates commercial and technological development.
- Competitors can be attractive and timely distribution channels.
- It is very useful for analyzing potential markets, locations, business formats, benefits, and pricing.
- Contributes to the self-regulation of prices.

Competition is an important benchmark for both benefits and pricing; if a product offers superior benefits, its price may exceed that of the competition. Comparisons with competitors are very important because they represent the other options available to customers; little or no differentiation leads to prices that are similar, or lower, than those of the competition.

Before establishing a pricing strategy the competition should be taken into account; its analysis involves the following steps[11]:

- Identify and locate the competitors.
- Determine their strengths and weaknesses (SWOT analysis[12]).
- Evaluate their financial, commercial and operational capacity.
- Examine their products: determine their features, benefits, competitive advantages, positioning and pricing structure.
- Identify their market segments, customers and distribution channels.
- Analyze their marketing strategy.

This same analysis can be applied to the firm, and once completed, it can facilitate deciding the most appropriate course of action, and establish its pricing policy.

---

[11] Donald R. Lehmann, R.S. Winer, "*Product Management*", McGraw-Hill, 2007, Ch. 5.

[12] SWOT is a planning method for analyzing *s*trengths, *w*eaknesses, *o*pportunities and *t*hreats.

Chapter 2

Marketing Concepts

2.1 Product Mix

Developing strategies and setting prices requires understanding key marketing concepts and how to apply them in highly competitive environments.

A product is anything offered in a market that satisfies a want or a need; a "product" is a set of characteristics, or attributes that can be physical, psychological, or symbolic; the product can be tangible, such as a car, or intangible, such as a health service. In fact, the product is constructed in the buyer´s own mind by the many inputs he receives.

While it is true that a product is described by its features, or specifications, what a customer really purchases is the benefits it offers. When a customer buys a product, he is actually sacrificing money and effort to obtain the set of benefits that satisfy his wants and needs.

For example, in a car with "ABS brakes", the customer is actually paying for obtaining the security offered. A well-trained car salesperson will focus on highlighting the benefits of security for the buyer's family, instead of spending too much time describing the intricacies of the braking system.

Companies generally sell a wide variety of products; the set of all products and services offered for sale is known in marketing as product mix.

The product mix is composed of product lines, which are groups of related products such as dairy foods, hardware, detergents, clothing, appliances, toys, etc.

The capital investments of firms (fixed assets and working capital) are geared towards increasing the profits obtained from their products; therefore, they must all be sold with a combination of quantity and price that maximizes profits. However, the best combination is determined not only by each product´s profit margin and by the quantity sold, but also by the level of commercial risk that each product carries.

A product with a stable level of sales carries lower risk than a product with highly volatile or variable sales; variability leads to uncertainty, which in turn increases the probability that an actual return (or profit) may be lower (or higher) than expected. Risk, therefore, reflects the degree of variability of outcomes; minimizing risk means reducing such variability. Risk may also refer to the ensuing damage or liability from a negative outcome.

For example, suppose ice cream is sold in hot days, and coffee is sold in cold days. This means that if only ice cream or coffee is sold, revenue would constantly change depending on the weather; however, if both products are sold, revenue is stabilized, as each product offsets the ups and downs of the other; this reduces variability in revenue, making it more predictable; this suggests that product diversification reduces risk.

Notice, however, that the sales of ice cream and coffee are not mutually exclusive: they can both be sold; the goal is to maximize revenue and profits. As mentioned earlier, pricing plays a key role in allocating goods efficiently by matching supply with demand; this suggests that the price of ice cream (or coffee) should not be the same when demand is low as when demand is high.

Does it really make sense to sell ice cream (or coffee) for the same price in winter as in summer? In addition to this, consider that these are perishable products, therefore their turnover must be constantly monitored to insure freshness and quality; prices play a key role here.

Pricing ice cream and coffee is no different from pricing drinks in bars depending upon the hour, or hotel rates and airfares, or even clothing, during season and off-season.

Suppose that the percentage profit margin of coffee is higher than that of ice cream. From a financial perspective it would appear that selling coffee would be always be more profitable than selling ice cream; however, when marketing is brought into play, customer needs and risk must be considered: they may want both products, even though the weather does indeed influence their desires and preferences; the sales driver must be customer satisfaction.

Product mix and pricing policy must be structured considering revenue maximization, product turnover, and risk.

Product mix pricing strategies must consider the following:

- The firm´s financial and marketing goals.
- Customers' needs, preferences and buying habits.
- The benefits offered to customers by the product mix.
- Competitors' products: benefits, features and prices.
- The extra costs of customizing, or adding accessory products.
- Revenue, profits, and the investments required.

2.2 Differentiation

This is a marketing strategy for the product to stand out in the customer's mind by virtue of its characteristics and benefits. The goal is to make the customer perceive that the benefits offered by the product satisfy his needs better than the competition. This is achieved not only by its design and other characteristics, but also by all the different messages conveyed by the company.

The degree of differentiation has important implications for the pricing criteria; when the product has a low level of differentiation, and its benefits do not play a key role, price is based on the competition.

If the product has no benefits to differentiate it, then price becomes the only differentiating element. Competing on price, however, requires very efficient cost management: It is crucial to achieve lower costs than the competition; otherwise, the firm finds itself at a disadvantage.

2.3 Segmentation[13]

This marketing strategy involves subdividing the market into different homogeneous groups whose members have similar characteristics, habits, preferences, behaviors and needs. Each segment responds uniformly to a given marketing strategy.

Identifying specific market segments that address specific customer needs and where there is little or no competition is ideal; these are known as niche markets; they carry great profit potential. Eventually, the firm selects a group of customers for the sale of their products; this is the *target market.* The goal is that the company´s messages trigger similar responses within each group.

The market can be subdivided, or segmented, according to criteria such as:

- Geographic: related to regions, zones, countries, locations, weather, etc.
- Demographic: age, gender, income, religion, race, profession, etc.
- Psychographic: concerning personality, values, lifestyle, etc.
- Behavioral: related to benefits sought, purchasing frequency, habits, brand loyalty, etc.

Proper segmentation facilitates:

- Reducing the cost of advertising and promotion by focusing on a specific group.
- Optimizing the use of company resources for marketing and sales.
- Adapting products and services according to the customers' specific needs.
- Setting prices that match the habits, preferences and purchasing power of the target segment.

---

[13] W.J. Stanton, M.J. Etzel, B.J. Walker, "*Marketing 13th edition*", McGraw-Hill, 2004, pp. 167- 180

The price of the product must be in line with regard to its target market. If it is a high-end segment with a highly differentiated product - or brand- by quality, status, exclusivity, etc., its price should reflect this. Products with low differentiation, aimed at less affluent segments, should carry a lower price.

2.4 Product Positioning

In marketing, positioning refers to the strategy that firms use to create an image or perception of their products –or brands– in the minds of their customers in order to encourage their purchase. Positioning is achieved by the various messages that are conveyed through advertising, sales force, brand, logos, slogans, distribution channels, promotions, packaging, price, etc.

The messages are aimed at the target market and are focused on the benefits offered, thereby differentiating the products from their competitors. Differentiation is used to position a product, service or brand.

Positioning must be consistent with:

- Pricing policies (goals, criteria, scope, responsibility, etc.).
- Target market (profile, habits, etc.).
- The symbols used (brand, slogans, logos, etc.).
- The communication strategy (advertising, messages, etc.).
- Packaging (design, functionality, etc.).
- Distribution channels (target market, coverage).
- Sales force (selection, training, motivation).

Market positioning of a product, or brand, must be in harmony with the targeted customer group; a "high" price, compared with competing products or services, projects an image of quality, exclusivity, elegance, status, prestige, etc.

In contrast, a comparatively "low" price reflects a lesser degree of product differentiation; however, this requires caution as prices that are too "low" can also convey a signal of low quality, and end up positioned as such.

The product´s package should reflect its positioning; a product intended to be a "gift", or a courtesy, requires a package–and a price–that reflects elegance and distinction. If a product is to be positioned as low-priced, its package should have a simple design; use low-cost packaging material; and, its price should appear on its package.

Understanding and developing the positioning of a product, or service, is crucial for:

- Communicating the product`s benefits to its target market.
- Differentiating the product against its competition.
- Influencing the customers` perception and expectations.
- Gaining and securing more customers.
- Advertising and promoting the product successfully.
- Developing a marketing strategy and a business plan.

2.5 Market Share

This term refers to the proportion (percentage) of sales of a product, or category, relative to total sales in its respective industry. It is often used as a measure of performance, because it distinguishes whether an increase in sales is a response to a growing market, or a response to a product´s preference over its competition.

When product sales increase in the same proportion as the market´s growth, market share remains constant; but, if they increase at a higher rate, this suggests a product is performing better than its competition. If sales are increasing but share is falling, this means the competition is gaining advantage.

2.6 Marketing mix

Businesses use a set of four tools to implement their marketing strategies; this is known as "marketing mix", or also as the "4P": Price, Promotion, Product and Place.

Price is the money that the customer must sacrifice to obtain the product´s benefits; *promotion* relates to the selling activities, such as advertising and personal sales; *product* relates to the product´s design, features and benefits; and *Place* relates to distribution channels, or where a product is sold.

These tools classify and describe reasonably well the marketing variables operating in a market. The methods used to promote and sell a product clearly have an effect on its demand. The role of branding, advertising and promotion can hardly be ignored. Similarly, design and product features are critical. The same is true of distribution channels and, of course, price.

The marketing mix (4P) also offers a very complete description of the marketing forces that influence the mechanisms of supply and demand; here, many variables come into play, not only micro and macroeconomic, but also psychological and sociological.

As will be discussed later, the marketing mix has important implications for product pricing.

2.7 Transactional Marketing[14]

The goal of transactional marketing is to maximize sales volume, serving as many customers as possible in the least amount of time; its purpose is to achieve sales quickly, without much concern for the individual needs of customers; it is commonly practiced in many businesses.

---

[14] Rosann L. Spiro, W.J. Stanton, G.A. Rich *"Management of Sales Force"*, McGraw-Hill Irwin, 2003, pp. 10-11

Transactional marketing can take place with any product and in any market, but tends to concentrate on convenience goods that are characterized by:

- Low differentiation.
- Relatively low prices.
- Little or no service is required.
- Customer loyalty is not particularly important or relevant.

This type of marketing focuses on:

- Indiscriminate acquisition of new customers.
- Selling to any potential customer.
- Obtaining purchase orders quickly.
- Maximizing short-term sales.
- Haggling or reducing prices in order to close the sale.

Prices tend to be comparatively low for several reasons:

- Warranties, if any, are minimized.
- Post sale service is low, or null.
- The sales force tends to be low skilled.
- Costs are kept low by offering minimum benefits.

Prices are set to achieve a profit goal without much regard towards developing customer loyalty.

This type of sale is often found in small informal businesses, or in places where customers probably will not return; for example, tourist zones.

2.8 Relationship Marketing[15]

[15] Ibid.

In contrast, relationship marketing focuses on meeting the needs of customers; this requires developing lasting relationships, and can only be achieved with employees that possess greater empowerment, training and accountability. It is also necessary to achieve teamwork with customers and facilitate their communication with the firm. The basic premise is that if this is properly executed, customer loyalty is achieved and this leads to higher sales and profits.

In this type of marketing, the customer is not simply received, or accepted, as in transactional marketing; here the customer is selected.

In relationship marketing, the approach with customers is to:

- Provide professional advice to match the customer's needs with the most appropriate products and services.
- Develop trust and friendship.
- Seek their loyalty in order to sustain long-term sales.
- Strive to become their only or main supplier.
- Deliver quality and service.
- Select profitable customers

In comparison with transactional marketing prices tend to be higher for the following reasons:

- Higher level of warranties.
- Improved post sales service.
- Increased cost of advertising and promotion.
- Superior customer benefits.
- The sales force is better selected, more qualified, skilled, specialized and motivated.
- Higher administration costs due to market research, surveys, development and database administration, communications, etc.

Customer loyalty and successful relationships are built with products that satisfy their needs by offering the best possible balance between benefits and prices.

2.9 Product Life Cycle

A product, like any living organism, has from its inception to its end, a life cycle that involves several stages, and its price is closely related to each one. Let us analyze each stage and how it relates to pricing and to the market´s competitive forces.

Price and strategy depend upon whether the product is radically new, or if it is an improvement of an existing one. The high cost of researching and developing new products is an important issue in each case; these factors will decisively influence the prices set.

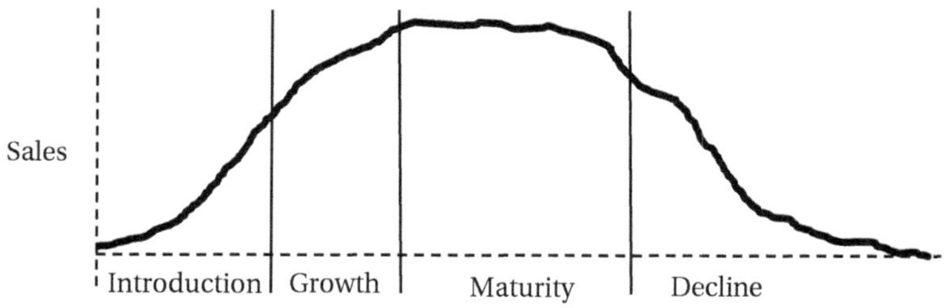

Fig. 2.1 Product Life Cycle

Market Introduction

This is the time to position the product and its brand in the market by means of the communication strategy; advertising and promotion expenses play an important role.

At this stage customers are not very price-sensitive, in particular if it is a new product; therefore, there is some flexibility to set prices with a relatively low risk of losing sales.

If the product is similar to an existing one, its price depends on the degree of differentiation with respect to its competition; if it is truly innovative, price considerations are more dependent on the benefits offered, the research and development costs, and the type of market it is aimed at. Such products often require at the outset high levels of educational advertising in order to make them known.

In most cases the introduction strategies range from penetration (low prices) to skimming (high prices), depending upon the product´s characteristics, the market and the firm´s priorities. For a radically new product, it is likely that a fast payback of research and development costs will be desired; this will point to a skimming strategy. A case in point being technology products such as computers, cell phones, TV's, etc.

On the other hand, if the aim is to cover the market and gain market share quickly, particularly if it is an improved product, then a penetration strategy will be favored, as competition will be a major threat from the outset.

Growth

This is the opportunity to create a solid market niche and lay out the foundations that will determine the future of the product. It is characterized by a rapidly growing market, and the emergence of competition in both benefits and prices. The sales volume achieved leads to higher purchasing quantities that will provide the company greater bargaining power with its suppliers; this may reduce costs, and the savings thus achieved can be reinvested in advertising to stimulate demand.

Expectations can play a key role here: if the product´s success is above expectations, it may be possible to increase the price further; but, if on the contrary, results are less than expected, there is less room for price flexibility.

Maturity

This is where most of the product´s life is located; sales growth slows down; customers are more familiar with all their options; and, prolonging this stage as long as possible is the key to success. The pressure on prices and benefits is even greater since the competition is also in a stronger position.

Differentiation is now less significant, and the price differential with the competition is narrower; the increased number of choices available makes buyers much more price-sensitive. This is a good opportunity for product improvement and for seeking new market niches.

It is advisable to:

- Develop new market segments.

- Reach new regions, zones, or countries.
- Develop new distribution systems and channels.
- Provide new product supporting services.
- Promote consumption through innovative packaging.
- Implement new pricing and promotion strategies to counter the competition.
- Invest in advertising to capture those segments that are not buying the product.

There are many products that have successfully remained at this stage for very long periods. Worthy of mention are Coca Cola and the Hewlett Packard 12C financial calculator[16]. The latter is of particular interest, since it is a product that was launched in 1981 and its production has continued uninterrupted for over 30 years, despite a market well known for its high rate of obsolescence, innovation and competition; the product´s design has been virtually unbeatable.

Coca Cola's successful marketing and advertising strategies have maintained this product at this stage for countless decades[17].

There are other products that may not only have a short maturity stage, but also a very short life cycle; a good example being toy sales during the Christmas season. Market introduction may take place somewhere at mid-year; maturity will peak between December 15 to 25; and thereon the decline sets in. Slow-moving inventory will soon be liquidated in January at low prices; the funds obtained are reinvested in products with higher turnover; perhaps school supplies and fashion clothing,

Decline

At this stage the weakness in demand begins to felt in prices; this prompts more frequent discount policies to encourage sales; the

[16] http://h30248.www3.hp.com/offers/12c/index.asp

[17] http://heritage.coca-cola.com/

product must be defended against a strong competition; it is now time to decide the end of the product's commercial life; prices fall and barely cover costs.

The decline can happen because there is a high degree of saturation in the market due to the proliferation of competitors and substitute products; it can also can be due to product obsolescence, or as the result of a new trends and fashion.

If the company has the financial capacity, it can prolong the product´s life by maintaining a very low pricing policy; this limits, or reduces, the number of competitors as many cannot withstand this economic pressure. The other option is to discontinue the product altogether and replace it with a new one.

2.10 Benefits

When a customer purchases a product, he is actually paying a price to obtain the benefits offered. A benefit in its broadest sense can be defined as any attribute, element, or action that may promote the purchase of a product and satisfy a need.

Benefits play a key role in pricing: they are the product´s differentiators and contribute towards reducing the sensitivity to price changes; they are regularly compared with those offered by the competition. Market share depends not only on price and competition, but also on the benefits that customers value.

Benefits can be classified into two categories: positive and negative; positive benefits push sales, but the negatives ones slow them down.

Positive benefits

Advertising

Advertising stimulates demand, and it may be the benefit with the greatest impact on price, due to its strong influence on the brand´s value and the product´s positioning.

Advice

The consumer needs to receive professional advice so that the product delivered satisfies his needs and he will therefore repurchase.

Branding

A well-known brand is valuable for several reasons: it sells by itself (herein lies the great value of a brand); customers´ trust in the brand is the basis for their loyalty; and, it makes them less sensitive to changes in price.

Channel

Addresses how adequate is the distribution channel of the product in relation to its positioning and target market; it is also related to the effort and time required by the customer to obtain the product.

Credit

Facilitates payment, increases purchasing frequency, builds trust and may increase the size of the target market.

Distribution, inventory and logistics

Reduces the effort required by customers to obtain the product.

Education

Facilitates understanding the use of the product; this is very important with new products and in the field of technology.

Entertainment

The Internet-generation shoppers, well armored against continuous advertising bombardment, are not just buying; they want more; they seek entertainment while shopping; their *purchasing experience* enhances their *buying pleasure*; it needs to be fun; this builds their brand loyalty.

Ethics / Honesty

Customer trust is a key sales driver, therefore the product must comply with its promises and benefits as advertised; the customer deserves to be treated honestly.

Information

This is, by far, the greatest benefit: information is what governs all markets; the knowledge the customer has about the product and its competition is the key that leads him to purchase. It is a major error to underestimate the customers´ knowledge and buying skills; this translates into lost sales.

Location

It addresses how easy it is to reach the target market and has a strong relationship with positioning.

Motivation (employee)

This is a powerful sales driver: work environment and compensation play a key role.

Packaging

It is an effective means of differentiating a product and making instantly visible its benefits to a potential buyer. It has a direct effect on price and must match the product´s positioning, its market segment, and the customer´s needs.

Personal Sales

A well-trained salesperson contributes, not only to sales volume, but also to build brand equity and customer loyalty. At the end of the value chain, all the marketing strategy ends up depending upon the sales force.

Physical and visual evidence

Corresponds to the architectural design, decor and ambience of the shop, store, office or premises; it also relates to the presentation and image projected by the firm and its employees; it plays an important role in building customer trust and thereby stimulate his desire to purchase.

Positioning

This refers to the image or perception customers have of a product, brand or firm. It is a key driver that prompts customers to prefer and purchase a product. See section "2.4 Product Positioning".

Price

This critical element suggests status and prestige. It relates to benefits as a sign of quality, either "high" or "low". If the price set is not in line with the product's positioning or benefits, it may seem either too "expensive" or "cheap"; this works against sales.

Product

Its design, features, specifications, functionality, and other intrinsic characteristics are key elements of its sale price and cost.

Purchasing experience

This is the "moment of truth": the interaction between seller and buyer carries a high emotional content. If this event is a "memorable moment", which the customer will happily remember, he will return as this builds his loyalty; the brand´s prestige is being gambled here; highly qualified and trained salespeople are required. The success, or failure, of the entire marketing strategy may totally depend upon this fleeting moment in time.

Quality

Must meet the customer's expectations and the product's specifications.

Sales promotions

Provide an incentive to stimulate sales quickly; these may include: contests, raffles, premiums (give away items), coupons (may be exchanged for a refund or rebate), prizes, samples, etc.

Savings

If a product helps save money, or generates a profit, this is clearly a very valuable benefit; in fact, it becomes an important component of the Value Proposition (a marketing statement for convincing customers to buy a product).

Service

Properly selected, trained and motivated human resources are the starting point for increased sales and customer loyalty.

Service hours

This has an important effect on purchasing frequency and sales level; extended hours with the right products and services tend to increase sales.

Sharing

The joint use of a product, service or resource, can be a valuable benefit as it may help reduce costs, improve the use of time, and strengthen bonds between people.

Social responsibility

This has an important effect on business image and is necessary for the firm's social contribution, acceptance and survival.

Status / prestige

This refers to a benefit that may provide exclusivity, elegance, luxury, distinction, cachet, etc. It raises the customers´ self-esteem, and highlights their image with their peers or community. It is generally associated with a high price.

Talent and expertise

This is necessary: society rewards creativity and talent with profits; but, it can also punish its absence; therefore, embarking on a new endeavor is not advisable, unless the necessary expertise and talent are present.

Time

This is a very valuable benefit that operates either way: less or more. In most services the customer wants them performed as quickly as possible (fast food), and the related benefit is time saved; in others, delay may be desired (a high-end restaurant), and the related benefit is exclusiveness, privilege, prestige, cachet, etc.

"Value Measurement"[18] / Quantity

This refers to the number of units, size, or quantity to which the price applies. It is the amount purchased in each retail unit of sale: serving size and number. Examples: 250g bar, 12 units per package, 6 servings, price per sq. ft., etc.

Variety

This is a powerful sales and price driver: it should focus on complementing the competitors´ product line; it must also respond to the needs and preferences of customers.

Warranty

It facilitates setting a higher price as it provides trust in the product, in its brand and in the firm that supports it.

This list illustrates many important examples of benefits that can be offered in a marketing strategy; undoubtedly, they can all increase the demand for a product.

Negative benefits

"Negative benefits" (pain points) are actions, activities, or situations that are unfavorable for business; they are a force that can adversely affect revenue, or at least delay the firm from reaching its goals. A brief list follows.

Misleading advertising, promotion, and pricing

A customer who feels cheated, rarely returns; his loyalty is lost. In general, the cost of replacing a customer is greater than the possible gain resulting from the deception.

Deceitful packaging

---

[18] Thomas Nagle, Reed K. Holden, "*The Strategy and Tactics of Pricing*", Pearson, Prentice Hall, 2002, p. 160

A package that does not contain the quantity specified, or in any way attempts to mislead the customer, is an open invitation for the customer to explore other purchasing alternatives with competing products, and certainly does not build his loyalty.

Employee selection, training and motivation

Human resources are the firms' most valuable asset; the mistakes here are paid with lost sales and profits.

Expectations

Products create expectations; in fact, they build them. If a product meets or exceeds expectations, the word spreads; but, if it fails, it goes "viral"; social networks, cell phones, and computers can easily set off a chain reaction against the product; its demise may be just around the corner.

Information

They say, "chance favors only the prepared mind"[19]; it comes from information; it can be the key to success and the lack of it the road to disaster. Markets are like reefs in the ocean: food floats and lurks everywhere; it is obtained through information. Success is largely based upon making decisions with proper information.

Physical and visual evidence

A negative effect on sales arises when the location, ambience, cleanliness, employee or business presentation, do not fit with the target market, or with the product´s positioning.

Price perception

A poorly set price works against sales because it sends wrong signals to buyers.

---

[19] Attributed to Louis Pasteur.

Risk[20]

The risk perceived in a product or service may arouse rejection against its price, or hinder its purchase. Risks inherently have a probability of occurrence and a degree of danger, threat or damage.

Five types of risk have been identified: financial, performance, physical, social and psychological[21]. *Financial:* Presupposes a monetary loss if the product does not perform properly. *Performance:* Refers to the possibility that the product may not function as expected. *Physical:* May cause personal or property damage due to a product malfunction. S*ocial:* Relates to a negative image that may result for the buyer from the purchase. P*sychological:* The buyer´s self-esteem may be adversely affected.

These risks need to be mitigated so that they will not have a negative impact on prices or on revenue. A few examples on how to mitigate risk follow.

Financial

Price lists, insurance policies, warranties, cash refunds, performance certifications, etc.

Performance

Testimonials from customers; control, safety, and quality certifications; precise user instructions, procedure manuals; employee selection, training, and motivation; service and safety standards, among others.

---

[20] K. Douglas Hoffman, J. E.G. Bateson, "*Essentials of Services Marketing*", 2nd, Harcourt College Publishers 2002, p. 91.

[21] L. Kaplan, G.J. Szybilo and J.Jacoby "*Components of Perceived Risk in Product Purchase; A Cross-Validation*", Journal of Applied Psychology 59 (1974) pp. 287-291.

Physical

Security such as surveillance cameras; first aid availability; damage insurance policies; proper lay-out and illumination; staff training certifications; protective apparel; safety signs, etc.

Social

Employees should project an image of status and prestige; elegant premises; admittance rights and restrictions; well selected and trained personnel; celebrity testimonials; VIP club, etc.

Psychological

Good service; clients must feel "important" and be well treated; educated and well-mannered employees; customer treatment should inspire trust and confidence; sales personnel should act as professional consultants.

Negative benefits should be avoided at all costs because they constrain sales and profits.

Chapter 3

The Value Concept

3.1 Definition of Value

The concept of Value bridges marketing and economics into one framework useful for developing strategy and setting prices.

From a marketing standpoint, Value can be defined as the set of benefits perceived by the customer in relation to the price and effort invested in obtaining it[22]. Consumers only buy products that have Value for them.

It is worth noting the difference between Value and positioning: Value expresses a logical relationship between benefits and price; and positioning, although it contains the same elements, simply refers to the image, or perception, of a product, brand or firm.

The current trend is that sales should not ignore the customer´s needs in a quick and fleeting exchange of money for product (transactional marketing); what is really sought is to establish a long-term relationship that simultaneously benefits the customer and the company (relationship marketing). The reason is that securing new customers costs more than retaining them[23]; it is not enough to just satisfy their needs, a step forward is required: retaining them long-term must be achieved (customer loyalty); this is the purpose that links relationship marketing with the concept of Value.

A key issue in relationship marketing is that a product´s price must achieve customer loyalty, and be justified by the benefits it offers. This is only possible with a clear understanding of his needs, habits and

---

[22] Thomas Nagle, Reed K. Holden, "*The Strategy and Tactics of Pricing*", Pearson, Prentice Hall, 2002, pp. 7-8

[23] M.W. Johnston, G. Marshall, "*Relationship Selling*", McGraw-Hill/Irwin, 2005, p. 79

preferences; thus, the product must satisfy them, without losing sight of the market context, the competition and the goals of the firm.

Value may be represented as follows[24]:

$$\text{Value} = \frac{\sum \text{Benefits}}{\text{Price} + \text{Effort}}$$

Value is the relationship between the sum of all the perceived benefits with the price and effort required to obtain the product. Value is the force that drives sales and market share and provides the customer with a strong incentive to make a purchase.

Effort is a subjective non-quantifiable variable, which points to the fact that obtaining a product consumes time, energy and work.

Value is also a way of representing the Value proposition: The firm promises customers a set of benefits at a given price. Value is aimed directly at customer satisfaction: it is the bull's-eye.

Consumers will always want to maximize their gains; this means to obtain the maximum while investing the least. The firm provides output in terms of benefits and consumers provide the input in terms of their economic sacrifice (price paid) and effort. Value is therefore a marketing output / input ratio which measures the consumer's gain, or "profitability" he obtains from his purchase.

This ratio suggests that Value increases when benefits increase or when the price and/or required effort decrease. If the price increases in greater proportion than the benefits offered, then Value decreases and the quantity demanded by the customer segment is reduced. Value remains unchanged if lower benefits are balanced by lower prices, or if higher benefits are balanced with higher prices. Negative benefits subtract from positive benefits; this reduces the Value of the product.

---

[24] Carlos Raúl Sánchez Sánchez, "*Administración del Precio en Mercadotecnia*", Thomson, 2003, pp. 51-56

This definition of "Value" can be equated with the definition of "Utility" in classical economics, which corresponds to the level satisfaction an individual obtains from a good or service. From a Marketing standpoint, Value or "Utility" may even be quantified, as will be shown in section "8.1 The Value Matrix".

Value is an orientation model that facilitates understanding the underlying mechanisms at play, and guides towards forging appropriate strategies.

Orientation models are useful in marketing and sales because responses tend to be non-linear, which means that a certain change in one variable will not necessarily trigger a proportional change in another. For example, a decrease in price may not trigger an instant, or even proportional increase in quantity sold: The market's response is loaded with uncertainty and time lags.

A thought experiment may come in handy here. Imagine an elastic string pulling a brick on a flat surface. A constant pulling force may be exerted on the string to pull the brick, but that does not necessarily mean that the brick will move steadily in proportion to the force applied. In fact, it probably will not move until a precise threshold force is applied; at that point, it may not even move slowly: it will jump abruptly and then stop, despite the constant force; then, after a little extra pull, another jump takes place, and this can go on indefinitely. This analogy illustrates the non-linear action-reaction situations commonly found in business.

It is easy to fall into the trap of applying too strong a force on the string to expedite results; but it may turn out to be excessive, leading to unwanted results; as may easily happen in pricing, or marketing in general. Each product is a universe in itself, so there are no solutions with fixed rules, or recipes; let alone magic formulae.

This can be hard to understand in business, because it may seem that the market does not respond to cause-effect. Just as this can apply to a price change, it applies to changes in Value: it may take some time, but the jump can occur at any moment; therefore, some patience is required because the response time, or lag, may be highly uncertain.

The brick analogy is of particular importance when making price changes, given that customers´ responses can be delayed; it takes time, perhaps months, or even years, until the market gradually responds and stabilizes itself. This makes it tempting to push up prices constantly with the expectation that somehow –as if by magic– this will also increase profits, when, in fact it may well have the opposite effect.

Non-linearity and lags are dangerous in business and need close attention: management can make truly logical and reasonable decisions, but, in a short-term managerial horizon an observable result may not be seen; in fact, even a negative result may appear; reactions can take time, or even years to materialize.

This is also a frequent pricing problem: when prices are too high and management reduces them, the result is an instant loss of revenue and profits. This prompts management to avoid reducing prices, despite the fact that signals like lower than average inventory turnover and loss of market share clearly indicate low Value (few benefits or a price too high); benchmarking with the competition can provide useful clues.

Management then wrongly believes that not much more can be done, and instead of solving the real problem (benefits and/or price), they attempt to compensate the loss of revenue by adding other products and diversifying the product line; this adds inventory and costs. Consequently, high prices are a common problem, which frequently paves the way for new competitors and further market share loss.

Many marketing opportunities appear because a given level of Value ("utility" or satisfaction) can be delivered in an almost limitless number of combinations of benefits and prices.

The Value relationship is static, dynamic, and relative. It is static because at any moment the customers must perceive that the benefits received outweigh the price and effort required to obtain the product. It is dynamic in the sense that a price change should be justified by a proportional change in benefits. It is relative because the Value of a product can be compared against its competition, or with different purchasing alternatives.

In fact, if the product´s Value is Vp, and the competing product´s Value is Vc, then its relative Value (or Value differential, Vr) is even more significant: Vr = Vp – Vc. This differential is the driver that will determine customer preference and the product´s behavior during its life cycle. This issue is explored further in section "7.3 Value Life Cycle".

Let us look at an example: If a Coke has a price of $ 1.00 at store X and $ 0.80 at store Y, which offers exactly the same benefits, then the Coke will have a greater Value (V) for the customer at store Y: Vy > Vx.

However, if X were to offer far greater benefits than Y, then the Coke would have a greater Value at X, then Vx > Vy.

If the price at store Y is increased, then its Value (Vy) decreases; the Coke now has a greater Value at X due to the price increase at Y, then Vx > Vy. Given the choice, the customer will very likely select the one with higher Value.

However, a Coke might even cost $ 5.00, or more, at an upscale restaurant that offers many more benefits than a store, such as status, service, prestige, etc. The higher price would be fully justified by the benefits.

Moreover, if the benefits offered by the restaurant are sufficiently attractive to the customer, then the Value of the Coke in the restaurant may be greater than its Value at the store. Given the choice, the customer may prefer to drink it at the restaurant even though it may cost more.

This example clearly illustrates how benefits may be more important than price in the demand for a product. (Notice that in the classical model of supply and demand quantity is determined only by price).

If another store offers the same Coke for $ 0.30 (very low price), then the customer might hesitate buying it, as he might think something is wrong: this would probably signal low quality in some way, thereby reducing its Value for him, or even lead him to abstain from purchasing altogether. This low price conveys to the customer confusing signals regarding the product´s positioning.

Prices function properly within the customer´s expected and reasonable price range. In this particular case, the price of the Coke is outside the price range expected by the customer and therefore he might doubt its quality (negative benefit); this reduces its Value despite the low price.

Effort has an interesting relationship with the time factor: if obtaining the product is too difficult, or involves an exaggerated investment in time, it might lose Value as it could easily be replaced it with another one that requires less effort.

The purchase of a product in the shortest time possible, or an agile service, can be highly valued; a good example lies in the fast food business that, as its name implies, requires fast service.

There are other cases, however, in which slowness may be highly valued, as may happen in an upscale restaurant; here the customer does not value or desire a fast service, in fact, he actually wants to prolong his purchasing experience; the benefit here is that slowness will be associated with status, elegance and prestige.

It may also happen that if the product, or service, is very "exclusive", the benefits associated with a greater effort may be prestige and a sense of belonging; hence the importance of user clubs, VIP cards, etc.; not everyone has the privilege of having them.

It should be noted, as in the prior Coke example, that care must be exercised with changes in the variables of Value, because they might send mixed signals to the client and alter the product´s positioning. A drastic reduction in price might negatively affect the associated benefits of quality, status and prestige; the positioning may change and probably reduce the customer´s trust in the brand; this can decrease the product's Value.

A product is purchased only if customers perceive Value in it; this means that the benefits offered must fully justify the price and effort sacrificed in order to obtain it; if Value is not perceived, then it will probably not be bought.

High Value is perceived when benefits outweigh price and effort; the consumer recognizes here a chance to "win" and his purchase therefore becomes an attractive deal; high Value induces greater demand.

Value is the real "engine" for increasing market share[25]. Sales volume is the direct result of the Value offered, and the higher it is, the faster the company can reach its earnings and profitability target.

The demand for a product is directly proportional to its Value.

A product ceases to have Value when the price is too high relative to its benefits, and therefore the customer may be unwilling to pay for it. If

[25] Donald R. Lehmann, R.S. Winer, "*Product Management*", McGraw-Hill, 2007. pp. 303-304

a product has no significant benefits relative to its competition, then the only possible differentiation is that given by its price.

A product may be very expensive, but, that does not mean that it necessarily has low Value; on the contrary, if its associated benefits are sufficiently attractive, then it can be a high Value product. A fine brandy or scotch provide good examples: their price may be very high, but their buyers attach great importance to the prestige that they provide in their social circles.

Similarly, a low quality product may have few benefits, but, if its price is low enough, it can also have a high Value. A cheap ball pen may do its writing job reasonably well, and if its price is sufficiently low to attract buyers, then it has Value for them.

As an example in the practical use of this concept, let us examine the reaction to a new competitor attempting to enter an established market with a low-pricing strategy; one obvious response would be to react with discounts, or even reduce prices. But, how about responding with a promotion that offers some extra benefit? One option is to add a free item to the product, which may be very pleasing to the consumer; this is likely to be more effective and cost less than reacting with discounts, or low prices.

Another option is to increase the quantity delivered without changing the price. This may have the same financial effect of a discount; but, it is perceived by the customer in a completely different way; it is clearly viewed as something better in the product; in fact, the customer is already used to the ongoing price; there is no need to confuse him.

These actions may thwart the efforts of competitors to gain entry into the market with low prices; indeed, this promotional strategy can be executed in precisely the same places where the competitor attempts to enter market, and thus avoid price erosion in other markets. The customer perceives something "better", the product´s positioning remains intact, and future earnings are not threatened; this may also help avert a "price war".

3.2 Resistance in sales

Value was previously defined as a force that drives sales. Nature, here comes to our rescue in order to understand the concept of force and apply it in marketing.

Sir Isaac Newton was first to understand a force and explain it in the language of science –mathematics. He concluded that force acting on a body not only moves it; it makes it go faster and faster; in other words, it accelerates it. However, he also noticed something else: larger bodies require more force to set them in motion. It seemed that matter somehow possesses a mysterious property, which makes it "resist" being moved.

As strange as this property was to him, it still is to us today, almost four centuries later. He described this property of matter in his first law of motion as an innate force of matter, or the power of resisting being moved; this is known as inertia.

If somehow inertia can be decreased, a body's resistance to being moved is reduced; therefore, it can increase its speed faster – acceleration. If resistance can be decreased, an object can move much faster in less time.

Newton also noticed that a body with more mass had more inertia; he expressed this in his second law of motion with his equation $F = ma$, or, force equals mass times acceleration: more force means more acceleration. For a given constant force, more mass leads to less acceleration, or conversely, less mass (less inertia and less resistance) leads to greater acceleration.

Interestingly, a similar law governs electricity. From Ohm's law: electromotive force (electric "pressure" or voltage) = resistance (ohms) x current (amperes), commonly expressed a $V = I \times R$; this simply means that more current flows through a circuit when it has less resistance.

Something similar happens with the flow of a fluid through a pipe: for a given amount of pressure, when there is less resistance more fluid flows.

This seems to be a universal law; marketing should be no exception.

Value is a force that pushes sales: more Value = more sales = more market share. Let us now apply this law of force to revenue (sales):

Value (force) = Resistance x Sales (Orientation model)

The relationship between sales and Value becomes clearer when presented as:

Sales = Value (force) / resistance

This indicates that as resistance increases, sales decrease; therefore, sales are inversely proportional to resistance: more resistance, less sales; and directly proportional to Value: more Value, more sales.

Evidently, Value cannot be delivered to its full potential if resistance does not allow it to act freely; it must act without it to increase sales and profits faster.

Therefore, the question is: What issues create resistance to sales and profits within and outside the firm? The first step is to identify them, and then propose solutions to mitigate or eliminate them.

It is important to identify resistances; otherwise, it is easy to fall into the trap of thinking that a sales –or profit– problem may be due to pricing, when in fact it may be for other reasons. From a pricing standpoint, resistances may originate from the market, the product, the economy, or the firm.

The following sections present some frequent sources of resistance.

Market resistance

Customer segmentation

Money, like time and energy, is a limited resource; no firm can concentrate on all markets simultaneously because this requires almost infinite resources; therefore, it must focus on the specific market segment that holds the best sales and profit potential; this is its target.

Advertising and promotion, in particular, must be aimed at the selected target in order to spend limited funds efficiently.

A profitable market segment must meet at least four requirements: it must have a clear need for the product; a sufficiently large number of customers; a minimum buying frequency, and the required purchasing power. If these requirements are not met, resistance is encountered (lower sales); therefore, a well-chosen target decreases resistance and allows Value to increase sales.

Brand or Product positioning

A strong brand is like an airplane on automatic pilot: it flies by itself and sells as if by magic; this reduces resistance and increases revenue. It not only carries customer trust and loyalty, but can also contribute towards selling other products.

If the product has a strong brand, it may be applied to other product categories that may benefit from it; this is known as "brand extension" or "brand stretching". The sale of these diverse products is leveraged by virtue of the brand's power.

The set of messages conveyed to the selected target must be sufficiently clear to highlight the product's competitive or complementary advantages.

The firm has two options: it can either attempt to capture the competition's customers with similar products, or it may seek to attract a slightly different market segment with products that somehow complement those offered by its competitors.

Either approach requires an effective positioning message, and a communications strategy that enhances the product's Value and its brand; this increases demand and revenue.

Distribution Channels

These are divided into two main categories: direct and indirect. Indirect channels include intermediaries such distributors, wholesalers, agents and retailers. Direct channels provide a direct means of selling from producer to consumer: these include manufacturers´ own retail stores, telemarketing, mail order, phone, Internet, or even company salesmen selling door to door.

A wide array of distribution channels increases sales, but it must be balanced against the investment required and its operating cost. Long distribution channels decrease the firm´s profit margin, or may pressure upward its prices, as each intermediary takes his share of the profit.

Global competition has placed intense downward pressure on prices; this has led to increased preference for direct distribution channels, with the Internet playing a major role.

The target customer segment, the product´s price and its positioning, must be aligned with the choice of the distribution channels; improper selection leads to sales resistance.

Competition

Revenue may decrease even though Value may remain unchanged; this is possible because competitors can also have high-Value products, as they may offer better benefits for an equivalent price, or similar benefits at a lower price; this can change customer preferences towards substitute products.

This reduction of revenue, and possibly of market share, suggests a resistance exists somewhere; its source needs to be identified and corrective action must be taken.

The first step to identify the source of the resistance is to analyze the product's Value; that is, its benefits to price combination, and compare it with the competition. This may require adjusting the price, or changing benefits, until a more competitive combination is found. If this has a cost implication, it also needs to be analyzed in order to maintain profitable sales.

This analysis may lead to an increase in benefits, a reduction in price, or a combination of both; either one is an increase in Value; the increase in Value should make the firm more competitive and increase sales (resistance reduction).

If a more profitable solution cannot be found, the product may be substituted, or complemented by additional product categories, in order to make up for the reduction in revenue.

Product resistance

Purchasing experience

Value is not limited to tangible products; it may also apply to intangible products (services). A high level of pleasure may be derived from the purchasing experience as if it is a product in itself; this relates not only the product and its brand, but also to the service delivered and its ancillary benefits.

This explains why the interest in a highly desired product may wear out after some time: the pleasure is not really obtained from the product; it is really derived from the purchasing experience itself.

An enhanced purchasing experience increases Value, decreases customer resistance, increases buying frequency and thereby sales. The lesson is that the interaction with the customer must be set up so that he obtains a high degree of pleasure and satisfaction from the act of purchasing.

This may explain the success of shopping malls; they have made great strides in improving the entertainment side of buying; evidently, pleasure decreases resistance.

Diminishing returns

Value remains unchanged as long as benefits and prices remain constant. The law of diminishing marginal utility in economics suggests that a consumer will continuously purchase a product as long as his additional (marginal) satisfaction is greater than the additional (marginal) cost of obtaining it (its price); in other words, the customer continues purchasing only as long as the pleasure exceeds its cost.

For example, a steak purchased at a restaurant provides the benefits the customer desires, but to receive them he must make a financial sacrifice by paying its price. However, if he desires a second steak, he would still have to pay the same amount, although one of the benefits (hunger satisfaction) is now less significant; this means its Value for him has somewhat decreased: fewer benefits at the same price. Therefore, it is quite likely he will not request the second steak and much less a third.

Resistance may set in, but that does not mean it cannot be mitigated: the fact is that the customer may still be hungry, yet he will not sacrifice more money for a marginal amount of pleasure. However, what happens if the restaurant has a "seconds" policy? The second order may then cost less, either by quantity or by price; this certainly adds Value; the customer may then feel enticed to go for seconds (more consumption); this, of course, not only enhances his buying experience (or pleasure), but also increases the restaurant's revenue.

Resistance can therefore be mitigated by continuously adding Value to the customer, either by additional benefits provided by added variety and service, or even by lower prices; this also builds customer loyalty and brand image.

The key is to properly identify the source of the resistance and then proceed to diminish or eliminate it.

Product packaging

Packages contribute significantly towards product differentiation and contain a substantial amount of information: brand, quality, price, quantity, instructions, etc.

The main marketing function of a package is to encourage buyers to purchase the product; this involves a package that conveys its positioning, and is specifically tailored for the target segment.

Humans are visual; therefore, the product´s packaging must exhibit the key signals that equate the product's benefits with the customers' needs.

Deceitful packaging prompts customer resistance; this leads to lost sales, which quite likely cost more than the short term gain from the deceit.

Price

In many cases, a product´s price may be the main source of resistance; that is why setting prices properly is such a high priority. A price out of line with the product's benefits, or with comparable substitutes, will discourage potential buyers and prompt them to pursue other alternatives, thereby leading to lost sales.

Customers are patient when it comes to searching for opportunities: when a high price entices them to shop for other alternatives, there is a good chance they will find them, especially if they believe the price is not justified by the product's benefits, or that better choices are available elsewhere.

It is not uncommon to see food spoil in supermarkets, restaurants, bakeries, butcheries, etc., simply because of poor pricing practices. This not only costs inventory money; it also takes its toll in customers and lost sales.

Businesspersons frequently fear price discounts because they do not realize that the price itself does not have to change; what really changes is the product´s Value. Discounts and promotions increase Value temporarily, until supply and demand come into balance; once the sales goal is met, price and Value remain unchanged.

Quality

From a marketing standpoint, quality is not only adherence to a product's specifications, but also how it compares with the customer's expectations.

The customer makes an appraisal of the product's Value: he weighs its features and benefits against the price; if he feels that it matches his expectations he interprets this as "good" quality.

If the customer is not satisfied and believes that the product or service has "low" quality, he voices his opinion via word of mouth to all his family and social circles; this has a very significant impact on the market as it spreads exponentially.

Sellers sometimes may not realize that a cost savings, which sacrifices the quality of a product, may be more than offset by the loss of sales to the customers that perceive low quality. This can happen because estimating savings is actually very simple: all it takes is determining the cost savings per unit and multiplying it by the number of units sold.

In contrast, estimating lost sales is a completely different story, because determining the number of disenchanted customers is almost impossible. If we add to this the exponential word of mouth effect, the numbers could be very large. Perhaps this can explain why sometimes a product, or a business, can fail so quickly.

In general, quality below customers' expectations leads to lost sales, as it decreases their purchasing frequency, and induces them to search for alternative options.

Negative benefits

As pointed out in Section "2.10 Benefits", just as positive benefits add Value, negative benefits reduce it. They work against sales by creating resistance and leading customers to reduce their purchasing frequency, or explore alternatives that are more competitive.

Resistance from the economy

Monopoly and oligopoly pricing

The lack of competition in monopolistic markets tends to drive up prices, which may prompt buyers to reduce or limit their purchases; this adds resistance to the free flow of goods and services.

In oligopolistic markets, competition exists among a few companies, but it may not be related to prices, as comparisons are relatively easy to make, and therefore they tend to be similar. The prices may be relatively high, but this is compensated by a wider selection of products; this promotes a greater flow of goods than in monopoly (less resistance).

When the price of a product is not justified by the benefits it offers, the customer segment (target) may feel it receives less Value, particularly if the price is perceived to be high, unfair, or abusive.

A customer may feel compelled to make the purchase anyway, but his buying frequency decreases, as he may have other needs, such as food, clothing, transportation, etc. The sellers may not realize that competition is not only amongst products in the market, but also for the customers` disposable income.

Customers can restrain themselves from buying, and perhaps may not even experience any pleasure from compulsory purchases, particularly when there are no other available alternatives. This resistance will not allow the sellers to achieve the full revenue potential that their target segment can deliver. Moreover, their financial statements may seem fine to them, but they will never know the amount of lost revenue and profits.

Taxes and tariffs

These are, unfortunately, interferences with the forces of supply and demand and with the free flow of goods worldwide; this, as was shown previously, leads to inefficiencies in the form of shortages or surpluses.

The purchase of a product that carries a high sales tax requires a greater financial sacrifice than the same product with no tax; this decreases its Value and creates resistance.

Tariffs and other taxes that increase costs, lead to price increases and therefore have a similar effect: they decrease Value and sales.

Resistance within the firm

Financial services

Inflexible credit policies may restrain revenue. Customers not only need products and services, they may need financing for various reasons: they may have reached a credit limit with their banks; perhaps they do not have credit available, or they may feel that supplier financing is more flexible, easier to obtain and less expensive (or perhaps even free!).

The firm can make loans, just like it can provide any other service that increases its capacity to compete in the market, and thereby increase revenue and profits.

Providing money in the form of "loans" is analogous to selling goods: money is “sold” to be repaid at some future date, and when payment is received, it includes "interest", which corresponds to the commission charged for the service rendered, or to the profit earned by the lender.

However, when a company provides credit, it does not deliver money: it delivers goods and services to be paid at some future date; this is termed "credit sales".

Credit increases revenue as it offers many alternative payment options; it can be tailored exactly to the customers´ needs; it increases their purchasing frequency, and may aid the firm in reaching other market segments. The credit service contributes to add Value to its products, and may increase its financial return on assets.

The firm, of course, must compute the financing cost. Since it is an additional benefit for the customer, it may or may not be added into the product´s selling price, depending upon the marketing strategy.

The firm may also offer support to its customers in obtaining credit from financial institutions; this may even leverage their capacity to obtain credit, not only due to the firm´s experience and connections, but also from its knowledge of the customers´ business.

Some customers may not have the administrative capacity to fulfill the credit requirements of banks, or may not even have the personnel needed; the firm can supply this. Its reward: less customer resistance and more sales.

Inventory turnover and logistics

“Sorry sir, we´re out of stock”. This phrase certainly does its job of discouraging any customer, and sends him flying directly into the open arms of competitors. This is not only a lost sale; it is a strong source of resistance in the selling battleground.

Inventory costs money in terms of the investment required, its carrying costs, financial and otherwise; therefore, inventory turnover is an important financial metric that needs to be tracked.

The slowest vehicle determines the speed of a convoy; something similar happens with inventory turnover; the slow-moving products drag down the total average inventory turnover, and therefore increase costs and logistical problems; this adds resistance and restrains sales.

If a high price is not accompanied by additional benefits, Value decreases and this has a negative impact on the product´s demand. Low inventory turnover is a signal indicating low product Value; that is, low benefits, or a price too high.

The term "low" inventory turnover relates to products whose inventory turnover is lower than the average turnover of the product line or category. This is very significant in perishable goods, food in particular.

There is a good chance that a product with relatively low turnover may not be fresh; once customers become aware of this, they may not wish to purchase it again; this further reduces turnover. A dangerous vicious circle looms overhead: this can kill a good product if corrective action on its price is not taken promptly.

If the company experiences low turnover, it may be tempted to extend a product´s expiration date in order to reduce returns. Customers, however, may perceive a lack of freshness and can confuse this with low quality; this arouses their resistance and decreases sales. The proper solution is to increase the product´s turnover by increasing its Value, either through improved benefits, or lower prices.

Service and warranties

Warranty and service support play a key role in building consumer confidence in the brand, and in their willingness to pay its price. Conversely, low quality service and insufficient warranties create purchasing resistance from customers.

Products may be copied or imitated; service is not so easy: it requires in-depth knowledge of the firm´s organization, its hiring practices, employee training, compensation and motivation. This has important implications for product quality, positioning, and manufacturing efficiency.

Service can be a very effective tool for differentiating a product or brand, as it may be a strong competitive advantage to reduce resistance and enhance customer loyalty.

Cost accounting methods and interpretation

A product´s cost may have an important influence on its selling price, as it is useful for determining its profit. A misinterpreted cost may lead to a high price that creates customer resistance, and it may even kill a profitable product.

Costs have a purpose: A cost used for determining a product´s profit may not necessarily be the same cost required for filing an income tax return, or for reporting financial results to stockholders.

Costs used for determining profits when setting prices must have a fair level of independence from sales volume, which may vary significantly throughout the product´s life cycle, and during normal business ups and downs.

This issue is analyzed further in *Chapter 5. Costs.*

Cooperation and teamwork

Teams tend to be better thinkers than individuals; perhaps that is the reason why companies have a board of directors; democracies function better than dictatorships, or even why free markets are more efficient than monopolies and oligopolies. However, serious danger may lurk inside the team, or the company for that matter.

Internal competition amongst employees may not exactly harmonize with cooperation, and this may create resistance to sales. A good example might be two sales representatives eagerly competing for a customer in an auto showroom: if they cooperate instead of competing, it is very likely that their joint sales effort will be much more productive. The outcome is beneficial for both of them in this win–win situation. This is also referred to as positive-sum game; the outcome for each player is positive. The firm´s compensation policy should be aimed at rewarding this selling strategy.

Another example is a restaurant in which a waiter will not tend a table that is not in his section; this projects a poor business image to the clientele, and certainly has a negative impact on its sales.

Many functional areas of companies tend to work independently of one another, thereby interfering with the coordination required to deliver the constant quality and service customers need; this can be another source of resistance in the selling process.

Human resources

Companies are no too different from sports teams: they need to win. However, getting good players is not easy: they must to be both capable and honest; no firm survives if its employees do not meet these two minimum requirements.

Competition also exists in the labor market; the best companies may get the top players. However, "best" may not refer only to pay; it is also closely related to the working environment and its organizational climate. There is hardly any possibility that demoralized workers can deliver constant quality and reliable service; in fact, they can even become a source of resistance.

Of particular importance is employee selection, training and motivation. This relates not only to sales personnel, but to all company employees as well. Lack of understanding of marketing and sales fundamentals by administration and production personnel, can lead to major restrictions that hinder the selling process.

A highly qualified salesperson has the capacity to turn a sale into a memorable moment for the customer; this reduces his resistance, increases purchasing frequency, and may increase the word of mouth activity –"free" advertising!

Selection, training and motivation play a key role. Winning in sales is not circumscribed to the sales and marketing departments; everyone in a company has a role to play for scoring points in the market; this is what the business game is all about.

Salespersons

A chain breaks at its weakest link; this is certainly true in business. Firms invest large sums of money on marketing plans; however, the entire strategy may end up depending on a single salesperson that may not be qualified to sell the product; at this point the chain breaks and all the money invested in this effort is lost. This is certainly a good source of resistance.

Machinery and equipment

Managing prices is a good method for matching supply with demand; however, a point may be reached when prices cannot be increased any further to cope with very high demand pressures. At that point, output capacity must be expanded; otherwise, a bottleneck will surface, thereby adding resistance to sales. This, of course, requires investment in fixed assets and working capital.

This outlay is feasible only if the additional quantity to be sold yields enough cash to pay for the added investment, within a timeframe in line with the firm`s financial goals.

All resistances have opportunity costs associated with them. If the opportunity costs can be identified and diminished, or eliminated, both sales and profits instantly increase.

3.3 Supply and Demand with Value

In section "1.1 Supply and Demand" the mechanism of supply and demand was analyzed; it was noted that the quantities supplied and demanded were balanced by virtue of price, which, if allowed to act freely, acts as a self-adjusting efficient mechanism for allocating and rationalizing the use of limited resources.

In contrast to “perfect competition” (compare with section “1.2 Markets and the Economy”), the market under the Value framework is characterized by:

- *Non-homogeneous products.* Substitute products, which are equivalent and directly compete with one another, are clearly distinguishable (differentiated) due to marketing mix (4P) strategies, such as branding, positioning, segmentation, benefits and price.
- *Large numbers of buyers and sellers.* Although there are indeed a large number of firms, markets have become “localized”, and in each locality there are firms that can individually influence the price of the goods and terms of sale; for example, stores in shopping malls.
- *Dependence.* Firms are apparently free to make decisions; but, in reality they are not, because they are being influenced by the media, and by the actions of their competitors.
- *Imperfect information.* Even though customers do possess very good market information, branding strategies may lead them to make subjective decisions that, from a pricing standpoint, may not seem economically “rational”. A well-positioned brand may sell successfully a product at a high price, although an equivalent

product, with the same quality, may be available from brand X at a lower price. In effect, the customer is paying a premium for enjoying the use of the brand.

- *Constrained entry and exit.* In fact, there are myriad barriers for entering or exiting a market: monopolies, oligopolies, red tape, business permits, complex tax and labor regulations, to name a few.
- *Transaction costs.* Buyers and sellers do incur many trading costs, mainly in the form of taxes: sales (value-added tax), banking, property, withholding, custom duties and tariffs, among many others.

All these market characteristics represent interferences that are reflected in the Value of the product, either in its benefits or in its price.

However, an unsolved problem remains: the truth is that the demand for a product depends not only on price as assumed by the law of supply and demand; from a marketing perspective, the supply and demand for a product depends mainly upon the marketing mix (4P).

The marketing solution requires developing a model that takes into account the marketing mix (4P) within the mechanism of supply and demand. The 4Ps have something in common: benefits. Upon review of the list of benefits suggested in section “2.10 Benefits" it can be seen that, one way or another, they are all included in the 4Ps.

The concept of Value and its relation to the demand for a product in terms of its benefits, price and effort was studied in the previous section. It was determined that the demand for a product is directly proportional to its Value.

$$\text{Value} = \frac{\sum \text{Benefits}}{\text{Price} + \text{Effort}}$$

This formula indicates that Value (benefits, price and effort) contains all the elements of the marketing mix (4Ps).

If the law of supply and demand is adapted to include Value as the key variable that determines the quantity sold, instead of price, it becomes a very practical tool for developing marketing and pricing strategies, as will be shown below.

In classical economics (see Figure 1.1) changes in the quantity (Q) demanded due to price are represented as *movements* along the demand curve; however, there are other determinants, aside from price, which can change demand; those changes are represented as *shifts* of the demand curve.

These shifts may result from changes in marketing variables such as advertising, branding, positioning, etc., as they increase the demand for a product at all price levels; changes in non-marketing variables such as the income level of consumers may also shift a price-based demand curve.

Similarly, in classical economics movements along the supply curve are due to price; however, the price-based supply curve itself may shift when there are changes in variables other than price that affect supply, for example: harvests, disasters, competition, seller expectations, costs, price of substitute products, etc.

From a marketing standpoint, demand reflects the desire or willingness to purchase a product; Value (4P, benefits/price) is a determinant that can clearly change demand: higher Value leads buyers to purchase more units (Q).

If Value is plotted along the horizontal scale instead of price, then changes in demand (Q) in response to marketing changes (Value) can be represented as movements along the Value-based demand curve (refer to Figure 3.1), instead of shifting curves. For example, more benefits, or lower price, increase Value; this increases the quantity demanded (or purchased) in a given period; benefits may include advertising, improved distribution, personal sales, branding, positioning, service, etc. Fewer benefits, or higher price, decrease Value; this decreases the quantity demanded.

If demand is determined more by Value than price, then it is possible to develop a demand function in which demand is directly proportional to the product´s Value; this indicates that as Value increases so does demand (Q).

This suggests for demand, as a function of Value, the following graph:

Figure 3.1

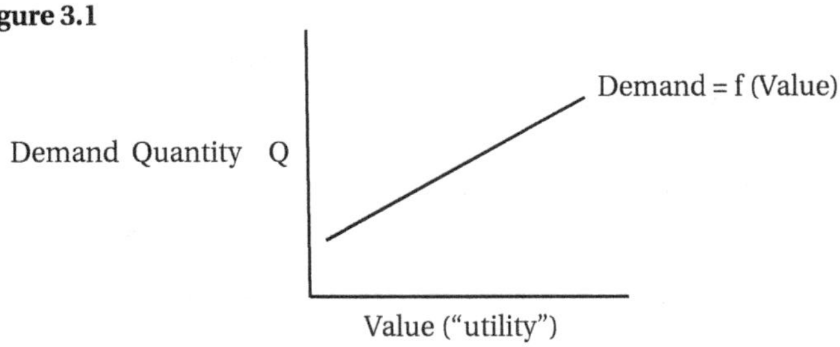

The quantity demanded (Q) is directly proportional to the product´s Value (or from economics, "utility"). Buyers are meticulous, well informed, and they react to changes in the marketing mix (benefits and price); in other words, they respond to Value.

A shift in the Value-based demand curve is possible when a change in demand is due to non-marketing variables; for example, changes in disposable income[26], demographics[27], competition, and expectations.

Movements along the price-based supply curve are due to price changes; the higher the price of a good, the greater the willingness of suppliers to produce a larger quantity and sell it; this is because sellers expect higher profits from higher prices.

From a marketing standpoint, the willingness to supply a product not only depends upon price: it is certainly a powerful incentive to make a profit, but, in order to sell (or supply) a product successfully, the seller also has to deliver benefits to his customers. Sellers know very well that they must convince their buyers; otherwise, they may go to the competition.

---

[26] Household after-tax income.

[27] Studies the composition of a population, such as age, race, sex, education, income, employment, etc.

A product can be sold at a higher price only if its benefits justify it; a seller will not be willing to market a product that has a low chance of being purchased; a high price necessarily requires benefits; this suggests that supply, like demand, also has a close association with Value; this makes it a useful concept in marketing.

However, nothing comes free: higher Value requires delivering more benefits, which adds costs, or setting lower prices; either way this reduces profits and therefore the willingness to supply or sell.

The more Value a seller delivers, the smaller the profit on each unit sold; this suggests an inverse relationship between supply and Value. If Value is plotted along the horizontal scale, then the changes in supply (Q) can be represented as movements along the Value-based supply curve (refer to Figure 3.2).

As a product´s Value increases, its unit profit decreases by virtue of the increased costs of the added benefits, and/or its price reduction. The result is that the firm will gradually reduce its output as the product´s attractiveness (profit) decreases; eventually, there will be a level of Value when production will cease altogether, simply because there is no longer profit in the units sold.

A shift in the Value-based supply curve is possible when a change in supply is due to changes in non-marketing variables; for example, harvests, disasters, weather, taxes, subsidies, substitute goods, production efficiency, costs, competition, and expectations.

This suggests that supply, based on Value, is function of the following type:

Figure 3.2 Quantity as a function of Value

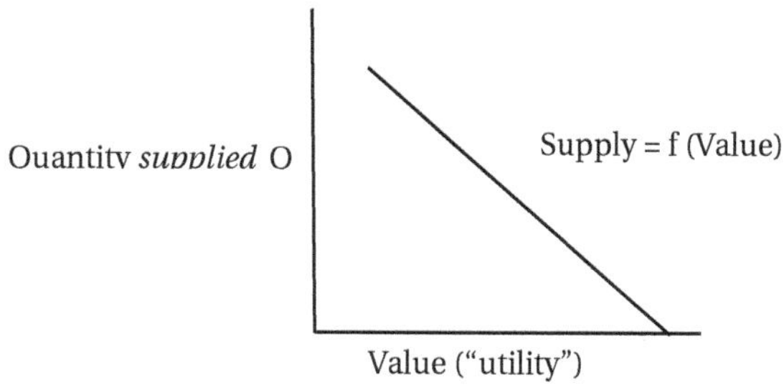

Notice that supply Q is inversely proportional to Value. There is a level of Value such that if it is too high, no quantity whatsoever is supplied to the market; its cost may equal, or even exceed, the selling price.

By overlaying both graphs, we obtain a representation of supply and demand in terms of Value, as follows:

Figure 3.3 Supply and demand based on

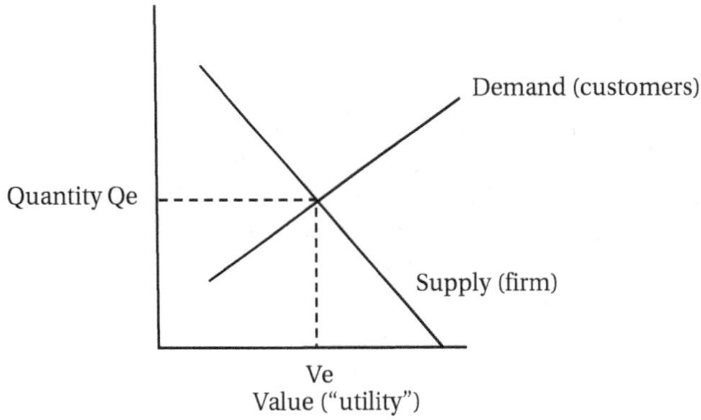

At a Value lower than Ve, supply exceeds demand; with this level of Value, the firm is interested in supplying the product to the market; but, the customers are not very interested in buying; this eventually leads to a surplus. This can happen because the Value offered may seem very low to them (few benefits in relation to the price).

It is worth noting that surplus product (at a Value less than Ve) indicates low inventory turnover, or "slow" sales (low purchasing frequency). This suggests either that the price is too high, or that the benefits being offered are insufficient; therefore, sales opportunities are lost. Customers may even refrain from buying at all, or possibly buy from the competition. This creates a pressure to increase Value.

When sales are slow, and an inventory surplus appears, this gives rise to an opportunity cost because the opportunity to sell more is lost and so are its corresponding profits. This creates pressure to increase Value.

To deliver greater value and increase sales requires improving the benefits and/or reducing the price, this puts pressure on the company to increase Value with greater benefits and/or lower price.

At a Value greater than Ve, customers are indeed interested in buying (many benefits in relation to price). They demand much more product than the firm may be willing to supply, because it is unprofitable to produce and sell it; this may be signaled by shortages and higher than average inventory turnover. Again, as in the previous case, the firm loses sales giving rise to the opportunity cost of lost profits; this puts pressure on the firm to decrease Value.

It may seem counterintuitive, but the model suggests that at this point the best solution is to raise prices, or, if more practical, cut back on benefits (less cost); this reduces Value until it returns to the Ve level.

These pressures, or forces, lead to a single level of Value (Ve), which makes it as attractive for customers to purchase, as it is for the company to sell. At this level of Value –marketing mix (4P)– supply and demand are in balance; the firm is willing to offer the maximum combination of quantity (Qe) and Value, which just matches the combination of quantity and Value (Ve) that customers are willing to buy. This is an equilibrium point, or the level of Value that balances supply and demand. It is the only point in which there are no opportunity costs; therefore, profits are maximum.

Given that this happens to all competitors simultaneously, they must make the same decisions regarding Value, in order to minimize shortages or surplus; any different level of Value reduces sales and income (profit).

This effect of aggregate demand and supply between sellers (competitors) and buyers (customers), gradually stabilizes a level of Value (Ve) that represents the multiple combinations of benefits and prices available in the market for a given product.

Success finally arises because not all competitors can achieve the Value (marketing mix, 4P) necessary to be profitable; only the survivors remain in the market.

Non-marketing changes can also be analyzed. Under the classical model of supply and demand, an increase in consumer disposable income leads to an upward shift in the demand curve; this increases the market price (equilibrium price); it makes sense: with more money, at every price level people are willing to buy more; or equivalently, more quantity is purchased at higher prices as customers have more money.

In Value-based demand, an increase in consumer disposable income should also shift upwards (left) the Value-based demand curve; at every level of Value more quantity is desired.

From Figure 3.3 it can be observed that an upward shift in the Value-based demand curve decreases the equilibrium level of Value (Ve); it also makes sense: with more money, people are willing to buy more quantity with fewer benefits, or with higher prices; this is equivalent to more quantity sold with lower Value. Affluent people are less concerned about prices and consume more.

The seller´s response to a general increase in income is to deliver lower Value by reducing benefits and/or raising prices. This is illustrated in Figure 3.3, when the demand curve is shifted upwards. His strategy will depend on how sensitive is his product mix is to price changes; this is known as the price elasticity of demand.

In products with high elasticity, a small increase in price may trigger a large decrease in the quantity sold. In contrast, in a product with low elasticity, an increase in price may have little or no effect on the quantity sold. (This subject is analyzed further in section 4.3 Price Elasticity.)

One thing is clear: raising prices or reducing benefits will increase the product´s unit profit. The seller will have to decide by how much to increase prices and by how much to reduce benefits. If his products are very sensitive to prices, his strategy will be not to increase them, and instead reduce benefits; on the other hand, if his products are not very sensitive to prices he can increase them, and add little or no benefits.

On the supply side, something similar happens with non-marketing changes. Under the classical model, an increase in production efficiency (just like a good harvest) leads to an upward shift in the price-based supply curve; this decreases the market price (equilibrium price); it makes sense: with more output, at every price level more quantity is offered; or equivalently, more quantity is sold at lower prices.

In Value-based supply, an increase in production efficiency should shift upwards (right) the Value-based supply curve; both Value and quantity increase. From Figure 3.3 it can be observed that an upward shift in the Value-based supply curve indeed increases the equilibrium level of Value (Ve); it also makes sense: with more quantity available, more quantity is sold.

At this point, the seller has to make an interesting decision: How is he going to deliver higher Value? He has to define a strategy with greater benefits, and/or with lower prices.

With a good harvest, he could simply go ahead and respond by cutting prices; but does it really make sense? What about the price elasticity of his product mix? Does he have other options?

Imagine for a moment, just for illustration purposes, that the seller is a corner store retailer that stocks food products with high price elasticity. This suggests that his response to a good harvest would probably be to lower prices and/or perhaps increase benefits.

Lowering prices is quite clear, but what about increasing benefits? Does this suggest that if he adds some extra benefits perhaps he need not lower his prices as much as would be expected? Certainly; this is what the Value model suggests; after all, customers seek “gains”; these can also be obtained through more benefits, and not necessarily through lower prices.

Customers may be willing to pay a little more, if they receive something valuable in return; for example, good service, variety, quality, etc. Adding some key benefits may be more effective, and perhaps even cost less than simply lowering prices.

The retailer may have to lower prices, but only to some extent, depending upon how creative are his compensating benefits. This strategy may even turn out to be more profitable; it can also help build customer loyalty.

In contrast to the retailer, suppose that the seller is a manufacturer of consumer goods. If, for some reason, an increase in production efficiency leads to much greater output (like a good harvest) he is then confronted by the same decision as the retailer.

His response to this good "harvest" may be entirely different from that of the retailer: Classic supply and demand dictates that under abundance prices tend to fall. In contrast, Value-based supply and demand suggests that under abundance Value increases, and this is probably what the manufacturer may do, but without touching prices. How?

The manufacturer will not lower prices; instead, he will promote his product through increased advertising, larger distribution, personal sales, etc. This will increase his volume of sales, and he will profitably benefit from greater production efficiency without sacrificing price.

Costs play an interesting role in the supply function (this subject is covered in Chapter 5). First, they can be classified into two major categories:

Fixed costs.

These are closely related to *time* and they bear no relation to sales volume. For example, rent, depreciation and wages are generally paid, or accrued, on a monthly basis. Independently of how much is sold, they tend to remain fixed in the short term; in the long run they may vary to the extent that the company requires more investment.

Variable costs.

In contrast to fixed costs, these are costs closely related to *sales volume* and they regularly increase in proportion to the quantity sold, although the unit variable cost tends to remain stable. Raw materials provide a good example: If sales double, the total cost of raw materials also doubles, but the unit cost remains constant.

Let us now return to the case of the manufacturer and examine how increases in costs can affect his willingness to supply. An increase in fixed costs may reduce his output capacity; an example of this could be an increase in taxes, wages, or rent; this may force him to reduce output due to his financial limitations (less inventory or fewer workers). This suggests a downward shift of the Value-based supply curve; less output at all levels of Value.

A downward shift of the Value-based supply curve leads to less output and less Value. This means that the manufacturer has two alternatives in response to higher fixed costs: either raise prices, which seems quite logical, as he can transfer to his customers his added costs, or he can reduce benefits, which would, of course, enable him to compensate to some extent the added costs. However, either course of action will constrain his selling capacity.

Conversely, a reduction of fixed costs might encourage him to increase output (supply); this would point to an upward shift of the Value-based supply curve, which would lead to higher output and higher Value: he can reduce prices or add benefits. In this case, either course of action will increase his selling capacity.

What happens when the change is in variable costs? Price is a marketing variable, and as such, its changes are movements along the supply curve. This begs the question: Is there any difference between a change in price and a change in variable costs? From the point of view of profit, there is no difference, since an increase in profit may arise from an increase in price or from a decrease in the variable costs; therefore, a change in variable costs would cause movement along the Value-based supply curve.

An increase in variable costs operates just like a price decrease; it leads the seller to either raise prices and/or reduce benefits. A decrease in variable costs stimulates the seller to increase output and increase Value: either lower prices and/or increase benefits. His final decision will be based on the product´s price elasticity: high elasticity will point to prices; low elasticity will point to benefits.

This analysis leads us to conclude that variable costs behave like marketing variables, as their changes can be represented as movements along the Value-based supply curve.

Fixed costs, on the other hand, behave as non-marketing variables given that they cause shifts, instead of movements, in the Value-based supply curve.

This links marketing strategies with variable costs. Let us again address the question of how the manufacturer can respond to an increase in fixed costs. The prior conclusion was that he could raise prices or reduce benefits. Since raising prices can be substituted by variable cost reductions, then the strategy might be to reduce benefits by decreasing their related variable costs, thereby avoiding price increases.

This option should always be open, as tinkering with sale prices is in general a risky move as they are difficult to implement; revenue is very sensitive to their changes; and, customers may react unpredictably. These pricing and cost issues are explored further in the next chapters.

This analysis indicates that price elasticity is the key for determining the best course of action; what is clear in all cases is that pricing is only a part of the strategy as benefits also play a major role. Again, these are orientation models, not success formulae; the final course of action depends upon the product, the company and the specific market circumstances.

It is interesting to see that when all the marketing variables come into play, the graphs of supply and demand seem to be the opposite of classical economics (see Figure 1.1). This, however, does not mean that the classical model is not valid; it merely reflects the special case of assuming that price determines quantities, or that quantities determine price. If in the Value-based demand and supply functions, the benefits remain constant, while varying only prices, the result is the same as in the classical model.

The demand function based on Value illustrates that when the price increases, while benefits are kept constant, Value decreases, and consequently demand also decreases; this means that it would still be inversely proportional to price, as in the classical model.

In the supply function based on Value it can also be observed that if the price is increased, while benefits are kept constant, Value decreases (higher profit) and, consequently supply increases (more output); this means that supply would still remain directly proportional to price (profit) as in the classical model.

The classical model of supply and demand describes the special case of analyzing the market, assuming that the price variable is the sole determinant of quantity (or vice versa). In Value-based supply and demand, this restriction is eliminated; therefore, the supply and demand functions include not only price, but also all the other marketing variables (4P) that influence the supply and demand of a product.

In fact, this model is a reflection of the world around us in which brands, advertising, distribution channels, discounts, promotions, and personal sales, among other things, decisively influence the market forces of supply and demand.

The model also indicates that there is a unique level of Value (Ve) that works for both the firm and its customers; at that precise level of Value there is no surplus or shortage of a product; but, at other levels there are shortages and surpluses; this translates into slow sales of some products and lost sales of others.

This also suggests that there must be a particular price which yields the precise level of Value required to maximize revenue and profits (this is discussed further in section 4.4 Optimum Price).

Today´s customers are keen at making comparisons of benefits and prices between different competitors, mainly due to the free flow of information available in the digital media such as the Internet, TV and cell phones; betting on the assumption that today´s consumer is uninformed can be very costly in terms of lost sales.

The use of this model is facilitated by classifying products into the following three categories:

Products with high elasticity

Generally, these are markets characterized by relatively low-priced products that can be easily substituted, and where brand loyalty plays a minor role. Included here, among others, are essential goods such as food, water, fuel, etc., in which price is an important consideration at the time of purchase; in these cases, in order to change Value, the strategy that might yield the fastest response is to adjust the price. (Applying the Value Matrix is suggested. Refer to "Chapter 8. The Value Matrix").

Products with low elasticity

These are markets characterized by products in which the brand and price play a key role in the product´s positioning; included here we mostly find, among others, luxury items in which the benefits offered are most important for the customers; in these cases the strategy with the greatest impact is to change the benefits. (See "Chapter 8. The Value Matrix").

Products with uncertain elasticity

Elasticity should be taken into account even though its interpretation may be more qualitative than quantitative; not knowing it does not mean it should be ignored. For practical purposes, it is sufficient to have an intuitive idea about whether it is high, medium or low. The first step is to classify the product in any of the previous categories. This task is facilitated by replying the following questions:

- Is the brand important at the moment of purchase?
- Does brand loyalty exist?
- Is it difficult to replace the product with one from another brand?
- Are prestige and status important benefits for the customer?

- Does the product have limited distribution to some stores, either owned or franchised?
- Does the customer spend time researching the product before purchasing?
- Is the product differentiated by quality?
- Does the sale of the product require well-trained salespeople?
- Does the client expect to be professionally advised by the seller?
- Does the sale of the product require any supporting services?
- Does the customer perceive in the price a signal of quality?

If the answer to most of these questions is yes, this means that the product probably has a low elasticity, and therefore benefits will predominate in the decisions. (See "Chapter 8. The Value Matrix"). If the answers are not conclusive, then the safest strategy to modify Value would be a combination of both benefits and prices.

In "Appendix 1. Optimization of the Demand Function" it can be observed that the level of sales is very sensitive to price changes; because of this, price adjustments require enormous caution. When modifying Value, changing benefits rather than prices should be considered first, as long as this is feasible.

This analysis suggests that the resource allocation mechanism in the economy is not really price; it is actually Value, as it involves all the marketing variables in addition to the competition. Clearly, there is a relationship between Value and price and it is provided by the benefits. Ultimately, it is Value and not price what gathers sellers and buyers in the market.

The Value-based supply and demand mechanics can be a valuable tool for analyzing how the firm should respond to market changes, and for determining its pricing and marketing strategy.

3.4 Value: Questions and Answers

Several questions need to be addressed in order to clarify the concept of Value.

Can Value be quantified?

Yes. The representation of Value = ∑ Benefits / (Price + effort) behaves like a regular fraction: the quotient is Value, the numerator is ∑ Benefits and the denominator is (Price + effort). If the denominator increases the quotient decreases, or if the numerator decreases the quotient also decreases and vice versa. A quantification method is presented in Chapter 8. *The Value Matrix*; this facilitates the use of Value for setting prices and developing strategies.

What is the effect on Value of a price increase?

A price increase without a proportional increase in benefits decreases Value.

What is the effect on Value of a price decrease?

A price decrease, without a proportional decrease in benefits, increases Value; however, if the price decrease has a negative impact on benefits, then Value may decrease. Example: a price decrease that diminishes the prestige of a product.

Can the actions of competitors change Value?

No. The Value of a product does not change unless its benefits, price and effort are changed; however, the actions of competitors may change customers´ preferences.

Is price the driver of market share?

Price is not the only driver of market share because it can never be isolated from the benefits attached to a product. A potential customer never loses sight of the benefit/price relationship; in fact, the best way to increase market share is to execute a benefit/price combination superior to that of the competition; this translates into offering greater Value; adding Value increases sales.

Is the economic concept of "utility" the same as Value?

Yes. "Utility" is an economic term that refers to the satisfaction derived from consuming a good or service. A customer will not be satisfied if he experiences the so-called "cognitive dissonance"[28]: a feeling of discomfort and skepticism about a purchase.

If a customer perceives a product as "expensive", he may abstain from buying it; but if he buys it anyway and feels he paid "too much", this means that a competing product would have provided him with greater satisfaction. He then understands he made the wrong choice and he feels unsatisfied; therefore "utility" is tied not only to the benefits of a product, but also to its price; the same as in Value.

Why use the word Value instead of "utility"? Simply because the term Value (noun) can be clearly related to something a person "values" (verb); on the other hand, "utility" (noun) can easily be confused with profits, or even with benefits, especially in other languages.

What is the role of "effort" in Value?

A customer not only sacrifices money when purchasing a product: he also expends "energy". This consumption of energy can be "good" or "bad". It is "good" if it provides the customer with an added benefit; for example, the prestige of belonging to a VIP club, or having a "Gold Card". Obtaining this takes trouble and effort, but it is desired, and it also provides self-esteem; it can be "bad" if the added effort does not provide any added benefit.

A product with inadequate distribution (requiring greater purchasing effort) will have less Value than one with a good distribution. A greater effort without any added benefit reduces Value.

Is Value constant?

Value changes only if benefits, price, or effort, change.

What are the Practical applications of Value?

Value is useful for devising marketing strategy and setting prices within the context of relationship marketing. The method and its development are covered in Chapter 8. *The Value Matrix.*

---

[28] K. Douglas Hoffman, J. E.G. Bateson, "Essentials *of Services Marketing*", 2nd, Harcourt College Publishers 2002, p. 87

It is also helpful for:

- Developing a strong and coherent Value Proposition.
- Redesigning a product when its benefits, or costs, need to be changed in order to achieve an acceptable profit.
- Structuring the communications strategy for positioning a product.
- Understanding what benefits customers truly need, desire and value.
- Analyzing the competition.
- Developing an optimum product mix.

Chapter 4

Price

4.1 Definition of Price

In marketing, there are several ways to understand the meaning of "price":

- What the customer pays for purchasing a product or service.
- The money he is willing to sacrifice to meet his wants and needs.
- It is an integral part of positioning and may be a signal associated with quality, prestige and status.
- It is the variable that determines the firm´s revenue, income and profitability.
- Price places a value on goods and services, thereby facilitating trade by avoiding the need for barter.
- Price plays a key role by matching supply with demand.
- Sets a trading value for the benefits offered by the product.
- A rising price may signal shortage or high demand.
- A falling price may signal surplus or low demand.
- A high price in relation to cost is a good indicator of a profitable product.

The customer has an economic value for the company, and it is represented by all the profits he generates through his purchases[29]. The set price should be able to achieve customer loyalty and yield the highest present value of the future stream of earnings.

---

[29] Thomas Nagle, Reed K. Holden, "*The Strategy and Tactics of Pricing*", Pearson, Prentice Hall, 2002, p. 160

4.2 The Dimensions of Price

In general, a product´s price should be set in the context of:

- The benefits it offers.
- The product's positioning (its image and perception).
- The target market (needs, profile, habits and preferences).
- The competition (prices and benefits).
- Market forces (supply and demand).
- Differentiation and / or competitive advantage.
- The product´s life cycle.
- Business trends.

In a high-end market segment, a high price is perceived as an indication of quality, prestige and status. When a price is too low, it is likely to be associated with lower quality and therefore have a negative effect on the product´s positioning; it may adversely affect the brand´s image.

Prices that do not fit with the target market, or with the product´s positioning, can be found frequently. A good example is a restaurant, where the food may be inexpensive but drinks expensive; beverage consumption will therefore be lower than what it could be. Another example might be a movie theater with very high prices in snacks and beverages, thereby reducing the sales potential within the target market.

Whenever the critical match between price, benefits, positioning, and target segment is lost, the sales volume, market share and profitability become adversely affected.

Price comparison with competitors

The Internet information revolution and its profound impact on global trade should not be underestimated: search engines provide all the necessary information so that modern consumers are well informed when it comes to comparing prices and benefits; therefore, when setting prices, the benefits and prices of the competition should be taken into account.

Previous Prices

Price changes are another dimension to be considered: sharp price reductions breed mistrust, lead consumers to suspect that either quality has decreased, or that previous prices were abusive. If this occurs as a response to a competitor´s low price, the negative effect is even more apparent, and this ends up benefiting the competitor´s image.

On the other hand, a sharp price increase can induce customers to explore other purchase alternatives; changes should be carried out gradually, and with a well-planned benefit strategy, to avoid sending unfavorable signals to the market.

Purchasing power and / or demand

The benefits to price ratio should be optimum for the target market: if the price is high and the benefits are too low, then demand will be low; if the price is low and the benefits are high, demand will be high.

The proposed price must take into account that the product is always competing for the customers´ financial resources; the customer may buy less, or even refrain from buying, depending upon his budget and priorities.

Transaction quantity

A common mistake is to sell in the unit (or amount) that the company wants, instead of what the customer may want, ignoring his buying patterns. Price measures the amount of product delivered in a transaction, and if this is not right, neither is the price. More mistakes are possibly made on quantity rather than on the price itself; this is frequently observed in new, little known or low-turnover products, which are sold in packages with large quantities that are neither attractive nor adequate.

If the amount delivered on each unit (or transaction) is too high, the purchasing frequency decreases; if the amount of each unit is too low, the customer has the option to purchase multiple units, or increase the purchasing frequency. What should remain clear is that it must be what the customer desires, and not what the manufacturer wants to impose. The customer´s desired purchasing frequency is what determines the amount (or servings) that the manufacturer must deliver on each unit sold.

Moreover, if the product is perishable, the customer is not going to risk buying an amount that can spoil before he consumes the quantity purchased; therefore, wrong quantities means lost sales; this illustrates why it is so important to know the target customers´ preferences and buying patterns.

Customers may not be willing to risk a relatively high sum in an unknown or low consumption product. In a trial purchase, the customer spends the least amount of money; therefore, the unit of sale (or serving size) must clearly match his needs and preferences.

Obsolescence

Products evolve as new customer needs, or new market niches, are discovered; this is frequently made possible due to inventions or new technologies. Good examples are computers, television and cellular phones. Product substitution becomes inevitable as new products and services with improved benefits enter the market; the remaining production, or inventory, must be eventually turned into cash for replacing those that are being phased out.

However, not all customers are prepared, or even willing, to substitute the products they have become accustomed to, perhaps due to habit, preference, or even financial reasons. This suggests that a profit potential may remain in the market; the question is how to tap it.

At some point products no longer enjoy the privileged market position they once had; therefore, their Value must have decreased; adding benefits may not be technically or financially feasible; therefore, their Value can only be increased through successive price reductions, until they no longer yield a profit; the product`s life cycle has effectively reached its end.

Fashion

Firms and individuals are constantly creating new means and ways to increase their wealth, and profits are powerful incentives for developing new products and services; in fact, this is the engine of the free enterprise system.

Fashion plays a key role in feeding this constant flow of goods that is powered by highly creative individuals who have the capacity to influence people´s tastes and preferences. As these evolve, firms strive to maximize profits from the dwindling sales of products running out of fashion; their Value can only be increased by means of price reductions.

Season

There are products that are tied to the time of the year in which they are sold; for example, toys, clothing, school supplies, sporting goods, etc. Ideally, at the end of the season, the remaining inventory should be zero; but, unfortunately, marketing tactics tend to be more static than dynamic; therefore, season and sales run out of synchronization, leading to slow-moving, or dead, low-Value inventory at the end of the season; liquidating these remaining goods becomes imperative.

Competition

A product may not yet be obsolete and still be in fashion; perhaps its timing is also favorable; but its inventory may be on the rise, or excessive, due to falling sales; this suggests that customers are obtaining Value elsewhere: the competition.

Falling sales, or low inventory turnover, in general, suggest low Value; this may be due to high prices, low benefits, or changing customer preferences stemming from competitors´ higher Value offers.

The speed with which information travels within the market leads customers to react very quickly to new opportunities; the firm must react to these competitive pressures by adding more Value to its products; otherwise, it stands to decrease or lose its market share.

Business cycle

There are indeed situations that are beyond the firm´s control: an economic, or political, event may certainly unleash negative expectations that lead customers to save money as a form of protection; this has an unfavorable impact on sales. A business downturn cannot be ignored, and if the firm does not protect its own cash reserves, it may not be able to cope with the momentum of its fixed costs.

Lower prices, fortunately, can act as a buffer against falling customer demand by stimulating further consumption, and thereby bring demand and supply back into balance; this is a major benefit of free markets. Profits may be lower, but, if pricing is properly handled, the cash flow may be saved.

In general, inventory turnover must be increased rapidly by liquidating goods of uncertain sale; otherwise, the firm´s cash flow may be insufficient to maintain an on-going business, or else the firm may easily fall into debt; this will further increase fixed costs, and erode profits by virtue of higher interest expenses.

One basic business principle must not be forgotten: the good times have to pay for the bad times; or, better said, during recovery, prices should be more than sufficient to offset prior losses; success must pay for failure.

The oil industry is well known as a risky business: many dry wells are constantly being drilled, and this leads to constant losses over time. If the success rate is, say, only ten percent, this means that 90% of the business is coping with losses. Therefore, when the ten percent eventually shows up, product prices must be more than sufficient to cover losses and yield a profit. The stockholders, just like any investor, expect returns that justify the risks, effort, time, and funds sacrificed in any endeavor.

This has an interesting mathematical background: the law of large numbers suggests that as the number of events (or trials) increases, results tend to approximate an average or expected value. For example, it is clear that when tossing a coin there is a 50% chance for each outcome; however, if a coin is tossed only a few times, the outcomes may not yield the 50% ratio; but, if the coin is tossed a very high number of times, the actual outcomes will very closely approximate the 50% expected ratio.

4.3 Price Elasticity

Each product, or brand, has its own customer segment and its reaction to price changes is known as "price elasticity". While it is true that price is not the only determinant of demand, it does clearly have an effect on it.

Price elasticity (of demand) measures the percentage change in quantity demanded relative to the percentage change in price.

Mathematically it can be expressed as:

$$\text{Price Elasticity (E)} = \frac{\text{\% change in quantity (Q)}}{\text{\% change in Price (P)}}$$

$$E = \frac{\Delta Q\%}{\Delta P\%}$$

Alternatively,

Solving for $\Delta Q\%$

$\Delta Q\% = E \times \Delta P\%$

This indicates that for a given percentage change in price, there is a corresponding percentage change in quantity demanded; the relationship between these changes is defined as price elasticity.

For example, if a price increases by 10% and the quantity demanded decreases by 20%, the relationship is:

$E = -20\% \; / \; 10\%$

$E = -2$

If a product has an elasticity of E = -0.5 and its price increases by 20%, then the percentage quantity ($\Delta Q\%$) demanded decreases by -0.5 x 20% = -10%, given that $\Delta Q\% = E \times \Delta P\%$

This is very practical when considering price changes and discounts. Businesspersons gradually acquire an intuitive sense of elasticity, based upon their experience and judgment; they can very likely anticipate their customers´ reactions to a price change; put another way, they can "sense" elasticity. It may be a rather difficult task to determine the precise elasticity of a product; however, in most circumstances, it is sufficient to rate it as high, medium or low. The following example illustrates this point.

Suppose a 10% price increase ($\Delta P\%$) will go into effect for three products with high, medium, and low elasticity (E). Let price P = 100, quantity Q = 100 and sales S = P X Q = 100 x 100 = $ 10,000, for all three products.

The expected sales response could very likely be as follows:

	Elasticity		
	High	***Medium***	***Low***
	E = -3	E = -1	E = -0.2
Price % change (ΔP%)	+10%	+10%	+10%
Quantity % change (ΔQ% = E x ΔP%)	-30%	-10%	-2%
Quantity change (ΔQ = 100 x ΔQ%)	-30	-10	-2
Sales before the price increase P x Q	$10,000	$10,000	$10,000
After 10% price increase:			
Price (P + 10%P)	$110	$110	$110
Quantity (Q - ΔQ)	70	90	98
Sales after price increase P x Q	$7,700	$9,900	$10,780

Notice that with "high" elasticity (E = –3) revenue (sales) falls because of the large loss in quantity; with "medium" elasticity (E = –1), there may be little impact on revenue; and, with "low" elasticity (E = –0.2), revenue may actually increase, as the loss in quantity is very small compared to the gain in price. Therefore, a price change may evidently have significant consequences on revenue, depending upon the product´s price elasticity.

When faced with a price increase customers may not react, but if they do, they have three options: first, and probably the most common, is simply to purchase a lower quantity, reduce their buying frequency, or even refrain completely from buying; second, they can purchase another brand; and third, replace the product type or category (premium for economy).

Let us see what happens with a decrease in price. Customers can react in two ways: the first is to buy a greater quantity, or increase the purchasing frequency; the second, however, can be surprising and unexpected: changing brands; this can happen if the usual brand is clearly associated with benefits such as status, exclusivity, prestige, etc. At a lower price, the customer can perceive the loss of these benefits; he is then likely to switch to the brand that will offer him what in his opinion he is losing.

Moreover, with prices that are too low, depending on elasticity, it is likely that the higher sales volume will not offset the sacrifice in price: successively lower prices may then work against sales by reducing income (profit), and even harm the product´s positioning.

The market is not a laboratory in which some variables can be isolated from others; it is rather chaotic, and this makes it difficult for experimentation. Customers do not respond instantaneously to price changes; there is a lag, or reaction time, which can be unknown or very long. In the course of this, a number of events can occur that are neither controllable nor measurable; in fact, it is very likely that price elasticity varies as the product advances in its life cycle.

There may also be price changes that are of no real concern to consumers; this is not because they are perceived as small or insignificant, but rather they just seem plain "normal", as they affect everyone equally: this is the case with price increases due to inflation.

We have seen that inflation in the end works as a form of taxation: it reduces purchasing power. Nonetheless, it has become a common reality of life; therefore, when prices change in response to inflationary pressures, no one is surprised. It is not unusual to see the price of food constantly increasing, or rent, or even wages (hopefully!). People are used to this.

How do sellers go about this? They can change prices by advertising with phrases such as "new", or "improved formula", etc. The truth is that the marketing mix (4P) strategies –advertising in particular– may have a "buffer effect" on elasticity: they reduce the impact of price changes on the quantity sold.

A benefit-related price increase may have unsuspected effects on the volume or quantity sold; in fact, sales volume may actually increase in response to a price increase. If a product has a price that is too low and lies below the price range rationally expected by the target market, it may not be purchased as customers may suspect low quality.

However, if the price is increased, and brought within the expected price boundary, then its sales volume may increase. A good example can be a cosmetic: if it is perceived as "too cheap" due to its low price, it probably will not have an acceptable level of sales; but, if its price is increased to what customers expect (as an indicator of quality), its sales volume increases.

Section "2.10 Benefits" indicates there are a myriad benefits that, if used creatively when the price increases, may actually increase the quantity sold. If the additional cost of benefits is carefully balanced with the additional price, then profits may also increase.

There are several circumstances, or effects, that may affect customers' price sensitivity (elasticity)[30]:

Reference price

Customers tend to be more price-sensitive when the price differential with a substitute product is high. Whenever possible, customers compare benefits and prices; if they find that the price differential amongst similar products is too high, they may feel reluctant to purchase the more expensive product. Therefore, high-priced products must reflect quality, prestige or status; this is mainly achievable by product design and packaging.

Benefits/features

Customers are less sensitive to price if the product has unique advantages and features, or multiple benefits. People are willing to sacrifice large sums for being exclusive or first with highly innovative products; this carries prestige, but it has its price. The product´s competitive advantage must be clearly emphasized in its communications strategy and in its packaging.

Comparison

Customers are less sensitive to prices when they cannot easily compare products. Some products are difficult to compare due to their packaging features; customers will not spend much too time trying to figure out their equivalent quantity and price; therefore, the price differences might not be very meaningful to them. This suggests that products which have significant competition must stand out from their substitutes, possibly by size, shape, packaging and other benefits such as the service offered.

---

30 Based on Thomas Nagle, Reed K. Holden, "*The Strategy* and *Tactics of Pricing*", Pearson, Prentice Hall, 2002. pp. 90-110

Substitution cost

Customers are less sensitive to a product's price if its substitute has a significant cost. If the next best alternative is too costly, the customers will not be very concerned with a product´s price; for example, another similar product can be offered with a much higher price to give the impression that the original product´s price is a real bargain. Moreover, the product´s package and its communication strategy should emphasize the benefit of its comparatively low price.

Substitutes

Customers are more sensitive to a price when the product has many substitutes. Whenever multiple alternatives with similar benefits are available, customers may quickly change brands. This clearly points to the importance of product differentiation; in as much as possible, products must enhance even subtle differences so that their substitution is less evident. This is the playing ground of brands: if the brand projects sufficient prestige and status, the product is less likely to be substituted.

Price-quality relationship

Customers are less sensitive to prices when they believe that they signal good quality. Delivering superior product quality justifies higher prices, as it requires higher costs; therefore, customers must be made aware of the product´s benefits, otherwise they may be reluctant to pay the price differential.

Brand image

Customers are less sensitive to the prices of well-known brands; customers are more sensitive to a product's price if it competes against a well-known brand. This is probably the best justification for investing in advertising and promotion for developing strong brands. Businesses frequently take a long time to become profitable precisely because developing a solid customer base goes hand in hand with building a strong brand. It takes time, energy and money convincing customers to trust the brand; entrepreneurs must be prepared for this before embarking on new endeavors, otherwise the risk of failure can be very high.

Expense

Customers are more sensitive to price if the expenditure represents a high proportion of their income. This is why proper market segmentation is a critical component of a marketing strategy; the target selected must have the purchasing power required by the product´s price.

Need

If, for whatever reason, the need for the product is high, the customer will have low sensitivity to its price. Again, a well-selected target must have a high need for the product.

Shared expense

Customers are less sensitive to a price if their proportion of a shared expense is low. Innovative or creative pricing can play a key role here: if, for any reason, the target segment cannot individually pay the full price, then sharing the product with others is an attractive option. A good example of this is time-sharing in hotels and resorts: instead of purchasing an expensive room or apartment, what is purchased is the right to a specific number of days per year, at a much lower price. This pricing concept can be also applied to many other services and high-price durable goods.

Fair price

Customers are more sensitive to a price if somehow they believe it is unfair or abusive. Monopolies may not attain their full sales potential if customer purchasing is restrained due to unfair price perception; this suggests that it is counterproductive to abuse pricing power.

Gain/loss

Customers are less sensitive to a price if they perceive it somehow reflects a gain. For example: if a customer is charged extra for paying with a credit card instead of cash, he will perceive a loss; however, if he is offered a discount for paying with cash, he perceives a gain, even though the disbursement may be exactly the same. Therefore, pricing negotiations must be presented to customers as gains instead of losses.

Purchasing frequency

Customers are more sensitive to a price change if the product is frequently purchased. Consumers are well aware of the prices of products they purchase on a daily basis; they are therefore very conscious of any change; in these products a price change needs to be justified very convincingly.

Product category

Customers are less sensitive to price in luxury items with high brand loyalty (low elasticity). They are more sensitive to price in basic necessities, where a price increase might easily prompt them to switch to another brand (high elasticity); medium elasticity may be found in products in which brand loyalty is neither too high nor too low, such as common home appliances (toasters, blenders, etc.).

Amazingly, price sensitivity also diminishes with advertising that alludes emotions such as friendship, beauty, love, tenderness, etc. This is significant because, in most cases, emotions rather than reason drive purchases. The product´s package plays a key role here. In contrast, if the goal is to advertise a low price, then a brief and concise message highlighting benefits such as savings, or purchasing more for less, will do the job.[31]

A price increase in luxury items may have little or no effect on their sales volume, since their elasticity may be relatively low; this is mainly because these goods usually represent a low percentage of an affluent segment´s income; and if brand loyalty is high, they may have few substitutes. A good example of this can be high-end perfumes, jewelry or cosmetics; the preferred brand offers a level of prestige difficult to substitute.

A price increase in low-priced essential goods may have a significant impact on their sales volume, as their elasticity can be relatively high. This is because these goods usually can be easily substituted; they may

---

[31] N. Braidot, *Neuro Marketing*, Ediciones Gestión 2000, 2009, p. 32.

have little differentiation; brand loyalty may be low; and they may represent a high percentage of the total income of a target segment with low purchasing power. A good example can be branded milk or eggs: if one brand increases its price, customers can substitute it for another one with a lower price.

In low-priced products with high elasticity, successive price increases, even while offering better benefits, may displace sales to higher market segments; although these may have a greater purchasing power, volume and frequency of purchase may become disproportionately lower.

In general, customers tend to be less sensitive (inelastic) to price changes when buyers:

- possess brand loyalty,
- believe that the product has few or no substitutes,
- are unaware of the price,
- are reluctant or slow to change their buying habits.
- think that high prices indicate high quality,
- believe that the product has a unique or many distinctive benefits and features,
- really need or desire the product,
- perceive a high ratio of benefits to price (Value).

This suggests that sellers should:

- be aware of the alternatives and substitutes available in the market,
- compare product benefits and prices with the competition,
- invest in advertising and promotion to increase demand and develop brand image and positioning,
- maintain quality and benefits above customers' expectations,
- develop highly differentiated products with significant competitive advantages,
- target specific customer segments,
- align the product's price with its benefits,

- use packaging creatively to differentiate products,
- justify, as much as possible, all price changes.

4.4 Optimum Price

Every product has a price such that if it is too high, sales volume (Q) is reduced; on the other hand, if it is too low, sales may be very high but they may not yield enough profit; in both cases, profits are lower than what they could be if the firm had an optimum price.

If a price decreases, the quantity demanded may increase, as long as there is an inverse relationship between quantity and price; this means that at a lower price a greater quantity is desired. For each price level (or market segment), high or low, a mechanism of supply and demand operates that yields an optimum price. This is true in high priced luxury goods, such as jewelry and cars, and also for low-priced essential goods.

The above can take place within the price range rationally expected by the target market, by virtue of the product´s positioning; outside this range, the customer´s response may be completely different.

As an example, a perfume with too low a price may lose its appeal for a woman: not only could she doubt its quality, but could also feel a negative effect on her self-esteem. If for any reason she were to buy it, her doubts would persist (cognitive dissonance); it is unlikely that customer loyalty can be achieved with such a low price.

If a price increases excessively, there is the risk of losing customers in the target market and sales volume may decrease; on the other hand, if the price is reduced by too much, profits will be too low and the product´s positioning may be adversely affected. This suggests that there is a price, which yields the highest sales and profits while maintaining consumer loyalty; otherwise, it would not be the best price.

For maximizing profits it is not necessary to reach a maximum sales volume (units) or a maximum price; what really counts is the most profitable combination of benefits, quantity and price. This may not even be related to efficient utilization of resources; they may even be underutilized. Moreover, depending on the type of product and market, it may even be possible to obtain more profits with a low volume and a high price than with a high volume and a low price.

A “wrong price” has the following characteristics:

- The benefits do not justify it.
- It does not match the product´s positioning.
- It aims at a segment different from the target segment.
- The amount or unit delivered (serving) has no logic in relation to other product presentations, or to other options available to customers.
- The purchasing frequency, or unit of sale, does not match the customers´ needs.
- It ignores the purchasing power of the target segment.
- The target customer may feel it is “unfair” if it is too high.
- The competition has better options in terms of benefits and price.
- Less than average turnover ("slow" sales), or lost sales within the target segment, are indicators of prices that may be too high (sub-optimal).
- In contrast, "excessive" inventory turnover with low profits may be indicative of a price that is too low (also sub-optimal).

Wrong prices reduce sales and profitability. Setting an optimal price ends up being a complex interplay between benefits, competition, resource availability and costs.

4.5 Pricing Policy

A pricing strategy requires a policy that governs pricing decisions; this is critical as a company can very easily to lose control over its prices. With the passage of time, vendors award discounts and special conditions to different customers, and quite often without adequate justification; eventually, employee turnover leads to confusion in the pricing structure.

The main elements of a Pricing Policy include:

Objectives[32]

A pricing policy must have a goal in line with the firm´s profitability target. Among possible objectives for prices, we may find:

- *Revenue and/or market share*: Aims at reaching a specific level of sales or target market share.
- *Income and profitability*: This is a clear target with firm numbers in terms of net income and profitability.
- *Social factors*: These may be especially low prices to serve some type of social objective; for example, subsidized medications, or housing for lower income groups.

Scope

It must be clearly established in what geographical areas and for what market segments the prices apply.

Discounts

Quite frequently, and for various reasons, discounts are offered. It must be clearly stated how they must be applied: justification and amount.

Method

The method used for setting prices must be defined: it determines under what circumstances they change and how to compute them.

Responsibility

Setting prices is a very critical task, which must be carried out by duly qualified personnel with proper empowerment and accountability.

---

[32] Carlos R. Sánchez S, "*Administración del Precio en Mercadotecnia*", Thomson, 2003, p. 28

Communication and Implementation

It must be clearly specified how prices are to be communicated and implemented. This refers to how, whom, when and where the price list applies.

Sales Terms

Sales transactions carry negotiation terms and conditions, such as delivery dates, payment form, warranty, etc.

Validity

A price list must include its effective and expiration dates (from... until*)*. Customers need to be aware that price lists are liable to change, with or without prior notice.

It should be remembered that a product´s positioning is clearly associated with its price, in particular because it is a sign of quality, status, or prestige.

A product must always be aimed at a specific market segment. Customer loyalty is lost if the price does not match the benefits expected by the target market.

4.6 Pricing Strategies

Prices and the methods commonly used to compute them can be classified into various categories, according to their purpose and objectives.

Supply and demand pricing

These apply in markets in which many sellers and buyers converge simultaneously; this is commonly known as "perfect competition", as described in section "1.2 Markets and the Economy"**.** All sellers respond to supply and demand by gradually adjusting their prices until a market price, which minimizes shortages and surpluses, is eventually set.

Each individual seller has little control over the market price; however, if he can somehow differentiate his product with added benefits, this may increase his sales and profits.

Competitive pricing

These prices are similar to those of the competition and are applied when there is little differentiation. They can be easily set by price comparisons and researching the market. These prices may also be aggressively low to deter or react to competitors´ threats. This method can be found in almost any market, except monopolies (no competition).

The set prices are similar to those of the competition because equivalent benefits are offered; that is, the same Value.

Cost-plus or profit-based pricing

Frequently prices are set based on product costs plus a preset profit target, as follows: Cost + expected Profit = Price. Cost should include all cost items that can be allocated to each individual unit.

This method is feasible under the following circumstances:

- The firm has a certain degree of control over prices in its surrounding market: Monopoly, oligopoly, monopolistic competition.
- Potential competition is not a significant or relevant issue.
- Customers do not have easy access to other purchasing alternatives.
- There is no benchmark price available in the surrounding market.
- Cost may be the only parameter at hand for setting a price.
- The target market has the purchasing power to pay the set price.
- The market potential is attractive.
- Customer loyalty is not a priority

Setting prices based only on costs is not optimal as it tends to ignore:

- Product benefits.
- Business environment.
- Product positioning.
- Brands.
- Competition.

- Product Life Cycle.
- The customer´s needs, characteristics, habits and preferences.

This pricing strategy is common in Transactional Marketing and in businesses subject to competitive bidding.

In contrast, when the product is offered in a market with little or no competition, the firm attempts to set the highest price that its market will "accept", although this can be very subjective. The price, as indicated in section "1.2 Markets and the Economy" cannot be too high or too low, otherwise the level of sales will be adversely affected.

Nevertheless, there must be sufficient benefits to justify the price charged; otherwise, the purchasing frequency will be too low, and the product will not have an optimal profitability.

Discount, liquidation or clearance pricing

This is a pricing strategy aimed at rewarding customers for: paying promptly or in advance; purchasing larger quantities; buying products that may be in the declining phase of their life cycles; or for stocking and reselling (dealers, wholesalers, and retailers).

Inventory has a carrying cost: it must be managed and controlled; this costs money, and additionally, it may have an opportunity cost, as there may be other investment alternatives with a greater profit potential. Discount or liquidation pricing facilitates reducing or clearing inventory over a short period; this means exchanging goods for cash to be reinvested in goods that are more profitable.

Discount pricing offers many advantages, for example:

Volume

Discounting the unit price entices buyers to purchase larger quantities; this benefits the firm as it executes a larger sale in just one transaction, and buyers in turn may also reap substantial savings on each unit purchased.

Prompt payment

Collecting cash promptly offers the firm the advantage of being able to anticipate its investments and thereby obtain profits faster. The savings achieved, in turn, reward the customer.

Trade discounts

These are price discounts extended to intermediaries such as dealers, wholesalers and retailers, to encourage them to stock and resell products with an attractive profit (the discount). The firm benefits from the expansion of its distribution network as this clearly increases its sales potential.

The intermediaries have the option to sell at the suggested list price provided by the manufacturer, or to add some extra profit into the selling price; this may be necessary as they carry high fixed costs such as rent and administration. In addition to this they provide added benefits for their suppliers and customers; for example, stocking and distributing a wide variety of products, advertising, extended warranties, record-keeping, personal selling, credit, customer relationship management (CRM), etc.

Promotions

Promotions are temporary incentives whose purpose is to boost sales by prompting a quick customer response; they often include discounts, prizes, samples, rebates, gifts, coupons, contests, raffles, etc.

Discounts

Discounts are types of sales promotions that are not actual price changes; the price itself remains the same and its positioning should remain unchanged. In general, a discount should be extended as a bonus in exchange for something the customer will give up at some point in time; he may sacrifice liquidity by paying in advance, or by purchasing a larger quantity. An unjustified discount should be avoided, as it can make the customer leery.

Survival pricing

This is a cost-based pricing method in which prices are low enough to just barely absorb variable and fixed costs, with very little or no profit. In general, it facilitates liquidating slow or dead inventory, and takes place with products that are in decline due to obsolescence, fashion, season, etc.

Generally the product is being replaced by another one preferred by the market, or it is in the declining phase of its life cycle and is being phased out. This method can be applied in any type of company or business.

The low price plays a key role: it increases Value and thereby prompts the customer to purchase the product.

Stability pricing

This mainly refers to products in the "business to business" (B2B) markets, in which pricing stability is paramount and requested by the buyer. "Stability" indicates that the supplier must not make sudden price changes, or changes without prior notice or acceptance by the buyer. Any change must be very well justified and informed well in advance. It may well be the case that the supplier´s profit is set by the buyer.

The prices set by the suppliers of large industries must be stable given that they request it, because they purchase very large quantities of supplies, parts, accessories, etc. A small price change can have a severe impact on their total costs. In general, these industries maintain strict cost controls.

This type of pricing applies in sales to monopolies, or large oligopolies in highly concentrated and capital-intensive markets in which one or very few companies dominate a particular industry. Government contractors may be a good example.

Any price change needs to be well justified in terms of benefits or cost increases.

Price discrimination

This is a pricing strategy aimed at maximizing revenue and increasing market share by charging different prices for the same product; this responds to marketing reasons and does not depend upon costs. Several discrimination criteria exist:

- *Age group*: Different prices are charged depending upon the age range of customers. Not all age groups have the same purchasing power, therefore charging each group according to his paying capacity enables the firm to reach a wider segment customer target. Movie theaters may have prices that depend on the age group of the customers.
- *Activity*: Prices are charged according to the activity of the customers. For example, students generally have low paying capacity; therefore, a special price for students allows the firm to reach this customer segment; museums generally offer this option.

- *Time*: Prices may vary depending upon the time of the day; maximum prices at peak hours; low prices in off-peak hours.
- *Type of user*: Generally, it may refer to domestic or industrial users; this is common in telephone or Internet services.
- *Supply and demand*: Prices are charged depending upon the level of demand. For example, the same product may cost more as Christmas approaches; car rentals are more expensive during weekends; airplane tickets purchased in advance are cheaper, etc.

Price discrimination is possible when:

- The market can be segmented.
- The different segments respond differently to the prices charged.
- The individual segments can be served separately.
- Customer arbitrage (buying at a low price and reselling at a higher price) is not possible.
- The firm has some degree of price leadership in its surrounding market.
- Revenue and profits can increase by virtue of the price discrimination.

This type of pricing increases revenue and profits as it captures many more market segments, and is able to benefit from different opportunities.

Penetration pricing

This strategy is used to rapidly enter a new market by offering high Value using low prices; the profits thereby obtained depend more from sales volume than price.

This strategy is useful when[33]:

- Achieving a high market share in a short period is a priority.
- Discouraging the competition is desired.
- A potential threat of competitors exists.
- The market has high price elasticity.
- The firm has a clear cost advantage against competitors.
- The high sales volume facilitates negotiating lower prices with suppliers, thereby reducing costs.
- The market is sufficiently large to absorb the high sales volume.
- The product may have little differentiation, or can be easily copied and sold.
- Arbitrage (buying and reselling elsewhere) is not possible.

Price Skimming

This is a strategy for entering a new market offering high Value with high benefits, but with high prices; the profits thereby obtained depend more from price than sales volume. High prices are feasible only if the product carries great benefits and has clear advantages against the competition.

This strategy seeks to ¨skim" the market by charging initial buyers a premium price for the privilege of being "exclusive" with the new product; it helps create an image of high quality, status, and prestige; however, it has the inconvenience that high profits attract new competitors to the market, and therefore tends to be a short-term strategy. It is quite common in the technology industry (computers, TV´s, cell phones, etc.).

---

[33] Carlos Raúl Sánchez Sánchez, "Administración *del Precio en Mercadotecnia*", Thomson, 2003, p. 129

As the product advances through its life cycle, competitors begin to enter the market and this leads to a gradual decrease of the price to maintain the product competitive.

This strategy is useful when[34]:

- Launching a new product into a new market with the aim of maximizing profit in the shortest possible time; this is necessary due to the risk of obsolescence, and for recouping quickly the product´s research and development costs.
- The strategy requires projecting an image of high quality, status and prestige.
- There is high certainty that the market will respond positively to the high benefits and prices.
- The firm has a fair degree of control over the surrounding market`s prices.
- The market has relatively low price elasticity, and its potential is high due to its size and customer purchasing power.
- Patent or license protection provides a legal barrier to ward off competitors.
- There is no significant competition; otherwise entering with high prices can be very difficult.
- Enough financial capacity exists to invest in advertising and promotion.

Captive product pricing

Some products require the use of auxiliary o "captive" products. Examples: printers sold at low prices with high priced printing cartridges; low priced shavers with high priced blade replacements. In these cases, the strategy is to compete aggressively with low prices on the primary or core product and recoup the profit with the captive

---

[34] Ibid.

products or accessories. This pricing strategy creates a forced brand loyalty.

The core product is a high Value item due to its low price. The captive product can be sold with a high price because of the high Value attached to the core product. It must be noted that the price of the core and captive product are not independent of one another: if the price of the captive product is too high it will adversely affect the sales of the core product, and may not reach the sales volume necessary to make a profit. The bait is the low price of the primary product; therefore, if it is too high the number of customers attracted will be too low.

A key issue to be considered is how long the customer will keep the core product, as this will determine the number of times that the captive product is purchased. A minimum number of purchases is required from the captive to product to offset the loss on the core product; after this breakeven point has been reached, the core/captive combination begins to be profitable.

Product-bundle Pricing

Frequently different products are combined into one unit (bundle) with a single price, which may be lower, higher, or the same as the sum of the prices of its individual components. This strategy is used with products that are regularly purchased simultaneously.

Consumers may be lured due to the potential savings, or because the bundle is very useful and attractive. A bundle can add to product variety, as it can be perceived as a product by itself. The most common examples are the "combos" in fast food restaurants, tool kits, toys, travel packages, communication services, etc.

Bundles offer several advantages:

- Speed-up customer service by saving decision-making and processing time.
- Offer the opportunity to sell several products at a lower price.
- Increase inventory turnover and revenue.
- Combinations of products can be marketed as single products.
- Increase sales of slow-moving inventory when bundled with high-turnover products.

Bundles with low sales prices increase sales quantity because customers can determine individual prices and easily compute the potential savings; this is equivalent to a discount on its individual components and rewards customers for purchasing a larger quantity.

Bundles may also be sold at prices higher than those of the individual components. If the product combination makes the bundle look attractive and can satisfy several needs simultaneously, then its price may be higher than the sum of its individual components.

A good example is home or office supplies bundled together in small packages, such as nails, rubber bands, clips, screws, etc. There is no question that this bundle is certainly more expensive than its individual components. Even if customers realize this, they do not mind, as it is convenient anyway; it has Value for them and increases profits. Bundling different products into one package to create attractive gifts is quite common.

This example can be extended to many other products and services; the trick lies in creating imaginative bundles with ingenious merchandizing that entice customers to purchase.

This pricing strategy can be used in many widely differing products, services and situations. Examples exist in tourism, hotels, restaurants, bars, airlines, beauty parlors, health clubs, automotive services, shopping malls, etc.

Block pricing

Every sale carries transaction costs such as salesperson time, invoicing, logistics, etc. Block pricing is similar to product-bundle pricing, except that the bundle is composed of several identical products, such as a six-pack of beer. The price of the block is less than the sum of its individual components. Its distinct advantage for the seller is that his sales increase, while saving costs: more units are sold in a single transaction.

The seller is, in effect, transferring his savings to the buyer, who, in turn, purchases more than what his buying frequency requires; he obtains savings, and even decreases his own logistical costs, as he will make fewer trips to the liquor store.

The price charged should be lower than that of the same quantity of individual products; this entices the consumer to make the block purchase.

In terms of Value, this means that for some customers the benefit to price relationship is sufficiently high to justify the purchase.

Geographic pricing

Companies may sometimes need to sell in different regions with different price levels, for various reasons:

- The product`s price needs to be competitive wherever it is sold.
- Customer habits, preferences, and purchasing power may vary in different locations.
- Demand may vary geographically, depending upon climate.
- There are other charges have to be absorbed in the sale price; for example, transportation, insurance, taxes, warehousing, packaging, etc.
- Cost structure: the same product may need to be manufactured in different locations in order to be competitive; for example, soft drinks require water, therefore they need to be bottled where it is available, and transported to their respective markets; this leads to cost differentials.

This type of pricing can take place domestically or abroad; it is of special significance to multinational corporations, as profit margins may widely differ, depending upon each market`s country, region or location.

"Creative" pricing

When a product is too expensive, setting an individual price not practical, but, there are other options available; for example:

- Renting or leasing instead of selling. This approach may be needed when it is not profitable to purchase the product; photocopiers are frequently rented or leased due to their high cost.
- Set a price for products or services shared by several customers. Time-share ownership is commonly used for vacation condominium property with rights to use it on specific dates; the cost is divided amongst several owners.
- Offer prices with trade-in or barter options. A customer may want to replace a product, but without discarding it, as it may have some value; however, finding a buyer may be difficult. In order to sell him

the new product, retailers may offer to trade-in the old one, or buy it for a low price, or reward the customer with a discount on the new one; this attracts customers and develops their loyalty as it keeps them returning. This is common with cars, printers, radios, television, appliances, furniture etc.

In essence, creative pricing increases Value by offering more favorable pricing options.

Psychological pricing

This pricing strategy focuses on buyer's perceptions and emotions rather than reason. For example, a price such as $ 9.99 instead of $ 10.00 may seem less costly; although the difference is in effect insignificant, customers prefer to pay $ 9.99. We read from left to right, so we tend to focus more on the first digits.

Visual effects can also be powerful: customers perceive 10 more favorably than $ 10.00.

Time is a limited non-replaceable resource; therefore, people respond favorably to time constraints. Numerous examples can be observed using time to spur demand and entice customers to purchase: for example, “the first 100 callers will receive a special price”, or “only today 50% off”, “call now”. A sense of urgency can also be created: “discounts 30% today, 20% tomorrow”, etc.

Simple arithmetic can also play with perception: “Buy one and get one free” seems much more attractive than a 50% discount, although they are equivalent. Just the idea of getting anything "free" seems quite attractive.

A discount of $10 on a $100 item seems easier to understand than 10% (math complication). However, a “high” discount of 50% seems better than a small number such as 5 in 10 as 50% seems a bigger number than $5.

Human psychology provides a universe of almost limitless possibilities for pricing options.

Value-based Pricing

The different pricing methods illustrate an important point: all the methods eventually lead the seller to justify prices with benefits, and to compare with the alternatives available to their customers, otherwise their revenue is negatively affected.

Value-based pricing is market-driven pricing; the goal is to provide the best benefits to price ratio for satisfying customers' needs with profitable products. This pricing strategy is applied en relationship marketing, and is developed further in section "7.8 Value-based pricing".

4.7 Services´ Pricing

Services can be very profitable products and they provide a powerful competitive advantage. Although they add value to the core business, pricing them is inherently more complex than pricing tangible products; this is precisely due to their *intangibility*; the customer cannot see, or even foresee, what he will receive in exchange for his money. He is therefore faced with uncertainty; this is the main obstacle the marketer must overcome; he needs to instill trust in his customer; this must be his goal, and his strategy must be aimed towards achieving it.

The intangibility of services has several consequences on prices: first-time users can have great difficulty understanding what they will get for their money. If the amount, or quantity, of tangible product sold concurrently with the service is low, the more customer-specific will be the price and the less standardized it will be.

Intangibility leads to another important distinction between services and tangible products: they cannot be stocked for sale or future consumption. Services are short-lived: There is a relatively short time span between their production and their consumption; in fact, it may even be simultaneous; upon consumption, they perish; they no longer exist.

Services are frequently sold prior to their production; this leads to the concept of *temporality*; services are inextricably tied to time in their production, consumption and payment.

The issue of temporality merits further discussion: Although a service cannot be stored in the physical sense of the word, it can indeed be stored, but as a source of *time*. For example, when a nightclub cannot serve any more customers at peak hour, this is simply because it runs out of the time available from its employees. It could make some extra time available by hiring temporary workers at peak hours; this increases its time inventory. These fluctuations between supply and demand have a direct effect on pricing.

An alternative option could be to restrict the consumption of time by raising prices ("cover" charge) at peak hours; this instantly increases sales and profits. At off-peak hours there is excess time inventory (idle employees, slow sales); to increase service turnover (number of services delivered per unit time), production and consumption must be stimulated; this is achieved by lowering the price ("happy hour"), and this also increases sales and profits. Airlines and hotels do something similar by varying seasonal prices.

The fluctuations between supply and demand are usually handled by:

- Prices: to level or smooth the peaks and off-peaks of the seasons or cycles.
- Time: to plan business activities.
- People: to anticipate their availability and use of time.
- Increasing the availability of limited resources (personnel, equipment, and space).

This leads a potential customer to foresee two future undesirable possibilities: either the service will be unavailable, or it will be more expensive if it is still available. The risk of unavailability is clearly unacceptable, and even having to pay more should also be avoided; therefore, he will prefer to make a reservation and pay in advance if necessary; this guarantees he will receive the service and it will also cost him less.

In other words, he is willing pay for something that, at that point in time, does not even exist; the service has not yet been produced. This instills many doubts and fears: Will the service be available? Will it be up to his expectations?

The service supplier also faces risks: Will he have the capacity to service all customers, or will he be constrained by his time or capacity limitations? What will happen if some customers do not show up? Are his prices adequate to compensate the risks? How will his competitors cope and react to these situations? Clearly, these uncertainties can lead to potential for conflict; this gives rise to many ways in which service markets structure themselves and set prices. Each vendor has its own specific pricing criteria, according to the type of product, customer, market and perceived risks.

In general, services can be classified for purposes of pricing as subject to:

- Two-part tariff pricing.
- Competitive pricing: monopolistic or "perfect" competition.
- Differential pricing by customer type: "what the market will bear"
- Cost-plus pricing: cost + expected profit.
- Value-based pricing: prices based on benefits.
- Formal self-regulation: professional associations, trade unions, guilds.
- Official prices: set by the government or legal authorities.

Let us analyze each pricing system.

Two-part tariff pricing

This is a pricing system mainly used when providing services: it involves a fixed and a variable component in the price charged.

The fixed component is an access fee (lump sum) charged at the outset that basically absorbs some fixed cost of the service. Examples include club memberships, credit card charges, cover charges in restaurants and bars, entrance fees at amusement parks, movie theaters, car rentals, utilities, hotels, etc.

The variable component is a usage fee that depends upon consumption, such as telephone use, number of rides, food and beverage, mileage, etc.

This pricing strategy is most commonly practiced when:

- The purchasing experience is more important than the individual product or service. For example: the customer at the bar is not just paying for drinks; he seeks pleasure from the purchasing experience itself; he is willing to pay the cover charge for the ambience, location, status, prestige, entertainment and service offered. If he were only interested in drinks, he could get them at the corner store, and at a much lower price.

- The target segment has a sufficiently large customer base with the necessary disposable income and buying frequency to make the service profitable.
- Customers are willing to pay an above-market price when their alternatives are limited and their demand is sufficiently strong.
- The firm has a relatively high degree of market leadership in its surrounding area.
- There is uncertainty as to the level of consumption or usage (for example, mileage); therefore, the fixed fee replaces the minimum level of consumption necessary to absorb some fixed costs.
- Profits are greater than with only lump-sum fees, or consumption charges.
- The seller has the power to control access to the service; a rather graphic example is the bouncer at a nightclub; another example is the cost of a club membership.

The fixed price must be computed to insure that the seller´s limiting or constraining resource is used to its full capacity; this means that the number of transactions, or customers served, is close to the maximum that the seller can handle.

The movie industry provides many good examples for analyzing this subject; the lessons are also applicable to other service businesses.

In a movie theater, the limiting resource is seating capacity; therefore, the benefit to price ratio (Value) must be high enough to guarantee nearly 100% occupancy. Given the benefits offered, if the price is too high, occupancy is low (customers lost), and if the price is too low, there will be many customers left unattended; both instances lead to foregone sales and earnings (opportunity costs). In other words, the fixed charge must be such that supply (available seats per show) exactly matches demand (moviegoers).

If this were not true, then the theater should have fewer seats; but then again, achieving 100% occupancy would still be desired. Moreover, the theater needs enough seating capacity to accommodate its average number of spectators, and still be able to handle occasional peak activity; it also needs some slack for future growth.

It is paramount to understand what drives customers to purchase the service offered. Examples:

- Do they want a privilege (VIP) that will make them stand out in their social circle?
- Status? Entertainment? A specific product? Socializing?
- Is the price itself the screening mechanism customers want to project their prestige?

An interesting question arises: Do health club members really want to exercise, or do they have an ulterior motive, such as socializing for example? The answer gives a clue as to how the club should price its service, and what services to offer. If they really want to spend time socializing, then the club must have areas adequate for enjoying the company of others, and should charge fees related to the time spent at the club; on the other hand, if the main concern is health, then charges should focus on equipment usage and personal trainers. The moral of the story would be: *know thy target customer.*

In physics the uncertainty principle in states that we can never measure anything with certainty because measurement, or the observation itself, alters the results. Uncertainty certainly has its place in marketing. Let us analyze an occupancy example from this perspective.

It would appear that to achieve a 100% occupancy all that is needed is to match supply and demand with the proper price. However, the very act of setting the price may change customer response: if the issue is with a movie theatre, it would seem that to reach full capacity with a bad film all that is needed is to set a sufficiently low ticket price. This is where uncertainty comes in: just by doing this, customer response is changed. If the public anticipates a bad film due to its low price, then this by itself is enough to change the expected result: attendance will be very low, and lowering the price would be pointless. Any clue customers receive that may hint lower quality changes the expected result.

Another example is an all-you-can-eat restaurant where the customer pays only the access fee and can eat as much as he wants. He already has an average consumption pattern, but, just by feeling that he can somehow "beat the system", his pattern changes: he wants more; and the more he is charged the more he wants! It becomes an uncertain self-feeding vicious circle. A reasonable price for reasonable consumption will not do: the customer will eat until satiety, and, of course, he will be priced accordingly. This pressures prices upward, thereby defeating the purpose of increasing customer traffic.

Alternatively, the restaurant could offer another extreme option: charge up front the expected profit (access fee) and then bill the consumption at cost; this would appear to attract many customers, as consumption would cost relatively little. The problem with this approach is that the consumption patterns of the customers may differ widely, and they would also change by virtue of the billing method; again, this adds uncertainty to the outcome, thereby pushing up prices to compensate for the added risk.

In many cases, prices can be charged without adding uncertainty, or risk, to the outcome; for example, hotels can offer low-season pricing, as customers do not perceive any problem; in fact, they respond positively to such lower prices. The key to two-part pricing lies in the product-bundling skills of hotels: their well-known "package deals" provide a good example. This significant marketing accomplishment can be applied in many other service industries.

This bundling concept is useful in two-part pricing because people seek entertainment, perhaps even more than the films themselves; therefore, the goal is to offer a memorable purchasing experience; this is applicable to the sale of almost any product or service.

We see coffee and sushi bars inside theaters; these all add to the experience; it just needs to be enhanced further. Certainly there is more to be offered, and with it comes the price… plus the extra profit.

If the purchasing experience is sufficiently attractive, it overshadows the product itself: people attend for the pleasure of the entertainment; this becomes the main product.

The variable fee has an interesting key psychological element: the customer feels that since he is in full control of his consumption, his total average cost will be less. This means that once he has paid his entrance fee, he may abstain from further spending, or only spend as much as he wants. He believes that his overall spending (admission plus consumption) will be low because *he* has the control; ironically, nothing could be further from reality.

The aim of the service supplier, or seller, is precisely to customize his service and design a pricing strategy that maximizes consumption. If the variable fee is too high, many target customers will abstain, or purchase less. If it is too low, many customers may go unattended, or profits will be too low. Either way, consumption is not maximized and earnings are foregone; therefore, the variable fee must approximate a price that the customer feels is "fair enough" (justified by benefits); otherwise, his emotional reaction from feeling abused will induce him to reduce his purchasing, and therefore consumption is sub-optimal.

In section "4.4 Optimum Price", the issue of optimal price was discussed: the variable fee must have a value that lies somewhere within the price range rationally expected by the target market; an abusive or "unfair" price is certainly outside this range.

The target segment very likely has a downward-sloping demand curve (quantity inversely proportional to price); this means that an optimum price exists (refer to Appendix 1. Optimization of the Demand Function). Market research and customer surveys may provide simple and inexpensive methods to establish reasonable price ranges. The Value Matrix (Chapter 8) may also be helpful.

The fixed and variable fees are not independent of one another because their sum is what the customer perceives as the total fee charged. This means that the variable fee is influenced to some extent by the fixed fee. If the fixed fee is high then the variable fee must be comparatively low and vice versa.

If the variable fee is perceived by the customer as "fair", that is, it is well justified by the purchasing experience, then the fixed fee can be adjusted to balance supply with demand, and thereby achieve a high occupancy rate. If the seller wants to improve his variable fee profit margin, then he needs to add more benefits to justify a higher price.

Competitive pricing

In perfect and in monopolistic competition, prices are subject to forces such as: economic conditions (inflation, interest, employment, etc.); price elasticity; degree of competition; substitute products; seasons, cycles, trends, etc.; market segmentation; level of demand or urge to obtain the service; buyer profile, habits and preferences; interferences affecting prices; barriers to enter or exit the business, among others.

Under perfect competition, no seller has the individual capacity to influence prices; however, they can influence buyers´ preferences by virtue of the services they provide. Although "perfect" competition hardly exists as such, there are services in markets where individual sellers do not have the ability to influence prices due to the intense competition; such is the case of many online sales, companies trading in commodities, currencies and stocks, among others.

In contrast, under monopolistic competition sellers do have the capacity to influence prices in their surrounding market, mainly due to the benefits they offer. Most services fall under this type of competition: accounting and law firms, medical services, consulting, education, etc.

Differential pricing by customer type

These are the maximum prices that the firm feels it can charge their customers; they are "what the market will bear". The sellers frequently have no clear idea, or basis, for charging their customers a given price, and their customers, in turn, do not really know how much they are willing to pay. The capacity to use differential pricing tactics depends on whether the market can be segmented based on price, or customer paying capacity.

The customer cannot easily compare the prices of different service suppliers given their intangibility and the particularities that each one may have. Given this uncertainty, the service supplier is inclined to overcharge the customer; in other words, charge the maximum that he will bear. However, the possibility exists that the client might take his business elsewhere; therefore, the service supplier may not only lose some customers, but, in his attempt to avoid this, he may end up undercharging others.

There is also the added risk that differential pricing may lead to frictions with customers as they may communicate amongst themselves. This points to the fact that by applying standard rates many pitfalls can be avoided.

Cost-plus Pricing

Under this particular method, prices are aimed at obtaining a specific profit on each unit sold: price or rate = cost + expected profit.

This practice is very common in services and tangible products. It can be very useful when there are no parameters for comparison. Trade or professional associations tend to set prices using this method. Prices relate to the minimum gain expected by the service supplier (lawyers, dentists, etc.).

Value-based pricing: prices based on benefits.

This is the most competitive pricing method: Prices are directly related to the benefits offered, such as brand, experience, tradition, skill, quality, level of competition, etc. The rates set are compared with those of substitute services offered by the competition. Prices are also related to the capacity and willingness of the client to pay for the particular service.

Formal self-regulation

Professional associations, trade unions, or guilds set prices. They are regulated by institutional arrangements; they depend on an appropriate regulatory body with the power and acceptance to set prices or rates; this power exists only as its members value the benefits of the association. It seeks to avoid "unfair" competition, or even price wars. Examples of such prices are those set by agreements of professional trade associations such as architects, dentists, doctors, etc.

Official prices

These are prices that are sometimes set by the government; this intervention occurs when the government needs to protect the interests of groups that may be in adversity (usually low income). Public education, health and transport may be instances in which the price is regulated officially; the government is thereby able to implement its policy, regularly with subsidized prices.

Pricing in social services

Such prices are used in non-profit organizations where the goal is not profit maximization; instead, they seek to achieve a level of earnings that absorbs variable and fixed costs, while obtaining a minimum surplus to fund future growth and development.

Not only are there different forms of pricing in services; there are also different ways to collect payment:

- The price charged may be related to the time it takes to deliver the service: hourly, daily, per unit, etc.
- There may also be a "flat" or fixed rate that has been agreed upon from the start, and regardless of its duration, or the number of times requested, it does not change.
- This flat rate is determined by applying a previously calculated rate to the time required to complete the service, and taking into account its frequency of use.
- If the seller takes less time than expected, his gain is higher; if he takes more time, his gain is lower.
- Charging in advance is common in those services where there is risk of default by the seller, or even by the customer.

The guiding principles of pricing services have some similarities with those used in tangible goods. The main forces that commonly influence the prices of services include costs (variable and fixed); competition (affecting customer preferences); demand for the service (need or urgency); the benefits offered by the service; the quality perceived by the customers, and the brand´s value, among others.

When setting pricing goals for services several factors must be considered.

Lifecycle stage of the service

The price of the service is directly related to its life cycle; it can be set low (penetration) to rapidly achieve market share. In general, this strategy is recommended when the brand is not well known; the product or service faces competition; and projecting an image of prestige is not an immediate priority. As the brand acquires value prices may gradually be increased.

Market entry can be achieved with high prices (skimming) if the brand is already well known; if it is a radically new service; competition is not imminent, and an image of prestige is desired from the outset. In the future, as the impact of novelty decreases, and competition sets in, this changes customer preferences and creates forces that lead to lower prices.

Elasticity of demand

The flexibility a firm has to set the price of its products and services is limited by their price elasticity of demand. An organization should know if the demand for its services is elastic or inelastic, in order to price them properly. Services have the fortunate advantage that they tend to be more inelastic than tangible products; that is, they are generally less sensitive to price changes.

Services are more responsive to changes in benefits rather than prices; this means that their perceived Value (benefits to price relationship) depends more on benefits than on prices. A service with a high Value is a powerful competitive advantage that can boost sales, market share and profits.

The added advantage is that services are relatively difficult to copy as competitors, very likely, ignore key issues used by a firm such as the employee selection process, training, compensation, motivation, and general administration.

The more exclusive a service is, the greater the vendor´s flexibility for pricing and the less sensitive customers are to price levels or changes. It is also possible that a high price in a service can be interpreted as a signal of quality. Although the idea may be somewhat subjective, this consideration adds another element of inelasticity to services; in fact, charging a higher price for a service can even boost its sales, as the public may think that by virtue of the high price the service is necessarily better, even if it is not.

The demand for a service tends to be inelastic (low sensitivity) when:

- There are few substitutes or competing services.
- There is an established official or trade union fee.
- Buyers believe that higher prices are justified by quality, experience, knowledge, etc.
- The brand or name of the service supplier is widely recognized and respected.
- The sacrifice needed to change the service supplier is high.
- We rely on personal sources to locate the supplier of a particular service.

Competitive situation

The firm´s market share and the strength of its competitors influence its pricing.

- When there is little differentiation between services, and competition is intense, the flexibility for setting prices is limited.
- This leads to similar prices amongst competitors.
- When the market share of the company is low in a very competitive market, its pricing power may be very limited.
- There is always the risk of "unfair" competition with rates close to or below cost.
- Tradition and habits influence prices: Luring customers away from the competition is a truly challenging task.

Pricing policies

The pricing policy has a strategic role in order to achieve the goals of the firm (commercial or financial). Thus, the pricing decision for a particular service must meet its strategic objectives. Any pricing strategy must fit within the overall marketing strategy (4P marketing mix).

Revenue, costs and profits

Cost-volume profit analysis for services resembles that of tangible products; the main difference, however, lies in service constraints imposed by time limitations. In services the "raw material" is time. The "inventory" of time is directly related to the number of people available, and the number of possible services in a given amount of time.

Sales, or revenue, from services arises from the number of services performed and the fee charged for each service provided. The number of services delivered are related to the number of services that a person can perform in a given time and the number of people providing it.

Variable costs in services:

1) Time-related costs.

a) Production costs: This is the cost of the time spent in the production or execution of the service; it includes costs related to payroll, or labor expenses such as salaries and other similar fees directly involved in the delivery of the service; if the service can be provided in less time its cost is therefore reduced.

b) Searching costs: This relates to the cost of the time spent in identifying, selecting and developing the type of service that the customer wants.

2) Physical costs: These are out-of-pocket expenses related to the direct effort required to provide the service such as transportation, communications, stationery, materials, etc.

Fixed costs are those that are not directly involved in the delivery of the service, such as management salaries, rent, utilities, etc.

Sales and profits

Service revenue = number of services rendered x rate

Number of services rendered = # Individuals x # Services / Individual

If R = service fee, Vc = variable cost, N = maximum volume or number of services rendered and Fc = fixed costs, then the operating profit is

$Op = N \times (R - Vc) - Fc$, where

Unit contribution margin $Cm = R - Vc$, and

Total contribution margin, $TCm = N \times (R - Vc)$, therefore

$Op = TCm - Fc$

Total contribution margin (TCm) is the real "engine" for creating profits in an enterprise.

The breakeven point occurs where the Op = 0, then

$0 = N \times (R - Vc) - Fc$

Solving N at breakeven (be)

$Nbe = Fc / (R - Vc)$

$Nbe = Fc / Cm$

In other words,

Nbe = Fixed Costs / Unit service margin, where the service margin (Cm) is the rate minus the variable costs associated with it (transportation, fees, billing, etc.).

If the expected profit that the service provider wishes to make Op (his "income"), the rate must charge can be found by solving for R in Op = N x (R – Vc) – Fc, thus:

R = (Op + N x Vc + Fc) / N

Example 1: A software company wishes to make $ 10,000/month in income from engineering technical service. The company has 5 engineers and each one regularly carries out an average of 2 calls per day for 20 days each month. The variable costs for each call (excluding the salaries of the engineers) is $ 15 per call. The fixed costs of the company (excluding the salaries of engineers) are $ 20,000/month. Each engineer's salary is $ 4,000/month. Question: What should be the minimum fee per call?

If the engineers can make 2 x 20 = 40 calls per month, the total number of monthly calls made by the engineering team is N = 5 x 40 = 200 calls/month. The engineering cost per call is $ 4,000 / 40 = $ 100.

The variable cost per call is Vc = 15 + 100 = $ 115

Substituting values in R = (Op + N x Vc + Fc) / N we obtain

R = (10,000 + 200 x 115 + 20.000) / 200

R = $ 265 per call

Proof:

10,000 = N x (R – Vc) – Fc, substituting values

10,000 = 200 x (265 – 115) – 20,000

10,000 = 10,000

Example 2: A law firm wishes to make a $ 250,000/month profit from its lawyers´ legal services. The firm has five attorneys and each one regularly serves its customers an average of 6 hours daily for 20 days per month (120 hours).

In this case, variable costs are not considered, or their cost is negligible and they can be included within fixed costs. The fixed costs of the firm are $ 20,000/month, excluding attorneys´ salaries. Each attorney expects a profit of $ 5,000/month. Question: What should be the minimum hourly fee charged to each customer?

If each lawyer spends 120 hours each month in customer calls, then the total number of hours is 120 x 5 = 600 hours.

Substituting values in R = (Op + Fc) / N we obtain

R = (250,000 + 20,000) / 600

R = $ 450/hr.

Proof:

250,000 = N x (R – Vc) – Fc, substituting values

250,000 = 600 x (450) - 20,000

250,000 = $ 250,000

Example 3: A service technician wishes to obtain an income of $ 3,000 / month. He makes an average of 6 calls per day to customers for 20 days a month (6 x 20 = 120 calls per month). His fixed costs are $ 1,200 / month (rent and utilities), and his estimated variable costs are $ 15 per visit (transportation and supplies). What should be his minimum rate per call?

R = (Op + N x Vc + Fc) / N, replacing values

R = (3,000 + 120 x 15 + 1.200) / 120

R = $ 50 per call.

Proof:

$ 3,000 = 120 (50-15) - 1,200

$ 3,000 = $ 3,000

4.8 Sales Velocity

Selling faster means selling more in the same period; this increases profits. "Sales Velocity" and "Sales" have exactly the same meaning; the emphasis is in taking the *time* factor into account, which is why it is necessary to highlight the word "*velocity*". Firms earn profits as a function of time: per year, month, day, or hour; similar to the concept of speed in a vehicle[35]. If money does not flow with the maximum possible velocity, profitability will be lower than what it could be.

It should be noted that financial statements only show what actually happened (history); but, they do not show what results could have been if different decisions had been made, as lost sales and profits don´t show up. This makes understanding the concept of sales velocity all the more important.

“Velocity” is a term that can be applied to a “*flow*”. A flow is measured between two points in time. Examples: “How much was sold between January 15 and February 15?”, “What was the cost of goods sold last year?”, and “How much is the monthly rent?” This means sales and costs are flows measured between two points in time.

The universal constraint is time: It is the only resource that can never be bought nor expanded; again, this emphasizes the importance of sales velocity. In other words, not only is it necessary to sell: Success is about doing it faster than the competition.

Value is the key determinant of sales velocity; superior Value contributes towards increasing sales velocity.

Sales velocity (S) can be expressed as:

Number of customers (Nc), multiplied by the

Quantity sold in each transaction (Qt), multiplied

Number of products offered (Np), multiplied by the

Purchasing frequency (Pf), multiplied by the

---

35 Eliyahu M. Goldratt, J. Cox, “*The Goal*”, North River Press. 1992, p. 74

Average price of products (P)

In algebraic notation: S = Nc x Qt x Np x Pf x P

Increasing any of these factors increases the sales of the company. This formula does not necessarily call for a numerical result: it is an orientation model. Suffice it to understand that these five factors determine sales velocity. If a numerical result were to be provided, then S has only one: the firm's sales, measured in currency terms per unit time (annual, monthly, or daily).

Following are some examples of strategic possibilities for each one of these factors.

1. Number of customers (Nc)

Focus: Market customers (aggregate demand)

Objective: Acquire new customers and retain existing ones.

- Proper market segmentation in order to focus marketing and sales resources to current and potential customers.
- Positioning must be aligned with the target market and convey a message that highlights the product´s differentiation and/or its competitive advantages.
- Develop new market segments (other types of customers).
- Reach out to new areas or regions.
- Develop new sales and distribution channels.
- Expand the distribution and sales network.
- Promote events, trade shows, conventions and sponsorships.
- Provide education and courses; for example, cooking in supermarkets, or carpentry in hardware stores for potential customers.
- Advertising geared towards attracting new customers and those of the competition.
- Emphasize competitive advantages.
- Institutional propaganda to stimulate demand and encourage consumption.

2. Quantity Sold (Qt)

Focus: target market (customers)

Objective: Increase the amount sold in each transaction.

- Clearly identify customer needs, habits and profile.
- Know very well the products and services of competitors.
- The products offered must satisfy the customers' needs.
- Packaging should be designed according to the needs and preferences of customers.
- Reposition the brand (new "life", tagline, logo, core message, etc.)
- Promote new uses and applications.
- Boost sales with promotional strategies.
- Offer volume discounts for purchases.
- Offer additional benefits.
- The quantity (Qt) sold in each transaction must be aligned with purchasing frequency (Pf), depending upon the customers' buying patterns.

3. Number of Products (Np)

Focus: The Firm

Objective: Increase and extend product lines.

- Products "improved" with new designs.
- Diversify with new products and/or brands.
- This has a favorable effect on the reduction of business risk.
- Create new products by combining existing ones.
- Offer products that *complement* those offered by competitors.
- Offer additional options of quality.
- Provide new services or add service to existing products.
- Extend the use of the brand to other products.

- Expand production capacity (plant and equipment) and human resources.
- Improve the quality and training of the sales force.

4. Purchasing frequency (Pf)

Focus: The Company

Objective: Increase the number of times customers purchase.

- Increase demand through advertising.
- Match supply with demand: in cycles of low activity through discounts and promotions, and in peak activity increase prices ("premium"), or increase output capacity and/or customer service.
- Optimize inventory management and logistics.
- Extend customer service hours.
- Reduce or increase, when needed, the time required to serve the customer.
- Promote customer loyalty through coupons, "miles", prizes, raffles, contests, etc.
- Locate and eliminate or mitigate any constraints ("bottlenecks") that may hinder production or sales.
- Extend warranties, financing and credit.
- Increase sales force and/or distribution capacity.
- Provide more payment options.
- Seek alternate sales channels; for example, Internet.
- Develop agreements with customers to supply them more frequently.
- Arrange distribution agreements with competitors.
- Improve the quality and management of customer databases (Customer Relationship Management).
- Develop/improve post sale service and customer tracking.
- Enhance computing and communications resources.

- Purchasing frequency (Pf) must be aligned with the quantity (Qt) sold in each transaction depending upon the customers' buying patterns.

5. Average Price (P)

Focus: The Company

Objective: Seek customer loyalty through pricing policy.

The price must:

- Be proportional to the amount delivered.
- Bear logic with the quantity contained in each unit of sale.
- Reflect the product's quality.
- Provide the benefits most valued by the target market.
- Comply with the company's financial goals.
- Be consistent with the product's positioning.
- Be properly focused towards the target market.

Additionally:

- The goals and policies of the company must be defined.
- The marketing objectives must be clearly established.
- The prices and benefits of competition must be clearly identified and compared.
- Product mix should complement the competition´s offerings.
- Product cost and profit must be in line with the firm´s profitability goals.
- Price changes should consider the product´s price elasticity.
- Understand the purchasing power of customers.
- Discounts and promotions should have a time framework, according to pricing policies, the economy and competition.
- Tiered pricing (different prices for different customers) should be focused on increasing sales.

This highlights something very important: all resources and activities of the company should be aimed at increasing sales velocity. These include not only all capital goods, but also human resources: everyone should be a potential salesperson!

It should be understood that the purpose of the firm, one way or another, is to increase its value for shareholders, customers, employees, suppliers and, in general, for society. This is made possible only through sales and, therefore, these five determinants of velocity are crucial to achieve the proposed goals and objectives of the firm in the shortest possible time.

Chapter 5
Costs

5.1 Variable Cost

Variable costs can be defined as all those costs that vary in direct proportion with the level of sales; that is, the number of units sold. When sales increase, these costs also increase; they are a relatively constant percentage of sales. The unit variable cost tends to be stable and does not decrease as volume increases, unless the cost of some component decreases.

Variable Cost includes:

- The cost of all direct materials that are part of finished goods and can be assigned to specific units.
- All labor costs directly traceable to specific products and actually paid based on units produced; that is, the amount paid for every shirt assembled in a garment factory ("piecework" payment). In contrast, if labor is paid on a monthly basis, independently of the level of sales or production, it would be considered a fixed cost.
- Production expenses that clearly vary in proportion to sales (or activity). Depending upon the production process these may include, for example, power, water, supplies, etc.
- Other administration, marketing and sales expenses that may have a variable component. This includes discounts, sales commissions, transportation and distribution expenses, etc. Again, this is true only if they can be traced directly to sales activity.

Example: An item is purchased for resale at a cost of $ 50 and a selling price of $ 80. The variable cost is therefore 62.5% of the sales price (50/80). If 100 units are sold, total sales would be $ 8,000 and the total variable cost would be $ 5,000.

If 10 additional units were sold, for a total of 110 units, total sales would be $ 8.800 and the total variable cost would be $ 5,500. Again, $ 5,500 is still 62.5% of $ 8,800. Total Variable cost is a constant percentage of total sales.

Variable cost may be allocated, or assigned, to each unit produced and sold; this is “unit variable cost”. Unit variable cost (Vc) remains unchanged with changes in quantity (Q); it may decrease if volume discounts can be negotiated with suppliers, or by virtue of greater efficiency and productivity; this makes it very practical for financial calculations.

Total Variable cost (TVc) = Quantity sold (Q) times unit Variable cost (Vc), or

TVc = Q x Vc

5.2 Variable Cost Velocity

In section "4.8 Sales Velocity" it was indicated how sales is a flow measured between two points in time. Variable Cost is also a flow. But it is not only a flow: it is a flow that is directly proportional to the number of units sold or to the sales flow; this means that as sales increase variable costs also increase and remain as a relatively constant percentage of sales; this is precisely why they are variable.

Sales velocity (S) was expressed as S = Nc x Qt x Np x Pf x P, where

Nc = Number of customers

Qt = Quantity sold in each transaction

Np = Number of products offered

Pf = Purchasing frequency

P = Average price of products

Variable cost can be analyzed in a similar fashion. Variable cost velocity (or Total Variable cost, TVc) is a function of:

Number of suppliers (Ns), multiplied by the

Quantity purchased in each transaction (Qt), multiplied by the

Number of purchased direct materials (Nm), multiplied by the

Purchase frequency (Pf), multiplied by the

Average cost of inputs (Vc)

In algebraic notation: TVc = Ns x Qt x Nm x Pf x Vc (orientation model).

Variable Cost Velocity = Total Variable cost (TVc)

Decreasing Variable Cost Velocity is equivalent to reducing Total Variable cost.

As in the case of sales velocity, decreasing any of these factors decreases the total variable cost. Less velocity means less Total Variable cost. Again, this formula does not necessarily call for a numerical result (orientation model). The emphasis is on velocity, that is, so much variable cost per year, month or day.

With the concept of velocity in mind, following are some examples of strategic options for each of these factors:

1. Number of suppliers (Ns)

Focus: Suppliers

Objective: Reduce the number of suppliers to decrease variable costs.

- Locate new suppliers in the market that have a greater capacity to serve the company.
- Reducing the number of suppliers may decrease administrative costs.
- This enhances purchasing efficiency through knowledge and experience.
- They become more specialized in service to satisfy better the firm´s requirements.
- Facilitates negotiating volume discounts to reduce variable cost.

2. Purchasing Quantity (Qt)

Focus: Suppliers

Objective: The purchased quantity must meet sales and inventory requirements.

- Set inventory policy such that purchases do not exceed needs.
- Packaged quantity must comply with the firm´s purchasing needs.
- The purchased quantity (Qt) must be aligned with purchasing frequency (Pf).
- Optimize inventory management and logistics; for example, EOC ("Economic Order Quantity").

3. Number of Direct Materials (Nm)

Focus: The Company

Objective: Reduce the number of different direct materials or parts required for production or sales.

- Explore the possibility of using the same raw materials, parts or components, in different products.
- Reducing the number or variety of direct materials reduces inventory cost.
- Seek other quality options.
- Order new services.
- Improve the quality and training of buyers.

4. Purchasing frequency (Pf)

Focus: The Company

Objective: Optimize purchasing frequency from each supplier

- Fewer purchasing transactions reduce the associated variable and fixed costs.
- Request from suppliers other payment options.
- Expand information resources: communications, databases.
- Purchasing frequency must be aligned with sales and inventory requirements.

5. Average Variable Cost (Vc)

Focus: The Company

Objective: Reduce direct material costs.

- Seek partnerships with suppliers to improve quality of direct materials.
- Cooperate with competitors to gain advantages in purchasing.
- Negotiate discounts with suppliers for purchasing volume or for advanced payments.
- Locate new suppliers who can offer better prices and/or purchasing terms.
- Vertical integration (manufacture or produce the firm´s own direct materials).
- Search for lower cost substitutes.
- Strive to improve yield or greater performance of direct materials.
- Control shrinkage, waste and losses within the inventory system.
- Outsource the production of goods whenever benefit/cost justifies it.

These are a few examples. The main idea is to take all the necessary actions to reduce variable costs, but without compromising sales.

5.3 Manufacturing Cost

In general accounting "Cost of Goods Sold", "Cost of Sales" and "Direct Costs" differ from Variable Cost in that they do not include in the product unit cost other variable cost items such as discounts, commissions and other operating expenses that may be variable, or contain variable components.

In the accounting of industrial enterprises, manufacturing cost (used for computing Cost of Goods Sold) includes:

a. Direct materials (DM): All materials that are part of the finished goods and can be traced to specific units.

b. Direct manufacturing labor (DL): All labor costs that can be allocated directly to specific products.

c. Overhead costs (OC): Includes fixed and variable costs such as depreciation, maintenance, repair, rent, insurance, supervisory salaries, indirect labor, power, water, supplies, etc.

d. A cost allocation method based on the number of units produced, person-hours, machine hours, etc. This is Q or the basis used to compute the unit manufacturing cost.

A method commonly used in computing the unit manufacturing cost is to divide the corresponding fixed cost by the number of units produced (Q), or man-hours, or machine-hours, as applicable.

Notice that "a-" has variable costs, but "b-" and "c-" may have variable as well as fixed costs.

The unit manufacturing cost can be computed as:

$$UMC = \frac{DM + DL + OC}{Q}$$

The effect of this is that the unit manufacturing cost (UMC) is reduced when Q increases. This is because when dividing DL and OC (which are mainly fixed) by Q, the value of UMC decreases due to the fixed cost components; with DM, this does not occur because it is a variable cost. The percentage of manufacturing cost related to the selling price (UCM/P) is also reduced if Q increases.

Logically, the opposite is also true: If the volume Q decreases the unit manufacturing cost increases. The percentage of manufacturing cost in relation to the price also increases when sales volume is reduced.

5.4 Other Variable Costs

Commissions on sales.

Sales commissions are commonly set as a fixed percentage of the sales achieved; this makes them a variable cost. The higher the sales level the greater the expense by way of commissions; this cost can also be assigned to each unit sold. This contrasts with the general accounting concept in which commissions are sales expenses and not product costs.

Commission example: Suppose that a computer has a retail price of $ 1,000. If salespeople are paid a commission of 5% on sales, then these would be a variable cost of $ 50 per unit. If 100 units were sold, sales would amount to $ 100,000 and the commissions would be a variable cost for $ 5,000. If 10 additional units were sold, then the variable cost would be $ 5,500. Commissions, therefore, constitute a variable cost and are a constant percentage of the sales level.

Discounts.

These are usually short-term, or temporary, incentives that reduce what the customer has to pay, but without changing the original price of the product, or its positioning. If the discount is a fixed percentage of the sales price, then, like commissions, it is a variable cost of the product, which can also be assigned to each unit sold.

Again, this differs from general accounting in which discounts are treated as a deduction from the sales price thereby yielding a “net price”. In the standard income statement, sales discounts are subtracted from sales to obtain net sales.

Advertising and promotions.

If advertising (or promotional) expenses are set as a fixed percentage of sales, they become a variable cost, which can be assigned to each unit sold. However, if they take place at a given moment, or are recurrent, and their amount does not correspond to a fixed percentage of sales, then they can be treated as a marketing expense ("fixed"). In accounting they are considered a marketing expense and not a product cost.

5.5 Fixed Costs

Fixed costs are also a flow. However, compared with variable costs, fixed costs are a function of time, rather than of sales activity; they are incurred, or paid at some point, or periodically, be it day, month or year; they are not affected, nor do they have any direct relationship with the volume of sales, at least not in the short term.

Revenue constantly varies over time and total variable costs change in direct proportion; therefore, any expense that is not a constant percentage of revenue can be treated as a fixed cost. Expenses such as depreciation, rent, salaries, insurance, office supplies, financial interest, etc., are classified in this category.

Fixed costs are incurred to increase sales and/or reduce variable costs; this is their only justification; there can be no other.

Following are some examples:

- Depreciation: Measures the rate at which the consumption of fixed assets (needed to create revenue) is recognized.
- Wages and labor: Measure the cost and quantity of the human resources required for manufacturing and selling goods.
- Rent and leases: Measure the amount of space needed for manufacturing and commercial activity.
- Maintenance and repairs: Like depreciation, they measure consumption in the use of fixed assets.
- General office expenses: They are also needed to create revenue. If a portion is a constant percentage of revenue it is considered a variable cost, the rest is fixed.
- Insurance premiums: Reflect the cost of insured assets and the probability of accidents (unexpected and instantaneous consumption of goods needed to create revenue).
- Property tax: Is an expense related to the use of property.
- Advertising and promotional expenses: They consume "cash" (a resource) and are clearly used to push sales. They are fixed expenses as long as their expenditure is not a constant percentage of revenue.
- Interest expense: measures the cost of the extra money needed to increase contribution margin by increasing sales and reducing variable or fixed costs. Example: working capital or fixed asset investment.

This interpretation of fixed costs is certainly practical for marketing and managerial purposes. Fixed costs create the benefits and conditions that induce and enable customers to buy products; in fact, any expenditure must fulfill this requirement; otherwise, it could be considered an inefficient use of resources.

Pleasant offices and premises attract customers. An employee cafeteria fosters their well-being and motivates them to produce and sell. In these examples fixed costs are spent for the specific purpose of building revenue; this illustrates how the marketing framework has a clear influence in all business activities and why they must all be subordinated to revenue and profit goals. (Needless to say, ethics and social responsibility are key benefits).

In the long run, all costs will eventually change, so that the term "fixed" is, in general, short and medium term. Fixed costs are directly related to the use of human resources and to the level of capital investment.

Given that fixed costs are spent to create contribution margin, it cannot be stated that a low level is "good" and a high level is "bad". High or low fixed costs are not significant: what is relevant is their impact on operating profit and profitability indexes.

From a marketing standpoint, it is very practical to treat all fixed costs as a single group, or block, and not as part of a product's unit cost. They must be absorbed by sales. If sales are not enough, then they will not be fully absorbed (not enough money to pay for them) and therefore a loss occurs.

If sales are just enough to absorb all variable and fixed costs, this is labeled as a "breakeven point". If sales are high enough to absorb all costs, and a surplus arises, this is known as "operating profit".

5.6 Other Costs

The case of "direct labor" presents two alternatives: If it is paid based on units produced ("piecework") it is treated as a variable cost; but, if it is paid on a monthly basis, it is treated as fixed; there may also be a combination of both, depending upon the payment method.

"Semi-variable" or "semi-fixed" costs are those that bear relationship, not only with the level of sales, but also with the time factor; this makes them somewhat difficult to use in financial computations. Expenses such as communications and office supplies fall into this category.

The proposed solution is to simply separate them into their variable and fixed components; this may be achieved by analyzing the type of expenditure and decomposing it on a logical basis: the time-based elements correspond to fixed components, and the activity, or sales-based elements, correspond to the variable components.

Alternatively, assumptions such as "x% variable and y% fixed" can be made, depending upon the type of expenditure and its magnitude. If the case warrants it, a linear regression[36] analysis can be performed over the expense with respect to the level of sales; in this way a function of the type TC = aQ + b is determined, where TC (Total Cost) is the sum total of the fixed and variable costs. The variable cost component corresponds to "a", the fixed cost component to "b", and Q is the number of units produced or sold.

The "overhead manufacturing costs" are a good example for the development of the proposed techniques: this includes costs such as indirect labor, power, communications, insurance, maintenance, repairs, depreciation, etc. Some of these are liable to be decomposed into fixed and variable costs one way or another.

[36] Linear regression is a mathematical method for determining the relationship between different variables.

Chapter 6

Contribution Margin

6.1 Contribution Margin Definition

The difference between selling price and variable cost is known as "contribution margin"[37]; this is what every unit of product sold contributes to the profit of the business. Contribution margin may also refer to the difference between total sales and total variable costs. This term will be used interchangeably with "total contribution margin", or "unit contribution margin", depending upon the context of its use.

Example: In a company that manufactures and markets clothing, a dress has the following price and cost structure:

Sales Price (P): $ 300

Variable costs:

Fabric and Buttons $ 100

10% for sales commissions, equivalent to $ 30 per dress.

Estimated additional supplies (yarn and stuffing), 5% (of the sales price), or $ 15

Variable cost Vc = Fabric and Buttons + Commissions + Supplies

Vc = $ 100 + 30 + 15 = $ 145 for each dress.

---

[37] Thomas Nagle, Reed K. Holden, "*The Strategy and Tactics of Pricing*", Pearson, Prentice Hall, 2002. pp. 33-36

If 100 dresses are sold monthly (Q), the following result is obtained:

Monthly sales of dresses: S = P x Q	S = $ 300 x 100 units =	$ 30.000
Less total variable cost: TVc = Vc x Q	TVc = $ 145 x 100 units =	14.500
Equals total contribution margin:	TCm = S – TVc =	$ 15.500

The contribution margin can also be calculated as follows:

Cm = Price – Variable cost = P – Vc

Cm = 300 – 145 = $ 155 for each dress

Total contribution margin is also a flow: TCm = Cm x Q.

TCm= $ 155 x 100 = $ 15.500 (same result as above).

This is the amount contributed to the profits of the company by all the dresses sold.

Suppose that the company has the following fixed monthly costs:

Rent: $ 2,000

Direct labor and other salaries: $ 4,000

Maintenance: $ 1,000

Insurance and other services: $ 3,000

Total fixed costs (Fc) = $ 2.000 + 4.000 + 1.000 + 3.000 = $ 10.000

Total contribution margin, TCm, computed from the sale of 100 dresses per month was $ 15,500. If the 100 dresses sold contribute to profits with $ 15.500 per month, then this is enough to absorb the $ 10,000 in fixed costs, thus leaving an operating profit (Op) of $ 5,500.

From this we can deduce that operating profit (Op) is:

Op = (sales – total variable cost) – fixed costs

Op = S – TVc – Fc, where Fc = Fixed Costs

Op = total contribution margin – fixed Costs

Op= TCm – Fc

Therefore,

Operating profit, Op = 15.500 – 10.000 = $ 5,500

Summary of the above calculations:

Contribution margin per unit: Cm = P – Vc

Total contribution margin, TCm:

TCm = Q x Cm

TCm = Q (P – Vc)

TCm = Q x P – Q x Vc

TCm = Total sales – total variable Costs

TCm = S – TVc

Operating profit can be computed as follows:

Operating profit = total contribution margin – fixed costs

Op = Q x Cm – Fc

Op = TCm – Fc

This computation technique is used to illustrate the logic of the analysis when a single product is involved. This is an exceptional situation, as in most businesses multiple products exist; however, the explanation is useful as it facilitates understanding the basic concept.

An ongoing business should generate with its sales enough contribution margin to absorb its fixed costs and yield an operating profit, in line with the profitability goals of the firm.

In other words, sufficient sales must be achieved to generate enough contribution margin so that fixed costs can be absorbed quickly, and thereby obtain the desired operating profit in the shortest possible time.

6.2 Optimum Value

The Value of a product reflects the desire of the customers for obtaining it. Customers are willing to purchase more quantities, or pay higher prices, for products with great benefits. However, adding more benefits costs more; in other words, too many benefits can make a product unprofitable; too few benefits can make a product undesirable; there is a precise level of benefits that makes a product sufficiently desirable for the customers and sufficiently profitable for the firm; therefore, Value cannot be too high nor too low.

The concepts of Value (benefits vs. price and effort) and total contribution margin (TCm) are closely related: to the extent that a product provides more benefits, the higher the price that customers are willing to pay for it, or the greater the amount they wish to purchase.

A good quality product, but with a relatively low price (high Value), will have greater demand than the same product with a high price (low Value); this increased demand translates into more Q units sold (in a given period), which multiplied by the product's contribution margin (Cm) yields the total contribution margin (TCm).

Cm = price – variable cost = P – Vc

TCm = Q x Cm

Customers are, ultimately, the real judges of the market: If they truly value a product, they will cast their "votes" for it just as they would for a political candidate; the market is similar to a complex electoral system in which some win and others lose. Their votes translate into sales (S = Q x P).

Although the customers may have other buying alternatives, they will cast their "votes" for the "candidate" that offers them the greatest benefits with regard to the sacrifice in price and effort required.

If clients have comparatively little preference for a product, because they may have many other options in terms of benefits, price and effort, then the price they are willing to pay may be low, or the amount they are willing to purchase may also be low; greater benefits allow a better price –contribution margin– or induce a higher sales volume.

This indicates that customers´ preferences are reflected in both Q and in P. The firm's product mix must deliver a total level of Value from all products (i) that maximizes sales (S) and the total contribution margin (TCm).

Cm = P – Vc

TCm = $\sum Q_i \times Cm_i$ The sum of Q x Cm of all the products (i)

For example, suppose the firm has the following product mix (average monthly sales):

Item (i)	**Quantity Q_i**	Price	Cost	**Cm_i**	**TCm**
Computers	50	1.200	700	500	25.000
Radios	100	300	200	100	10.000
Televisions	30	700	500	200	6.000
					TCm = $ 41.000

The quantities sold depend on the Value of each product, that is, its benefits to price ratio. Determining the optimal product mix requires properly balancing all these variables in order to maximize the total contribution margin (TCm) of the product mix.

If Value is too high, then Cm is too low due to the added variable costs (or the lower price); and, if Value is too low, then Q will be low as well. The product mix may be visualized as if it is a single product with its own Value; this set of products is what is eventually delivered to the customers; and it must have an optimum level of Value; not too high and not too low; the same as prices, not too high and not too low.

There is therefore a specific level of Value for each product, that maximizes the Value of the product mix and the total contribution margin (TCm); this in turn maximizes the operating profit (Op), after deducting the fixed costs (Fc). In other words, Op = TCm – Fc.

J. von Neumann and O. Morgenstern stated in the *Theory of Games and Economic Behavior* that is not mathematically possible to maximize for two (or more) variables at the same time. This certainly seems true in this case, given that what is to be maximized is the Value and profit from the *product mix*, and not necessarily that of each product. In many cases, selling a specific product may require sacrificing the prices and contribution margins of others; some products depend upon others for their sale.

Loss leaders[38] are products sold at a low price (or even given away freely) in order to attract (lead) customers into the store with the aim of selling to them other more profitable products. Their low price makes them very high Value; therefore, the product mix has more Value with them than without them.

For example, staple foods such as milk or eggs may be sold at low prices (high Value) to attract customers; they act as "bait". The underlying assumption is, of course, that customers will also purchase other more expensive and profitable products.

The success of the strategy is to adjust selectively the Value of all individual items in order to maximize the total contribution margin (TCm) of the product mix. Optimizing the Value of the product mix supersedes optimizing the Value of each individual product.

In general, this can be achieved as follows:

- Accept setting relatively low prices (low margin) for products with high elasticity; this adds Value to them. Given that they are frequently purchased, and their prices are well known, they can be advertised to attract customers, promote the brand, and lead to more customer traffic. Prices must not be too low, otherwise they may not yield enough profit. It is sufficient to have their Value somewhat higher than that of the competition by means of lower prices. (Refer to Chapter 8. *The Value Matrix*).
- Set relatively high prices (high margin) on items with low elasticity. These are high-end products that are purchased less frequently, customers are less aware of their prices and they are more sensitive to their benefits, particularly advertising, brand and quality. If market share is a priority, then their Value should be greater than that of the competition through their benefits or their price.
- The prices of products with medium elasticity can be treated either way, depending upon their quality, brand awareness, availability and competition.

---

[38] Thomas Nagle, Reed K. Holden, "*The Strategy and Tactics of Pricing*", Pearson, Prentice Hall, 2002, p. 277

"Appendix 3. *Value and Contribution Margin*" indicates that there is an optimum Value, which maximizes total contribution margin (TCm).

6.3 Breakeven Analysis

When the total contribution margin achieved can only absorb fixed costs, with no Operating profit (Op), the level of sales (S) is at the "breakeven" point.

Op = S – TVc – Fc

When Op = 0, then

0 = S – TVc – Fc

S = TVc + Fc

This level of sales (S) is at breakeven.

Op = 0 = Q x Cm – Fc

Q x Cm = Fc,

Solving for Q,

Q = Fc / Cm

The breakeven point is achieved just when the volume of sales (Q units) multiplied by the unit contribution margin (Cm = P – Vc) is equal to the fixed costs (Fc) and operating profit is zero: Fc = Q x Cm.

"Breakeven" suggests that sales are just balancing all costs (variable and fixed) and there is no operating profit; if sales have not reached this point, losses occur; with sales above the breakeven point, profits are generated.

Example

A business that sells hamburgers has the following price and cost structure:

Price, P = $ 5.00

Variable Costs:

Meat, bread, vegetables = $ 2.00

Sauces, power, napkins, etc., estimated at 20% of sales.

20% x 5.00 = $ 1.00

Variable Cost (Vc) = $ 2.00 + 1.00 = $ 3.00 per unit

Fixed costs (Fc) = $ 3,000 (rent, payroll, etc.)

Contribution margin (Cm) = P – Vc = $ 5.00 – 3.00 = $ 2.00

Question: How many hamburgers need to be sold just to absorb fixed costs, that is, to reach the breakeven point?

Solution:

At breakeven (be), Q x Cm = Fc

Therefore,

Qbe = Fc / Cm

Since Fc = $ 3,000

Q = 3,000 / 2.00 = 1,500 units (hamburgers) required to achieve breakeven (absorbing the fixed cost of $ 3,000 without obtaining any operating income).

Proof:

S = 1,500 x 5.00 = $ 7,500

TVc = 1,500 x 3.00 = $ 4.500

TCm = 7.500 – 4.500 = $ 3,000

Operating Profit = TCm – Fc = $ 3,000 – 3,000 = 0, (breakeven)

A variant of this example would be: How many burgers have to be sold to make a profit of $ 1,000?

Solution:

If profit Op = \$ 1000, then

\$ 1,000 = Q x Cm - Fc and

\$ 1,000 = Q x 2.00 - 3.000

Therefore, \$ 4,000 = Q x 2.00

Solving for Q

Q = 4,000 / 2.00 = 2,000 units (burgers) sold to absorb the fixed costs of \$ 3,000 and yield a profit of \$ 1,000.

Notice that 2,000 burgers (units) are equivalent to a sales level (*in money)* of:

S = 2,000 x 5.00 = \$ 10,000

Breakeven analysis illustrates something very important: when the firm can reduce its fixed cost and/or increase its contribution margin its breakeven point is reduced; this implies it takes less Q to achieve the balance between total contribution margin and fixed costs.

In periods of low activity the risk of running into losses is lower because relatively low sales are required to absorb fixed costs; in periods of high activity, profits can increase very quickly as fixed costs are easily absorbed.

One of the greatest uncertainties in a new business venture is when will the breakeven point be reached. If it is achieved earlier than expected, this is a success. But, what if it takes longer than expected? This can be a serious financial drain as the constant losses require more funds to keep the business going. In fact, the longer it takes, the greater the risks that the business will fall into debt and incur additional interest expenses, or even fail altogether; therefore, reaching breakeven quickly is a critical priority.

An optimum Value, with the best benefit to price combination, increases demand and revenue; therefore, the breakeven point can be reached faster when prices have been set using the concept of Value. The specific method is covered in section "7.8 Value-based pricing".

6.4 Applying Contribution Margin

Contribution margin (Cm) can be expressed as a percentage of the sale price (P); this has several practical applications.

From the previous example: P = 5.00 and Cm = 2.00

Cm% is the contribution margin (Cm) divided by the sale price (P).

Cm% = Cm / P

Cm% = 2.00 / 5.00 = 0.40 equivalent to 40%

If we know beforehand the Cm%, then solving for Cm we obtain

Cm = Cm% x P

If the Cm% of a product is known beforehand and a price P is suggested, then the expected contribution margin will be Cm=Cm% x P.

Multiplying both sides of the equation by Q we obtain:

Cm x Q = Cm% x P x Q, therefore, since TCm = Cm x Q, then

TCm = Cm% x P x Q

Given that sales S = P x Q then

TCm = Cm% x S

An alternative formula for computing operating profit (Op) can be developed as follows:

Recall that Op = TCm - Fc

Therefore, if TCm = Cm% x S, then

Op = Cm% x S - Fc

Operating profit is obtained by multiplying the percent contribution margin (Cm%) by sales S and subtracting the fixed costs Fc.

The main advantage of using the formula with the percentage contribution margin (Op = S x Cm% - Fc) is that it can be applied in scenarios with multiple products, in which Cm% may be an average of several products.

An example of this can be found in "Appendix 6. Solved Problems in Pricing", exercise # 7.

Note that breakeven occurs when operating profit is zero; that is, when

Op = 0 = Cm% x S - Fc

Rearranging terms, we obtain Fc = Cm% x S and solving for the level of sales in S at the breakeven point (be):

Sbe = Fc / Cm%

(Very similar to Qbe = Fc / Cm, used for single products). The sales Sbe level can be computed by just dividing the Fixed costs (Fc) by the percent contribution margin (Cm%).

In the previous example of the burgers,

P = 5.00 Vc = 3.00 and therefore Cm = 5.00 – 3.00 = 2.00

Cm% = 2.00 / 5.00 = 0.40 equivalent to 40%.

To compute the sales level required to cover fixed costs of $ 3,000 and obtain a profit of $ 1,000, apply Op = S x Cm% – Fc, where S is the level sales, and Cm% is the percent contribution margin.

Replacing the respective values obtain

Op = $ 1000 = S x 40% – 3,000

4.000 = S x 40% and solving for S

S = 4,000 / 0.40 = $ 10,000 is the money sales amount (not units) required to obtain a profit of $ 1,000 and absorb fixed costs of $ 3,000

Proof:

$ 1,000 = $ 10,000 x 40% - $ 3,000

$ 1,000 = $ 4,000 - $ 3,000

$ 1,000 = $ 1,000

Notice that this is exactly the same result previously obtained, with the computation made using Op = Q x Cm - Fc, where Q was the quantity sold in units and Cm the contribution margin of each unit.

6.5 Variable Cost Percentage

Variable Cost% is determined similar to Cm%, as follows:

Vc% = variable cost / selling price

Vc% = Vc / P

In the hamburger example:

Cm% = 2.00 / 5.00 = 0.40 = 40%, and

Vc% = 3.00 / 5.00 = 0.60 = 60%

Note that since Cm = P – Vc, then P = Cm + Vc.

If we proceed to divide all these terms by P, we obtain

P / P = Cm / P + Vc / P

Given that

P / P = 100%, Cm / P = Cm% y Vc / P = Vc%, therefore

100% = Cm% + Vc%

This means that the addition of Vc% and Cm% should always equal 100%. By simply subtracting from 100%, either one can be obtained if the other one is known.

Example, if Vc% = 60%, then Cm% = 100% - 60% = 40%.

These percentages are critical control variables, not only in marketing, but also in general business administration. We can say that for almost any business, product, or product line, the Vc% and Cm% should always be known for planning and internal control purposes.

The main benefit of this is that given any sales level (S), be it estimated or actual, by applying the Cm% the total contribution margin is easily obtained (TCm = Cm% x S).

For example, if the average Cm% of a business (or a product line) is 40%, then, with expected sales of $ 10,000, the *most probable* contribution margin will be TCm = $ 10,000 x 40% = $ 4,000.

The term "most probable" is used because it assumes that for a given line of business it is highly probable that in the short or medium term this percentage may be relatively stable, assuming that the product mix maintains its composition. The underlying assumption is that product mix, and other cost components, will not change significantly in an on-going well-established business; at least not in a short period of time.

Even if the percentage does change, or exhibits some variance, it still needs to be investigated, as an explanation is required anyway; this is precisely what makes it a powerful marketing and administration tool.

In the same example, if fixed costs are $ 3,000, then the business will have an *expected* operating profit of $ 1,000 ($ 4,000 total contribution margin less fixed costs of $ 3,000).

The Vc% works the same way as Cm%, except that it operates with the variable cost instead of the contribution margin. Another example follows.

XYZ Company has an established profit plan, or "business plan", in which Vc% is planned at 70% of sales.

Suppose that for the month of January sales were forecasted at $ 100,000; therefore, the expected TVc should be TVc = Vc% x S = 70% x 100,000 = $ 70,000.

In the accounting period the following result is obtained with actual sales of $ 90,000

Beginning inventory	$ 150.000
+ Purchases of the month	60.000
= Cost of goods available for sale	210.000
– Ending inventory	130.000
= Cost of goods sold	80.000

If sales were actually $ 90,000, the cost of goods sold (COGS) must have been something close to 70% x 90.000 = $ 63,000; but no, the cost was exceeded by $ 17,000 = 80.000 – 63.000; a significant amount with regard to the level of sales.

If the firm is controlling its Vc%, which must have been about 70%, but ended up with Vc% = 89% ($ 80,000/90,000), this means that something unusual must have happened and requires management´s attention. This illustrates how the Vc% goes beyond marketing calculations: it is also a very important management control variable.

As a product progresses through its life cycle, the Vc% is gradually stabilized. In general, when the product is already well known, and has a solid customer base, with well-established buying patterns, then (short-term) changes in Vc% are relatively small. As the Vc% settles, so does the Cm% since Vc% + Cm% = 100%.

There are several factors that may alter the Vc%, for example:

- The product mix may vary significantly, meaning that products are being sold in different proportions. (See "Appendix 6. Solved Problems in Pricing", exercise # 7).
- Price and/or cost changes.
- Shrinkage or inefficiencies.
- Losses (theft) in sales, production, purchasing or inventory.

Each one of these issues needs to be closely monitored; this, by itself, illustrates the importance of Vc% and Cm%.

When using Cm% and Vc% as forecasting parameters, it is therefore convenient to use the terms "expected", "estimated", "approximate", etc., because it assumes that the above factors do not vary significantly in the short term. If Vc%, or Cm%, exhibit a significant variation, then a proper investigation might be in order.

6.6 Product Categories

Different product categories respond differently to price increases; the key issue to understand is the product´s price elasticity: high, medium, or low. The impact on total contribution margin is given by $\Delta TCm = \Delta Q \times \Delta Cm$; this means that the change in total contribution margin is given by the change in quantity times the change in unit contribution margin.

If the product is highly sensitive to price (high price elasticity), then an increase in price not supported by a corresponding increase in benefits, might not be sufficient to offset the resulting disproportionate decrease in quantity sold; this will very likely drive down total contribution margin (TCm) and profits.

If the product is not very sensitive to price (low price elasticity), then an increase in price not supported by a corresponding change in benefits, might be more than enough to compensate a possible decrease in quantity sold; this may drive up total contribution margin (TCm) and profits.

In general, if an increase in price is accompanied by increased benefits, it is very likely that the quantity sold will not decrease. Depending upon the product type, its benefits and elasticity, a price increase may even drive up the quantity sold, yielding a positive impact on total contribution margin and profits; this may happen when a higher price is associated with benefits such as status and prestige.

Let us analyze different product categories.

Convenience Goods

These are low-priced products used in everyday life for personal consumption, very easy to purchase and with minimum effort. Good examples are milk, eggs, bread, candy, aspirin, toothpaste, light bulbs, batteries, newspapers, etc. The product´s brand is not particularly important; little time is spent on their purchase; they have widespread distribution.

The majority of these products are very sensitive to price; their elasticity tends to be from medium to high, therefore price increases should preferably be accompanied by additional benefits to avoid drastic falls in sales volume.

Shopping Goods

These types of goods tend to be medium priced and their consumers compare quality, price, brand, design, etc. They devote a moderate amount of time in planning and in executing the purchase. Examples include furniture, clothing, appliances, tools, cars, etc. Brand loyalty may exist, but it is not particularly strong. Their distribution is somewhat more specialized than in convenience goods.

Their elasticity tends to be from medium to low, therefore price increases may not have a significant impact on sales volume, depending upon benefits and competitive conditions. It might be expected that a 10% increase in price will not decrease sales volume by more than 10%, and therefore there may be no significant impact on total contribution margin and profits. Again, what may tip the balance are the benefits offered.

Specialty Goods

These are the next level of goods in which prices are higher and brand loyalty is strong. Consumers devote a great deal of time and effort in searching and buying their favorite brand. Examples include high-end cars, cell phones, computers, designer clothing, health services, cosmetics, etc. In these goods, prestige and status are very important benefits; these goods tend to distributed through brand-name stores or franchises.

Their elasticity tends to be low, therefore price increases may not have a significant impact on volume; but, again, this depends upon benefits and competitive conditions.

Unsought goods

These are unusual products and their need is not urgent, unless it is for some special occasion. Good examples may be tool kits that can be used as presents, new inventions or fancy gadgets, a new sauce or new food ingredients, life insurance, funeral services, etc. There is no major brand loyalty and their purchase is rarely planned.

Their price elasticity tends to be very low, as customers would hardly know what a "fair" price might mean; perhaps not even the manufacturer knows! Benchmarking with the competition is unlikely as these are not common goods. They tend to be very high profit items, although their turnover might be questionable.

Price increases, within reasonable limits, probably will not have a negative impact on sales volume; therefore it is likely that their total contribution margin and profits may increase. Benefits, as always, cannot be overlooked, as they must justify the price charged.

6.7 Inventory Profitability

Inventory turnover is a critical pricing variable as it can gauge the effectiveness of a pricing strategy. It is useful because increasing the turnover of any specific product increases the average turnover of the entire inventory, and this leads to greater revenue and profits.

Turnover indicates the number of times an inventory is sold over a given period.

Inventory turnover (It) may be computed as:

It = Total variable cost (TVc) ÷ average inventory (Ia).

It = TVc ÷ Ia

For example:

Suppose that the month-end inventory averaged over the last 12 months is:

Ia = $ 10,000 (valued at cost)

TVc (annual) = $240,000

It = 240,000 ÷ 10,000

It = 24 (times per year.)

Inventory turnover can also be expressed in inventory days (Id) by dividing 365 days by the inventory turnover (It). From the above example, as follows:

Id = 365 days / It

Id = 365 days / 24 = 15 days

This means the inventory is sold, on average, every 15 days.

It is also possible to compute inventory turnover by using sales statistics instead of cost data, as follows:

It = sales (S) / inventory average (Ia)

It = S / Ia

The advantage of this method is that it facilitates comparison with other firms, or industries, as this type of information is obtainable from public records.

In section “3.3 Supply and Demand with Value” it was shown that providing Value plays a key role in increasing sales, which in turn leads to higher inventory turnover and profits.

An interesting question arises: What exactly does "low" or "high" inventory turnover mean? A good starting point is to compare a product's turnover with the average turnover of its product line or category, or even with the firm's average inventory turnover, computed as previously described.

A slow-moving inventory has two main causes:

a. The product has low Value because its price is too high in relation to its benefits.

b. The competition offers a substitute product of higher Value that has a more favorable benefits to price ratio; this shifts customers´ preferences.

If a product has low turnover, the strategy to increase it can be by providing higher Value through added benefits and lower prices, or by lowering the inventory average (Ia). This decision, however, requires taking into account the product's price elasticity.

Recall: Sales = Price x Quantity, or S = P x Q

A price increase in a high-elasticity product can yield a significant reduction in its resulting sales volume; this volume loss may not be compensated by the price increase and therefore revenue and profits may decrease. In contrast, a price decrease may have a favorable impact on sales volume, and if its elasticity is high enough, revenue and profits may increase.

A price increase in a low-elasticity product may have little or no impact, in its resulting sales volume. The price increase will not be offset by a lower sales volume, and therefore revenue and profits may increase. In contrast, a price decrease may not increase sales volume significantly, but it may decrease revenue and profits.

A price increase in a product with medium elasticity may have a moderately low impact on its sales volume. A lower sales volume will offset the price increase, and therefore there may not be any significant effect on sales and profits. The same can happen with a price decrease.

High-end products tend to have high brand loyalty and relatively low price elasticity; therefore, lowering prices might not be the best strategy for increasing sales and turnover; improving benefits presents a better option, as this adds prestige and status to the product.

Low-end products tend to be more sensitive to price; therefore, lowering prices may be a reasonable alternative for increasing turnover and market share. Inventory with goods in poor condition is often a symptom of low turnover; customers are lost because they perceive this as poor product quality. This problem is commonly found in restaurants, and in other businesses that stock food.

If a product has a higher-than-average turnover, this may suggest that the product is quite successful; in other words, it delivers high Value; or perhaps, that its price may be somewhat low and there may be some room for improvement. Again, price elasticity plays a key role in this decision.

Inventory turnover is an important performance metric because it increases if sales increase, or if inventory decreases. Despite the fact that accounting treats inventory as an asset, it is nevertheless a cash outlay; therefore, firms should strive to minimize their inventory level, but without sacrificing sales or customer service.

Inventory is an investment that must be profitable, as it is the most critical resource needed to create revenue and profits. A reasonable measure of inventory profitability (Ip) would be a ratio that relates total contribution margin (TCm) with inventory average (Ia), as follows:

Ip = TCm / Ia

The Ip ratio indicates the product mix´s profitability. It is a measure of financial efficiency; that is, how much profit the product contributes in a given period, in relation to its inventory. Inventory profitability plays a major role in the profitability of the firm.

Increasing inventory turnover (It) would appear to be a good financial goal for profit improvement. Since inventory turnover can be increased by lowering prices, there seems to a trade-off between these two variables. This is illustrated as follows:

If It = S / Ia, and Cm% = TCm / S then

It x Cm% = S / Ia x TCm / S = TCm / Ia

Since Ip = TCm / Ia, it follows that

Ip = It x Cm%

This means that inventory profitability (Ip) is equal to inventory turnover (It) times contribution margin (Cm%).

Inventory profitability is indeed a trade-off between margins and turnover: higher prices (high Cm%) may lead to lower inventory turnover (It); similarly, lower prices may lead to higher inventory turnover.

This trade-off indicates that what really counts is inventory profitability, and not turnover or contribution margin, as these two really play against each other. In Section "6.2 Optimum Value", it was shown that the goal is to maximize the total contribution margin of the product mix, as opposed to maximizing the contribution margin of each individual product. If a product´s price needs to be sacrificed (low Cm%) in order to sell other more profitable products, it needs to be offset by higher inventory turnover.

In other words, if a product carries a very low price, its higher sales volume would offset this in order to maintain its profitability. If it does not sell in larger quantities, then it would not make sense to keep in the inventory, unless it is needed for some very specific reason. In general, all products need to be profitable, even though some may be more profitable than others. Selling an unprofitable product is reasonable only if it serves a specific tactical purpose within the firm´s overall pricing strategy.

A key point to understand is that price is not the only determinant of sales and turnover; what really determines them is Value; this means that depending upon the product´s elasticity, its profitability is achieved by managing its benefits and/or price.

The goal is to maximize the profitability of the entire product mix. Evaluating the strategy´s success requires keeping statistics, which include tracking sales (S), volume (Q), price (P), variable cost (Vc), contribution margin (Cm), inventory average (Ia), and inventory profitability (Ip = TCm / Ia).

Actions to increase inventory profitability (Ip) include:

- Reducing the inventory average (Ia), as long as this does not hinder product sales or customer service.
- Reducing the variable cost, as long it does not interfere significantly with the product´s benefits; if it does, the price may have to be readjusted.
- Increasing the product´s benefits, as long as the increase in sales justifies any added variable cost.
- Increasing prices in low elasticity high-end products, as long as this will not adversely affect sales; if it does, consider increasing benefits.
- Decreasing prices in high elasticity low-end products, if this will significantly increase sales volume; if it does not, abstain.
- Increasing sales volume (Q), as long as its benefit exceeds its cost; for example, increasing demand through advertising and promotion.

The strategy´s success is measured by the increase in inventory profitability, as benefits and prices are tactically managed to achieve the firm´s goals.

Chapter 7

Applying Value

7.1 Strategy

The Value concept can be very useful for understanding and planning strategies under monopolistic competition; in this type of market commercial firms have a certain degree of control over prices despite nearby competition; this attracts customers by adding options and variety.

The representation of Value is:

$$\text{Value} = \frac{\sum \text{Benefits}}{\text{Price} + \text{Effort}}$$

Value, with regard to the competition, works in two basic ways in order to increase sales:

a. Higher Value: *Confrontation* strategy

- More benefits with the same or lower price.
- The same benefits at a lower price.

b. Same Value: *Complementation* strategy

- More benefits at a higher price.
- Fewer benefits at a lower price.

Let us analyze each one.

Confrontation strategy

Under this strategy, the firm focuses mainly on gaining market share by offering higher Value through similar (or superior) benefits, but at lower prices. This confrontation poses a clear threat to its competitors; it is a zero-sum game: the gain of one participant is offset by the loss of the other participant; one firm´s gain is its competitor´s loss.

This strategy carries a relatively high degree of risk and uncertainty, as it is difficult to predict the competitions' reaction and/or the customers' acceptance, as they may respond negatively to the actions of both competitors attempting to outsell each other. It is even likely that they may withhold from purchasing altogether and search elsewhere.

Suggested recommendations for this strategy:

- It needs clear competitive advantages; without this, the risk of failure can be high.
- Adding benefits and/or lowering prices reduces the contribution margin (Cm); the volume (Q) response and effect on net profit (Q x Cm) will depend upon the overall marketing strategy (Value) and the product´s price elasticity.
- Cost advantages are necessary when higher benefits or lower prices are used to compete, as the risk of a price war can be high.
- Sufficient financial resources are required in case a price war ensues.
- A team of highly skilled and well-motivated salespeople is needed to face an aggressive sales environment.
- If brand loyalty is important, focus on benefits; if it is not, concentrate on price.

Complementation Strategy

Under this strategy, the firm aims at complementing its competitors, rather than confronting them. When more benefits are offered at higher prices, or fewer benefits at *lower* prices, the proportion of benefits to price remains constant and therefore Value seems unchanged. For example, a firm can compete in the shoe business by selling better quality at higher prices, and when the opportunity arises, the competitors may even end up recommending the more expensive shoes (!).

Value may also seem unchanged when selling inferior quality at lower prices; this is also a complementation strategy. Once again, if lower quality shoes are sold at lower prices, competitors may not feel threatened, as this aims at a different market segment.

Complementation strategy can be described as a Pareto improvement; that is, an action that benefits someone without harming anyone else. It is an adaptation and specialization strategy that holds great marketing potential; it is a positive-sum game: all participants win with this arrangement; the customers, the competition and the firm. In the end, greater variety is offered and society as a whole wins; there is room for everyone; of course, this requires imagination, creativity and persistence, as in any business.

Suggested recommendations for this strategy:

- Thorough marketing research is needed to determine the market's profit potential.
- The target market must be clearly identified and segmented.
- The competition should be thoroughly analyzed.
- The firm´s compensation policy should reward collaborative behavior amongst its employees.
- Added benefits carry higher costs that may be offset by higher prices; lower benefits carry lower costs that may be offset by lower prices; therefore, contribution margin may remain unchanged; again, the volume response and its effect on net profit will also depend upon the overall marketing strategy (Value) and the product´s price elasticity.
- The selling strategy should concentrate on the product´s Value (its benefits to price relationship).

Another Complementation alternative is to enter a new market with new products, or with the same products; or enter a new segment with little or no competition.

This is not too different from how international trade works: each country specializes on what it can do best; that is its comparative advantage. Everyone is better off by doing what he can do best; each participant tailors his product mix according to his ability and opportunity. In the end, all nations are better off as long as interferences can be avoided; this is precisely why free trade agreements are actively sought.

Complementation strategy is also very similar to how nature works: the adaptation and specialization of each species to its niche ensures survival. One way or another, nature creates haphazard variety; it reaches the point where symbiotic relationships are developed, meaning that some species depend on others for survival. In this process, some survive and evolve adapting to a changing environment; just like a market.

These two strategies are not mutually exclusive; some products may complement the competition while others may confront it. The strategy depends upon the balance selected.

7.2 Acceleration

In section "3.1 Definition of Value" it was shown that the demand for a product is directly proportional to its Value: higher Value leads to higher revenue through a better price x quantity combination.

Recall:

$$\text{Value} = \frac{\sum \text{Benefits}}{\text{Price} + \text{Effort}}$$

Herein lies the key to the firm´s profitability: Value-based pricing is the fastest way for the firm to achieve its profitability goal in the shortest possible time.

An interesting question arises here: Can Value explain changes in sales? How? Let us analyze Value a little further.

"Sales", as mentioned earlier, is a velocity (or flow); that is, so much in money sales per year. If sales velocity is determined by Value, this means that the longer (time) we apply Value to a product, the greater will be its sales. This suggests the following relationship, or link, between sales (S), Value (Va) and time (T):

Sales = Va x T (orientation model)

If sales increase from one period Si to the next Sf, during time T, then sales in the final period Sf will be:

Sf = Si + Va x T

This is better understood by using a familiar concept of physics: If a vehicle is moving at 50 kph and it starts accelerating at average of 10 kph every hour, this means that after one hour it would be moving at 60 kph.

Final velocity = Initial velocity + Acceleration (A) x Time elapsed (T).

Vf = Vi + A x T

After 2 hours, it would be moving at:

Final velocity = 50 + 10 x 2 = 70 mph.

Value behaves in the same fashion. If Sf = Si + Va x T, then we can say that Value is a force that accelerates sales. (Acceleration is the change in velocity with respect to time.)

Put in simple words, Value accelerates sales. This explains why the sales of a successful business or product seem to be explosive; this is why we see long lines of people for gaining entry into a fashionable restaurant, or for buying the latest model cell phone. Business just seems to bloom all of a sudden; the trick lies in Value, as it accelerates sales and therefore profits increase.

This can also explain why businesses may fall into bankruptcy so quickly: acceleration can also be negative (deceleration). Simple: when a business delivers negative Value to its customers (negative benefits surpass positive benefits), it accelerates negatively and quickly recedes away from its profitability target.

7.3 Value Life Cycle

How does Value evolve throughout the product´s life cycle? Section "2.7 Product Life Cycle" indicated how a product evolved during its life cycle. The ultimate judge for a product is the market; therefore, the level of sales is in fact an indicator of how the market values a product. The product life cycle may just as well be labeled the Value life cycle.

Let us analyze each of its phases in the following graph:

Figure 7.1 Product Life Cycle

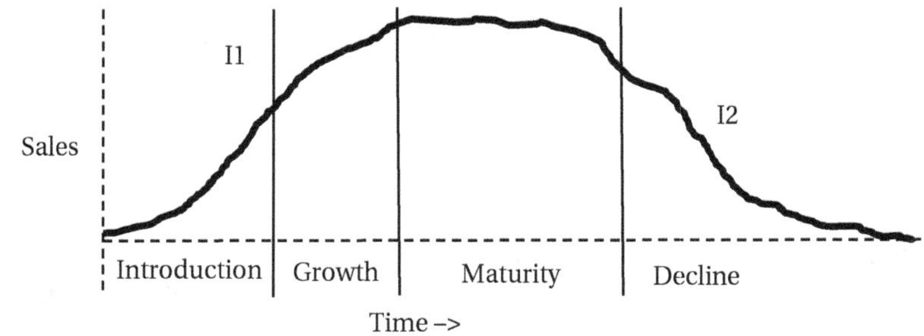

Notice that sales increase quickly during the introduction phase, and then they slow down during the growth phase; subsequently they level off during the maturity phase and remain relatively stable; thereon they gradually start slowing down during the decline phase until they eventually reach a zero level.

Figure 7.2 Value Life Cycle (Vr)

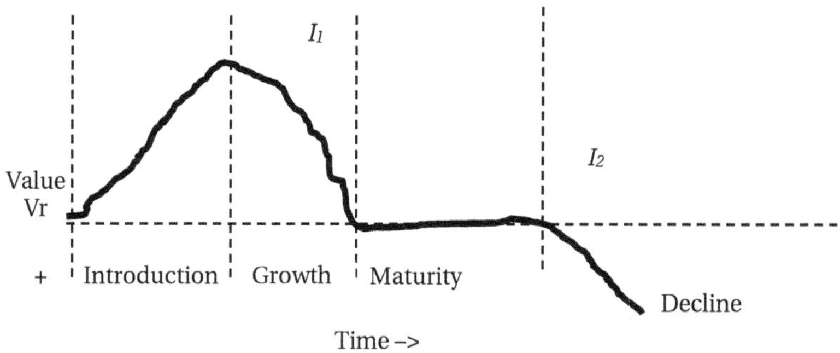

The "Value Life Cycle" graph shows the product´s rate of change in its sales level; that is, its acceleration or relative Value (Vr) with respect to its competition. Recall from section "3.1 Definition of Value" that the product´s relative Value is Vr = Vp – Vc, where Vp is the product´s Value and Vc is the competing´s product Value (orientation model).

Therefore, the above graph actually reflects how the product´s Value is perceived, or compared, during its life cycle.

Since Value is the force that pushes sales, then the change in sales per unit time is a clear indicator of Value. The product has Value during all of its life cycle, but the customers perceive different levels of Value in each phase; this is similar to a vehicle that advances at different speeds during a journey.

During the introduction phase, the product is highly valued due to its novelty and sales accelerate; they increase very quickly; the Value differential (Vr) is certainly pushing.

In the growth phase, there is an inflection (*I1*) point in which product sales start to slow down; this is the product´s peak moment in its life cycle; this point offers a great marketing opportunity for firmly positioning its brand. Thereon, its appeal begins to fade as substitutes or other options begin to appear. Although sales are still increasing, they are slowing down; they are not growing as fast; Vr is decreasing as competition ensues.

This inflection point suggests something very important: customer preferences are changing; the benefits and price combination is not being valued as it used to be; the effect of the emerging competition is taking its toll on sales: something has to be done… and fast. This is the moment to stop and think about what is happening; the course of action must change; otherwise, the inevitable may arrive, and perhaps sooner than expected.

This stage still enjoys low price elasticity due to the product´s novelty; therefore, management´s efforts should focus on improving benefits; never mind price, yet. The high profits can be reinvested in adding benefits, so as to maintain growth as long as possible.

It should be pointed out that products begin the introductory stage with insufficient sales to absorb fixed costs, including the amortization of their research and development costs; this translates into losses. Eventually, a sales level is reached in which enough contribution margin is obtained to absorb the fixed costs; the breakeven point has been reached.

As the high profits gradually attract more competition, the maturity phase inevitably sets in; there is no longer acceleration; there is some degree of indifference due to the wide array of options available; the relative Value is practically nil (Vr =0) as there are there are now probably many other competing (or substitute) products offering a similar level of Value.

What is happening? Have customer preferences changed? Are the potential sales being taken over by competitors? Have differentiation and competitive advantage disappeared? Is the market saturated? ¿Is the product obsolete? These issues need to be addressed and require action.

In this phase it is likely that the capacity to add significant benefits is somewhat diminished, but it is still possible: improved distribution, expanding into new markets, advertising and promotion, etc., are feasible benefits that may contribute to add Value and prolong the maturity stage; perhaps even indefinitely.

If the previous strategy eventually wears out, the decline phase sets in, and Value is lost at flashing speed. Relative Value (Vr) is actually negative as customer preferences shift to competing products offering greater Value (Vc > Vp); then, suddenly, as sales taper off, its relative Value picks up some momentum (in the second inflection point I2) as many other competing products have already exited the market, and the going low prices yield a small increase in Value.

Since adding benefits at this stage is probably no longer possible, then the only available option for increasing Value is through price reductions, or by implementing very aggressive discounts and promotions; this enables Vr to rise again.

All this points to one conclusion: The key to success is managing Value throughout the product´s life cycle.

7.4 Value Model

In section "3.2 Supply and Demand with Value", we noted that a firm`s revenue (S = P x Q) is not a random result; it clearly obeys forces of supply and demand with Value. These forces result from the interaction of the 4P´s with the market and the overall economy. If we take into account that the 4P´s originate in the marketing strategy devised by the firm, then we can complete the Value Model from the flow perspective (revenue and income) as follows:

Customers (needs) => 4P => Value => S - TvC - Fc => Profits / Investment => Profitability

The customers´ needs drive the marketing mix (4P´s), which in turn determines the level of Value (benefits and prices) with which a product is offered to the market; this level of Value defines the rate (TCm – Fc = Operating profit) at which the company makes money and approaches its profitability goal.

The three flows, sales (S), total variable cost (TVc), and fixed costs (Fc), summarize all the activities that determine the rate at which a firm advances towards its profitability goal, and that are effectively under the direct control of the firm´s management.

Managing Value can be accomplished by visualizing the company as a *system* composed of three subsystems with functional areas that are responsible for the firm´s profit velocity:

- Sales: Marketing and Sales.
- Variable costs: Manufacturing, Purchasing, Quality Control.
- Fixed costs: Administration, Finance, Accounting, Human Resources, etc.

Functional areas are interdependent and each provides its own contribution to the Value the firm delivers to its customers.

7.5 Profitability

The firm also requires that its products have economic value (profit); otherwise, it will have no interest in producing or selling them. The firm obtains its profits by virtue of the Value delivered to its customers through its products and services; Value for the customer and profitability for the firm must therefore coexist.

Profitability is commonly referred to as "Return on Investment" (ROI); this is a metric used to measure the money-creating efficiency of an investment by comparing the profits (income) it yields with the capital invested.

$$\text{ROI} = \frac{\text{Profits}}{\text{Investment}}$$

Financial value for the firm may be expressed as:

$$\text{Profitability} = \frac{\text{Sales} - \text{Variable Costs} - \text{Fixed Costs}}{\text{Investment}}$$

Income tax is the only expense that bears no relationship with business operations: it is the government´s share of the profits. If this tax issue is not considered relevant, or is too complex, it may be excluded from the analysis altogether, as it is not a variable directly related to the marketing activity.

Profit after tax or Net Income (NI), is undoubtedly necessary so that stockholders know how much profit remains for reinvestment and/or dividends; it is also used to compute profitability.

"Investment" can be measured in two ways:

a. Total assets.

This is the firm´s total investment in assets; in this case "Profitability" measures profits earned in relation to the assets used; this is known as Return on Assets, ROA = NI / Total assets. This metric does not take into account liabilities; it is very useful for comparing companies across the same industry, independently of their debt structure.

b. Shareholders' Equity

It is equivalent to Total assets less Liabilities; in this case "Profitability" measures profits earned in relation to shareholders equity; this is known as Return on Equity, ROE = NI / Equity. This metric includes the "leverage" effect of debt (liabilities), thereby making ROE > ROA, and reflects efficiency in the use of investment funds to generate earnings.

Since marketing decisions have a direct impact on profits, its targets must be aligned with the firm´s financial goals. ROA and ROE are both used as profitability metrics as they complement each other very well; a high ROA indicates Management is using assets very productively to generate profits without resorting to debt; and a high ROE indicates a productive use of both assets and liabilities (debt).

It may be stated that investors (or shareholders) would like to reach their profitability goal in the shortest possible time. What then needs to be done in order to achieve it quickly?

The net flow of profits into the firm is given by its contribution margin less its fixed costs.

Upon subtracting fixed costs from the total contribution margin, operating profit is obtained:

Op = TCm – Fc

The total contribution margin (TCm) minus the fixed costs (Fc) is the profit velocity (Op), or rate at which the company really advances; that is, makes money[39]. The goal is to move fast in order to reach the profitability goal in the shortest possible time; this is better explained with an analogy.

Imagine a person climbing up a down-moving escalator. In order to be able to climb up, the escalator has to be outrun. The person (or firm) ascends the escalator with a speed S (sales), but the escalator descends with a speed TVc (total variable cost).

To reach the top (the goal), the ascent rate (sales) of the climber must exceed the descent rate (variable costs) of the escalator. In terms of speed, ascent velocity (sales) must exceed descent velocity (variable costs). Energy, of course, is expended to move the escalator and the climber. Let us think of the energy used in the system as the fixed costs: they are also consumed at a given rate.

The company´s management should strive to increase the rate of climb and decrease the rate of descent of the escalator, but consuming the least possible amount of energy. Revenue (sales) less variable costs less fixed costs (S – TVc – Fc) is the net rate at which the firm advances towards its profitability goal, Op = TCm – Fc.

This managerial effort requires "fuel" or fixed costs (Fc); these measure the rate at which the available resources are consumed. Fixed costs are the "fuel" that moves the firm towards its profitability target; therefore, they must be used efficiently. In the escalator analogy, (S – TVc) measures the "distance traveled" (total contribution margin) over a period, and fixed costs (Fc) are the "fuel" consumed in the same period.

If the ascent rate S is equal to the rate of descent TVc, then the person (or company) is stalled; it neither ascends nor descends, but it is still consuming "fuel" (fixed costs); this gives it a negative velocity, which is in fact a loss; in this case it is receding from its goal. Conversely, the higher S with respect to TVc and Fc the faster the firm approaches its profitability goal.

---

[39] This is based on the seventh chapter of "*The Haystack Syndrome*" by Eliyahu M. Goldratt, The North River Press, 1990

In "Appendix 3. Contribution Margin and Value", it can be observed that there is an optimum combination of benefits and price (Value) that maximizes the total contribution margin (TCm): too much, or too little Value, effectively decreases the TCm.

Section “6.7 Inventory Profitability”, outlined the strategy for maximizing the inventory´s profitability; this is paramount towards increasing ROA and ROE.

In order to reach the profitability goal in the least amount of time, it is necessary to develop and operate an efficient firm that can reach its goal quickly, with minimum “fuel” consumption; this requires management that can achieve many "miles per gallon", which is equivalent to high total contribution margin (TCm) with minimum investment and low fixed costs.

7.6 Income Statements

We have seen that in marketing, for purposes of pricing and strategy, it is very practical to separate all costs into fixed and variable. The product`s unit cost (unit variable cost, Vc) is computed with all the variable costs. When enough units (Q) are sold, sufficient total contribution margin (TCm = Q x Cm) must be generated to absorb fixed costs (Fc) and yield profits (Op).

Operating Profit, Op = Q x Cm – Fc

This method can also be taken to the gross sales level (S) using the percentage contribution margin (Cm%) as follows:

Operating Profit, Op = Cm% x S – Fc (refer to section “6.4 Applying Contribution Margin”).

It was also shown that this approach facilitates not only setting prices but also understanding the concept of velocity in sales and costs; this is crucial for advancing towards the firm`s profitability goal in the shortest possible time.

In contrast, in cost accounting a different approach is taken**:** the manufacturing overhead costs (depreciation, indirect labor, supervision, insurance, maintenance and repairs, etc.) are assigned to the unit cost of the product, independently of whether they are fixed or variable. Direct labor is also assigned to the manufacturing unit cost, even if it may be a fixed cost regularly paid on a monthly basis. (See section "5.3 Manufacturing Cost").

The allocation criteria for doing this can be the number of units produced, person-hours, machine hours, etc. With this method, both variable and fixed costs become part of the manufacturing unit cost.

"Cost of goods sold" is computed using the manufacturing unit cost, which in turn is subtracted from net sales to obtain the "Gross profit on sales"; thereupon, the administrative, marketing and sales expenses are deducted in order to obtain "operating income".

The value of in-process and finished inventory is also computed with the manufacturing unit cost; therefore, both variable and fixed costs are "stored" in inventory, until the goods are finally sold; this is when they are recognized and flow into the income statement as "Cost of Goods Sold".

Manufacturing unit cost may appear "high" as it includes the allocated or assigned fixed costs. If sales volume is low, the manufacturing unit cost is high and this tends to pressure price increases; if the price increase reduces the sales volume, the problem is aggravated as the manufacturing unit cost of will be even higher; this can become a dangerous vicious circle, particularly from a marketing and sales standpoint.

If we analyze the product Life Cycle (section "2.9 Product Life Cycle") we notice that sales volume changes as the product progresses in the market; this has the effect of changing the unit manufacturing cost throughout the life cycle.

If prices were to be set, or analyzed, based upon the unit manufacturing cost, this would tend to inflate or deflate them depending upon the sales volume and the allocation criteria; this can become a constraint towards achieving sales velocity, and attain profitability in the least possible time.

In comparison, the unit variable cost tends to remain stable throughout the entire life cycle.

Cost accounting is geared mainly towards the presentation of financial statements; their practical application in marketing and sales is limited for the following reasons:

- It is tempting to set prices based upon unit manufacturing costs.
- It is possible that the financial and accounting personnel will ignore the competition, the benefits of the product, and the marketing variables (4P).
- A low sales level, particularly during the introduction phase, yields a high unit manufacturing cost, which may induce setting high prices and adversely impact the product´s sales growth; this decreases its market penetration potential.
- Accounting classifies costs by category and not by their variable or fixed nature.
- This may create confusion and complicates the analysis required to set prices and develop strategies.
- Accounting costs thereby lose their effectiveness as a useful tool in making marketing and sales decisions[40].

This does not mean that the accounting information is not useful; not at all, it serves its purpose very well: it correctly indicates what costs are contained in each category; this is very handy for accounting and finance, no doubt.

In marketing, however, the separation of fixed and variable costs facilitates the analysis required for making management decisions; this mainly includes pricing decisions that directly affect the firm´s profitability.

A tractor is not going to perform well in a Formula-1 race simply because it is not designed for this; the same happens here: the accounting system is designed for finance. What needs to be done is to

---

[40] Thomas Nagle, Reed K. Holden, "*The* Strategy *and Tactics of Pricing*", Pearson, Prentice Hall, 2002. pp. 26-28

extract the information from accounting and adapt it to the needs of marketing and sales (Management Information System, MIS).

For illustration, two different examples of an Income Statement are presented.

The objective is to:

- Highlight the importance of the contribution margin.
- Illustrate the importance of separating variable and fixed costs.

Income Statement – Accounting

Gross Sales	$ 1,000,000	100%
Sales Discounts	100.000	10%
Net sales	900.000	
Cost of Goods sold	600.000	60%
Gross profit on sales	300.000	30%
Operating Expenses	200.000	
Operating Profit	100.000	

In the "Income Statement – Accounting" the following items stand out:

- Sales discounts are presented as a deduction to gross sales, not as a variable cost.
- Cost of goods sold includes both fixed costs and variable costs.
- Developing projections is difficult because manufacturing unit cost may increase or decrease depending upon fluctuations in sales, production and inventory.
- Cost of goods sold as a percentage of sales can seem very high due to the effect of fixed costs on manufacturing unit cost and inventory.
- Operating expenses also include a mix of fixed and variable costs.

Income Statement - Contribution Margin

Gross sales	$ 1,000,000	100%
Variable costs	500.000	50%
Contribution margin	500.000	50%
Fixed costs	400.000	
Operating profit	100.000	

In the "Income Statement - Contribution Margin" the following items stand out:

- The contribution margin includes gross sales minus all variable costs, such as direct materials, supplies, discounts, commissions and other variable costs coming from operating expenses (administration, marketing and sales).
- It is very convenient to see clearly the contribution margin, as this is the key determinant of profitability.
- The contribution margin excludes all indirect manufacturing costs that are fixed in nature; that is, do not vary with sales.
- Fixed costs include only the operating expenses that are fixed.
- The variable cost and contribution margin percentages can be easily observed; these are key variables for financial and administrative control.
- Enables developing quickly profit projections and sensitivity analysis.
- Clearly separates variable and fixed costs; this facilitates financial analysis and marketing decision-making.

The "Income Statement - Contribution Margin" supplements the "Income Statement – Accounting" with valuable management information.

7.7 Sources and Resources

Section "4.8 Sales Velocity" introduced the concept of flow and its relation to velocity. Notice, for example, that water flows from one reservoir to another: from a lake to a river and then to the ocean. The lakes and ocean are reservoirs and water flows through rivers (with velocity); reservoirs also represent something very important: resources.

The firm's reservoirs are divided into two main groups: one is a source of funds known as "Liabilities and Equity", and the other, known as "Assets", is the set of resources into which these funds are invested. These resources are specifically used to transform goods and services into valuable products that provide benefits (Value) for the firms´ customers.

In accounting and economics, these reservoirs are termed *stock* accounts and they are exhibited in a financial report known as "Balance Sheet". The purpose of the firm is to increase the money reservoir of its stockholders (Equity) through the sale of goods and services that satisfy the needs of its customers.

Let us analyze some examples of stock accounts.

"Inventory" (an asset) is a stock account that changes by virtue of two flows: it increases with purchases from suppliers and decreases with the cost of the goods that are sold and exit inventory. Similarly, "accounts receivable" (an asset) is a stock account that changes by virtue of sales on account to customers and decreases through their payments; "accounts payable to suppliers" (a liability) is a stock account that increases with purchases on account from suppliers and decreases when they are paid.

Sales, variable and fixed costs are flow accounts: they grow day by day as the firm executes its commercial activities; they only decrease at year-end when their added balances (profits) are transferred to stockholders' equity; this is done in order to reset these accounts to zero for starting the new accounting period. All flow accounts belong to a financial report known as the Income Statement.

In the previous sections it was indicated how Value leads to sales and profit velocity; delivering Value makes the stockholders´ reservoir

(Equity) increase fast; this is what they want and this is precisely why they set up the firm in the first place; it delivers Value to its stockholders through profits.

Stockholders always want to know how fast their reservoir is increasing: this is measured by ROE, which measures the *rate* at which the firm accumulates profits. They also have the capacity to deplete this reservoir for their own personal use: this is known as dividends, which are money outflows from the firm to its stockholders.

Shareholders actually have two options with their profits: request dividends and withdraw money from the company (thus decreasing the value of their equity), or allow this money to be reinvested in additional resources to promote further growth of the company; this increases their equity account.

Reinvesting profits has important consequences: the firm´s share value increases and so does their demand in the stock markets, thereby attracting new investors with funds to further drive the company´s growth. These increased resources do not go unnoticed: banks and other credit agencies see additional opportunities for investment; this means even more funds and resources can become available for the company.

The question now is, how does Value Model fit with the resources needed to deliver Value to customers with the products and services offered by the firm?

Just as an altimeter is useful for flying an airplane, the accounting balance sheet can viewed as an instrument for managing sources and resources, as follows:

1. "Liabilities and equity" are the sources of funds for the resources.

2. "Assets" represent the resources available for transforming goods and services into benefits aimed at satisfying customers´ needs.

From this perspective, the right side of the balance sheet can viewed as "sources" and the left side as "resources".

The firm is funded by its creditors (liabilities) and stockholders (equity). Each one of these groups expects a return on the funds they provide.

The stockholders bear the highest risk: If the firm fails, they may lose their investment, because all creditors are paid first and whatever remains is distributed amongst them, depending upon the amount and type of stock held. Stockholders expect returns in proportion to their level of risk and to their investment alternatives.

The creditors expect to receive compensation for the funds provided in agreement with the Law and the contracts that bind the firm; their expected return and level of risk is lower than that of the stockholders and is reflected in the cost of the funds they provide (interest rate).

The funds received are invested into resources (assets) used for transforming goods to deliver products with Value (benefits/price); this is how income is created for meeting the stockholders´ expectations (ROE).

The Value Model can be summarized as follows:

- The customers´ needs drive strategy, which in turn defines Value (marketing mix, 4P).
- Value determines revenue or sales (S = Q x P).
- The revenue level determines the resources required.
- If resources are insufficient, Value may not be delivered and excessive resources will lower profitability.
- This indicates that there exists an optimal level of resources: no too much, no too little.
- The cost of using resources to transform goods capable of delivering Value (benefits/price) to customers is reflected in fixed and variable costs.
- Fixed and variable costs are determined from the benefits offered.
- Contribution margin is obtained from the selling price less variable costs (Cm = P – Vc).
- Total contribution margin is obtained from the sales volume (Q) and the contribution margin Cm. (TCm = Q x Cm).

The total contribution margin thus obtained must be sufficient to:

- Absorb fixed costs (Fc), including the cost of funds from creditors (interest expense).
- Pay income taxes.
- Yield the surplus (profit) necessary to meet the stockholders expected returns (ROE).

The Value Model complete with stocks and flows can therefore be represented as follows:

Customers (needs)=> Strategy => 4P => Sources => Resources => Value

=> Q (P – Vc) - Fc => Profits / Investment => Profitability (ROA, ROE)

The stockholders deliver Value to the customers through the firm's products and services. Value measures the profitability of the products for the customers and ROE measures their profitability for the stockholders.

7.8 Value-based pricing

The procedure for setting prices with Value requires establishing a pricing policy (see section "4.6 Pricing Policy") and a financial goal for the firm. This method takes into account the product´s perceived benefits and the reality of a competitive environment.

It is not a question of finding the highest, or the lowest price; it is a price that:

- Meets the firm´s overall marketing goals.
- Reflects the product's benefits.
- Compares favorably against the competition, taking into account benefits and prices.
- Considers the target customer´s purchasing power.
- Achieves customer loyalty.
- Satisfies key marketing elements such as positioning and segmentation.

- Yields an operating profit that meets the firm's financial goals (ROA, ROE).

The steps for setting a Value-based price are:

1. Compare the product´s benefits and the proposed price with the competition.
2. If the product's benefits are superior to those of the competition, then the price may be the same or higher, depending upon the strategy desired.
3. If the product's benefits are inferior to those of the competition, then the price should be lower.
4. If it is a new product, or if comparisons with the competition are not relevant, or possible, the set price must meet the following requirements:

   a) Justify the benefits offered.

   b) Select the pricing strategy: penetration, if the product is easy to copy and competition is imminent; skimming, if it is difficult to copy, competition is not imminent, and an image of status and quality is to be projected.

   c) Match the target customer´s purchasing power.

   d) Achieve customer loyalty.

   e) Comply with the marketing strategy.

   f) Meet the firm´s financial goals (ROA, ROE).

Once the price (P) of each product has been set, the next step is to analyze it:

1. Estimate the *probable* sales volume (Q) of each product, using conventional sales forecasting methods, benchmarking and experience. (If it is a price change, considering elasticity may come in handy).
2. For the entire firm's product mix compute for each product "*i*" the total contribution margin: $TCm = \sum Q_i (P_i - Vc_i)$.

3. Determine the fixed costs (Fc) to obtain operating profit, Op = TCm – Fc.
4. With this data build an "Income Statement - Contribution Margin".
5. If the resulting operating profit from the Income Statement is acceptable with the firm´s profitability target, then the prices are firmly set.
6. If the operating profit (Op) is not acceptable there are several alternatives:
   - Carry out negotiations, partnerships, etc., to reduce variable costs.
   - Explore vertical or horizontal integration (see section "1.2 Markets and the Economy", *Oligopoly*, footnotes 1,2).
   - Explore opportunities for reducing fixed costs.
   - If possible, redesign the product to decrease its variable cost (Vc), without significantly changing benefits.
   - Improve prices by increasing benefits and verify the new Operating profit (Op) with the new variable costs (Vc), or the fixed costs (Fc) resulting from the added benefits.
   - Reduce benefits, decrease the price and verify the new Op with the new Vc or Fc resulting from the diminished benefits.
   - A final option is to change the pricing system "creatively": that is, explore the possibility of renting, leasing, sharing, etc.

Prices are set once an operating profit that meets the firm´s financial goals has been reached. The Value Matrix (Chapter 8) provides a tool for setting prices by quantifying benefits, and thereby obtain a numerical measure for Value, which can be used for developing and analyzing different strategies.

7.9 Practical Application Cases

The Value Model can be applied to various management questions; let us analyze each case.

Case 1. Downsizing.

Downsizing is a drastic cost reduction measure aimed at improving profits in a short period.

Let us first begin with the service provided by the firm´s human resources**.** The Value Model is based upon the principle that the price of a product must reflect its benefits. Similarly, the Value of an employee reflects the benefits he provides in relation to his cost.

Employees offer benefits by virtue of their characteristics, which may include their level of training, skills, experience, education, character, honesty, personality, etc. Their expected returns, directly or indirectly, improve contribution margin (TCm) and/or reduce fixed costs (Fc).

Examples:

- A salesperson increases TCm by increasing sales, (S).
- A buyer increases TCm by reducing variable costs, (TVc).
- A managing director increases the Value delivered to customers (thereby yielding profitability).
- An accountant provides the information necessary to increase TCm or and/or reduce Fc.
- The controller, or auditor, controls and/or monitors revenue, fixed and variable costs, assets, liabilities and equity.
- The human resources director must locate, select, hire and train the employees necessary to increase TCm and/or reduce Fc.
- The Marketing Director increases TCm by increasing sales and Value to customers.
- A receptionist channels the flow of communications to increase TCm and/or reduce Fc.
- The General Services clerk must ensure that all supplies and office goods are available in the workplace to increase TCm and/or reduce Fc.

- The Information Technology Manager channels the flow of information to increase TCm and/or reduce Fc.

All positions in a company can be similarly described. It is then clear that management mainly revolves around contribution margin (TCm) and fixed costs (Fc); therefore, every employee is hired to achieve a positive contribution towards TCm and/or Fc.

This also suggests that if employees add value to the company (capacity to generate profits), then their price (salary or compensation) must be set according to the benefits contributed; otherwise, the same will happen as with any product in the market: they might abstain from providing their services (lose motivation or resign), or they may sell them to a competitor.

Downsizing instantly reduces fixed costs and profits may actually increase in the short term; however, a reduction in fixed costs may have a negative impact on contribution margin; what is not known is how, when, or by how much. The reaction to any action may actually take days, months, or even years.

The real question is what will happen, sooner or later, to the contribution margin as a result of the downsizing. Let us recall that the market is not a science laboratory with immediate answers: causality may have delayed effects, as customers and competitors do not react instantaneously.

The contribution margin response may be delayed, but it arrives. It should be no wonder that a company may eventually find itself in a situation even worse than what it was before the downsizing. Employees that are necessary to improve or maintain TCm and Fc may be lost; in other words, the company may actually slow down rather than move faster towards its profitability goal.

Nevertheless, a fundamental question remains: Is downsizing the inevitable consequence in a company that does not deliver proper Value to its customers? If its competition offers greater Value, will downsizing solve this? Evidently, it will not, therefore it should be clear that the recovery strategy should concentrate on delivering better Value, rather than on "burning the barn".

Downsizing may be necessary due to changes in economic conditions, actions of competitors, obsolescence, customer preferences, etc. It may decrease revenue, but it can be successful as long as a careful assessment of the available resources is made, and after analyzing the effect of each alternative on profits.

The Value Model illustrates how pricing policies and costs have a direct impact on the decisions that affect human resources.

Case 2. Prices and Margins

Management sometimes pursues the goal of achieving higher profits with more "margin"; that is, raising prices; this resembles a mirage because as they attempt to approach it, it fades away; it may even lead the firm to price itself out of the market.

Why? Because sales are more sensitive to prices than what they appear to be. Pricing works in two ways simultaneously: first, it has a direct impact on sales volume, because Q is a function of Value, which in turn is a function of benefits and price; second, because sales S is the product of the resulting volume Q times the price itself (S = P x Q).

A price increase may be offset by a volume decrease, depending upon the product´s price-elasticity. If the price increase (P) reduces the total contribution margin (TCm) due to its negative effect on sales volume (Q), then the price increase will not achieve anything, or may even end up reducing profits.

What really counts is not whether margin is "high" or "low"; the key point is to understand that what is really relevant in the end is profits. Profit is given by Op = Q x Cm – Fc, where Cm = P – Vc. Note that P, Vc and Fc are directly related to the benefits offered.

Once the price (P) of each product has been set, then Sales (S = Q x P) is the market´s natural response.

The profit goal (Op) of the firm is given by the sum of the profits that each product yields, minus the fixed costs.

Algebraically, for each product "i":

$$Op = \sum Qi\,(Pi - Vci) - Fc$$

What needs to be accomplished is a combination of Qi and Pi that meets, or exceeds, the firms profit goal after deducting the variable and fixed costs; therefore, there is no such thing as a Cm% target for each product: each product has its own Cm and Cm% that results from its price. The goal is to maximize the profits generated by the product mix, as opposed to attempting to maximize the profit of each individual product.

Recall from Section 6.2 “Optimum Value” that in many cases selling a specific product frequently requires sacrificing others by means of their prices; some products depend upon others for their sale; this is why attempting to have maximum margin on each individual product leads to sub-optimal sales and profits.

Setting prices with Value is described in section "7.8 Value-based pricing". The issue of pricing effects is further analyzed in "Appendix 1. Optimization of the Demand Function”.

Case 3. Market Share

It is generally thought that to increase market share *per se* is "good", even with lower prices. What does the Value Model suggest?

The Model indicates that market share may be increased by increasing Value: more benefits, lower prices, or a combination of both.

Several issues need to be considered.

a. Benefits

Changing benefits may seem to be a fail-safe choice, but it requires taking into account the following:

- They may carry additional variable and fixed costs that decrease contribution margin Cm and operating profit.
- If volume Q does not increase sufficiently to offset the reduction in contribution margin, profits will decrease.
- Added benefits work best in products preferred by perceived high quality and in which brand loyalty and image play a major role (low elasticity).
- Adding benefits to price-sensitive goods (high elasticity) may not yield enough additional volume to compensate for the extra cost.

b. Prices

Lowering prices to drive up sales volume has several consequences:

- A price decrease lowers unit contribution margin (Cm).
- It may represent a potential threat to the product´s positioning.
- Increased working capital may be required to handle larger inventories and added trade receivables; this carries additional financing costs.
- Additional human resources may be required to manage increased sales activity, collections, and logistical costs.
- More physical space may be necessary to accommodate more resources, both human and material.
- Variable costs may increase due to transportation, handling, supplies, stationery, communications, etc.
- More fixed assets such as furniture and equipment, vehicles, etc., may be needed.
- Other Fixed costs might increase.
- Lower price works best in products preferred more by price (high elasticity) and convenience than by brand.

The firm's purpose is not to win a race with a certain "percentage" of market share *per se*; the goal is to increase the total contribution margin (TCm) with a minimum consumption of resources (Fc), in order to achieve the profit that meets, or exceeds, the firm´s financial goal: Op = TCm – Fc.

There is only one optimal Value level: any different level reduces sales and profits; therefore, higher market share does not necessarily lead to higher profits.

A market share loss is an important warning signal: it invariably indicates that the product´s Value (Vp) is lower than the competition´s (Vc); therefore the product Value differential (Vr = Vp – Vc) is negative, and this inevitably leads to a market share loss.

This reflects the following possibilities: benefits are too low; prices are too high, or a combination of both. If this situation is not promptly corrected, the product –or even the firm– may eventually price itself out of the market; this is a frequent reason for business failure.

Case 4. Performance Indexes

What does the Value Model have to say about management indexes such as "Gross Margin Percentage" and "Revenue per Employee"? These two indexes have some drawbacks. Let us analyze each one.

"Gross Margin Percentage" = 100% x (Revenue – Cost of Goods Sold) / Revenue

As explained previously, in cost accounting "Cost of Goods Sold" contains a mix of fixed and variable costs; this makes it possible to overestimate the cost and underestimate the "Margin Percentage" depending on the level of income (sales), fixed costs and inventory fluctuations; it may also lead to sub-optimal marketing and sales decisions.

"Revenue per Employee" = Revenue / number of employees.

The "Revenue per Employee" index does not consider the functional link between employees, contribution margin and fixed costs. "Fewer" employees may lead to believe that this will increase "productivity", when in fact it can actually decrease it. (See Case1. Downsizing).

Case 5. Volume vs. Price

Businesspersons often wonder if they can increase their profits by reducing prices in order to capture a higher sales volume, or if instead they should increase prices to obtain a greater "margin". This is similar to the argument over what is best: a large sales volume with low prices, or a low sales volume with high prices.

It would appear that since Sales = Q x P, it might not make much difference since many combinations of Q and P will yield the same level of sales. This is not that simple: it is not possible to generalize because all products and businesses have their own peculiarities; nonetheless, there are several issues that need be taken into account:

Price elasticity

Management needs to be aware of product elasticity, even if it is an intuitive "feeling" of whether it is high, medium or low.

If the product (or its category) is highly elastic, a small price increase may drive down its sales volume significantly, in particular if it can be easily replaced by another brand; thus, a price increase may have a negative impact on profits.

A price reduction may drive up volume, but it may also add variable and fixed costs.

If the product has low elasticity stemming from high brand loyalty, a small price increase probably will not have much impact on volume; but, the price level and possible response of competitors still needs to be taken into account.

A small price decrease may not have much impact its sales volume, so it is unlikely that it would reduce profits.

If the product has a medium elasticity, it is likely that a small price increase will yield a small volume reduction, with perhaps no major impact on profits. However, if it is a priority for the brand to be widely known, then it might be preferable to stick with a lower price and a higher volume, as many more customers will be made aware of it.

Positioning

A product's price is a key component of its positioning; therefore, any change in price must consider this. If it is a high-end product, a price reduction might send confusing signals to its market, thereby decreasing its status and prestige.

Low-end products are purchased frequently and are preferred for their price; therefore, these products should not appear "expensive" and this should be reflected in their packaging.

Costs and business size

In small businesses, fixed costs represent a high percentage of revenue because they have many limitations in output or production capacity. Its variable costs tend to be high because their relatively low volumes do not allow for negotiating large discounts with suppliers; their prices must be geared to absorb fixed costs with low sales volume in comparison with a large business; this generally suggests a high-Value (Vp) high-margin (Cm%) strategy.

These are the main reasons why retailers frequently have percentage profit margins higher than that of the manufacturers which supply them.

A small business may not be able to cope with large sales volumes due to the added costs and its limitations in output capacity; large volumes (Q) require more fixed assets and working capital, personnel, space, inventory, transportation, etc. All this adds extra costs.

In contrast, large businesses have greater output, and this enables them to absorb fixed costs over a larger sales volume. They also have a greater capacity for negotiating volume discounts with suppliers, thereby reducing variable costs; these advantages enable them to operate with lower prices as compared to small businesses.

Competition

The competition is a key benchmark; therefore, it has to be closely monitored, particularly in what regards benefits, prices and market share.

In all of the above cases the Value Model will provide support for setting prices (refer to Chapter 8).

In order to evaluate the quantitative impact of decisions with multiple products taking into account fixed costs, the Operating profit formula is recommended:

Operating profit $Op = \sum Q_i (P_i - Vc_i) - Fc$

If it is a single product without considering fixed costs, apply:

$TCm = Q (P - Vc)$

These formulae are useful for comparing the "before" and "after" scenarios when setting prices and taking into account the competition.

The "crowd" effect[41]

Humans are gregarious beings that depend upon society for survival; socialization and teamwork enabled our ancestors to hunt large prey and fend off predators.

Individual survival depended on group acceptance; we are instinctively drawn to people; we avoid lonely places that might place us in peril; we feel vulnerable alone; so naturally, crowds give us a sense of security.

This has some interesting repercussions in marketing: it explains why, in most cases, we avoid restaurants, bars, stores, etc., that seem to be

---

[41] N. Braidot, *Neuro* Marketing, Ediciones Gestión 2000, 2009, p. 123.

solitary; we prefer places where we see other people. This gives the feeling that there is something "good"; that is why there are other people there. If they are buying a product, or service, then we instinctively think it is probably good.

Prices play a key role here: low prices attract customers, and when potential buyers see a crowd, it acts like a magnet; instinct stimulates our urge to join others for the "hunt"; once these forces have been unleashed, the price itself becomes secondary.

Customers are lured with low prices to a product or service with valuable benefits. The product thereby makes headway in the market in a relatively short time: it soon reaches a self-sustaining critical mass of customers that under other circumstances might have taken years to build; the time required to reach the breakeven point may be significantly shortened.

Low prices increase product turnover and increase the number of clients that flow through the business (traffic); this benefits the brand´s awareness and its value. The sacrifice in price is the cost of this strategy.

Case 6. How much should be produced and sold.

In many businesses, the question lingers concerning how much output is advisable. Economic theory provides a simple answer based on price: sell more, as long as the revenue from selling more is greater than the cost. Example: if a product is sold for $ 10 and it costs $ 9 to produce it, then sell more.

However, if a point comes when it can be sold for $ 10 but it costs $ 10 or more, then its production must be stopped as no additional revenue is obtained from selling more; the quantity sold at $ 10 is the maximum output.

In more "technical" terms this is defined as the point in which marginal revenue equals marginal cost (MR = MC). This means that if the cost of producing an additional unit exceeds the revenue generated by the additional unit, then production should be stopped at that point. It seems reasonable, but how practical is it for solving business problems?

This concept, translated into a real business example can be illustrated as follows: For a manufacturing firm selling more means producing more, until the output capacity at some point reaches a cost limitation. For example, to produce an additional unit the firm has to either hire a new employee, or buy a new machine, and this will increase the manufacturing cost of the extra unit; this increase in unit cost is the result of allocating fixed cost to unit manufacturing cost.

In this case, salary or machine depreciation is allocated to the additional unit. The additional (marginal) cost of the unit sold will surpass the additional (marginal) revenue, and at that point MC > MR; therefore production must be stopped. But, what if the fixed cost is pulled out of the equation? This presents a completely different situation: in this case MR > MC, therefore production and sales may continue!

The Value Model does not allocate fixed costs to unit costs; the contribution margin arises from the difference between the selling price and the variable cost (no fixed cost). So in this case the extra salary, or the additional depreciation, will not add to unit cost: the variable unit cost remains the same. This does not imply that fixed costs are ignored: fixed costs are flow accounts that must be recognized and properly accounted for when they are incurred.

This means that despite the added fixed costs, the firm can still continue producing and selling, provided the expected sales volume will be sufficient to absorb them. The unit variable cost will very likely go down, not up. The higher production level will eventually enable the firm to negotiate greater volume discounts and more favorable payment terms from suppliers.

A few issues stand out:

- The benefits offered reflect the marketing strategy: marketing mix (4P).
- The selling price (P) reflects the benefits, and should not be any different (within a certain range), unless the benefits are changed.
- Both benefits and prices must be compared against the competition.
- The benefits offered determine the fixed (Fc) and variable costs (Vc).
- The benefits and price combination determines the product's Value.
- Value in turn facilitates estimating the quantity (Q) customers are willing to purchase; this can be carried out using conventional sales forecasting methods, benchmarking and experience.

- The estimated sales volume (Q) must be sufficiently high to absorb all fixed and variable costs and yield an operating profit that meets financial goals (ROA/ROE); if not, then a different combination of benefits, price and costs has to be proposed (a different Value).
- Once fixed costs are excluded from the unit product cost, it becomes a variable cost.
- A larger sales volume may reduce unit costs, only if they can be decreased by virtue of greater manufacturing productivity, efficiency, or lower supplier costs.
- Selling "more" is not necessarily more profitable (ROA / ROE) than selling "less"; this depends upon the operating profit and the investment.
- Profits can never be isolated from the investment required to generate them.

Evidently, the Value Model approach provides a more practical solution than the MR/MC economic analysis for solving common business problems. However, some of its consequences, depending upon price and strategy, may seem unexpected:

- Maximum profitability is possible in a firm even if its resources operate at less than full capacity, as profits depend on Value more than anything else.
- For example, a restaurant owner might be surprised to discover that, depending upon his benefits and price combinations, it may be possible to make more money with a few customers than with many.
- It might be more profitable to operate many small outlets rather than one single large store.

These are examples of the possible consequences predicted by the Value Model. Every product or market is, of course, unique, therefore, there are no set of rules or "recipes"; each requires its own individual analysis.

Case 7. Credit Policy

A credit policy sets the guidelines that indicate which customers are sold on open account, their limits, the payment terms, and how to handle past-due accounts.

Firms commonly extend credit as part of their service in regular selling activities; this facilitates trade as it may offer convenient payment arrangements.

Credit policies must be geared as a service that supports sales and marketing activities in order to avoid constraining them. The key point is that credit decisions should avoid constraining sales, or more specifically, the firm's target profitability; this requires a decision-making method compatible with the marketing strategy (positioning and segmentation) and with financial goals such as sales and ROA.

The market needs to be properly segmented, so that the selected target market offers an attractive revenue potential and the financial capacity to purchase the firm's products.

Customer credit is an investment that must be profitable; this requires a procedure for estimating its profitability, and which in turn must be aligned with the firm's financial goals.

The profit (total margin contribution) of each individual customer is given by:

$TCm = \sum Q_i (P_i - Vc_i)$, for each product i pertaining to his purchase product mix.

The quantity Q_i is the sales volume expected to be sold.

The asset amount to be invested in the customer is the expected credit outstanding, or the average accounts receivable balance (AR).

Since ROA = Profit / Assets, then the expected ROA for customer *c* is:

ROAc = TCm / AR

This ROAc must greater or equal to the firm's ROA target (computed as TCm/AR) if sales velocity is to be surpassed, or at least maintained. A lower ROAc (within certain limits) could be financially acceptable, but it may slow down the rate at which the firm approaches its profit target.

If a non-payment risk is to be considered, then AR can be adjusted to deduct an allowance for doubtful receivables; this increases the required ROA.

Since the firm always has limited resources, a good practice is to rank customers by ROA potential and thereby establish an order of priorities for credit allocation and approval.

These cases illustrate how all functional areas are interrelated, and why they must be subordinated to a marketing and Value framework.

Case 8. Pricing products with intensive man- or machine-hours and output capacity limitations.

A major question is how to price products whose manufacture requires many man or machine-hours and output capacity is limited. These are products, or services, which usually require for their production expensive equipment; they carry high fixed costs in terms of depreciation and/or direct labor.

The key point to understand is that the goal is not to determine the product's price or cost; the true goal is to reach the ROA and ROE targets; therefore, the price and cost determination must be subordinated to this goal.

There is no doubt that if the manufacture of a product requires many man or machine hours, it must provide very special benefits to its customers and therefore they will be willing to pay a relatively "high" price. Notice that the price arises from these benefits and not because of its cost; costs are used to determine profits.

If high processing times lead to a low output capacity (Q), this must be balanced with a higher price (P), as described in section "7.8 Value-based pricing". If the price thus obtained is too high and the market does not respond (low Value), then the product is not profitable; with such a high price the purchasing frequency would not be enough to sustain an acceptable sales volume (Q).

Once the output capacity limit is reached (Q cannot increase further), and supply is still short of demand, this suggests that the product´s Value still allows a higher price.

Once production capacity is overwhelmed, the company can still increase its price (P) further, until supply is balanced with demand. If the market will not accept it, then the alternative is to invest in additional resources and expand output capacity to continue selling at a lower price.

This is very similar to the entrance fee ("cover") charged at bars and nightclubs at peak hours: Value-based supply and demand will establish the proper fee. If success justifies it, the next step is to increase output capacity; the opposite takes place in the off-peak hours: this is when “happy hour” discount prices go into effect to increase frequency and sales velocity.

These actions in peak and off-peak hours fulfill a major objective: they increase average sales velocity (S = P x Q). This illustrates how using price to balance supply with demand increases revenue and profits.

What happens in the case of two products with similar variable unit costs, but with different machine or labor hours? Their unit variable costs (Vc) would be the same, the only difference would be their price (P) and sales quantity (Q). Again, and as previously explained, price would be used precisely to balance supply with demand; the product most highly valued by the customers would carry the highest price (P) and the highest contribution margin (P – Vc).

Their fixed costs would differ because of labor costs and/or equipment depreciation; however, these costs flow correctly through the income statement accounts anyway; therefore, from the point of view of pricing, there is no need to allocate fixed costs to the unit cost of each product.

However, the interplay between quantity (Q), price (P), and variable unit cost (Vc) must be sufficient to absorb the fixed costs and yield an Operating profit, Op = Q (P – Vc) – Fc, which meets the firm´s financial goals.

Case 9. Price Increases

During a product´s life cycle, there is frequently need to effect price changes; most of them are necessary to increase revenue by balancing supply with demand.

The market always has a strong resistance against price increases and this makes them difficult to implement; therefore, it is important to have an effective Value strategy, in order to counteract the customers´ possible reactions.

Price increases may be due to multiple circumstances, among which the following stand out:

Inflation

This pushes up costs and affects all market participants equally. In general, it is customary to raise prices in proportion to the increase in costs; this does not affect customer preferences, as long as the competition responds in a similar fashion.

The increases may be carried out selectively to avoid negative reactions from customers; in some products they may be higher or lower, depending upon the implementation strategy.

Expectations

It is possible that the acceptance of customers to a new product may be much higher than expected; this means that the product has some benefit, which the market values beyond expectations, and presents an opportunity to increase price and profit without affecting the quantity demanded (Q). This occurs most likely during the introduction and growth phases of the product's life cycle.

Competition

The preference for a product may increase if competitors raise the price of substitute products; this increases the product´s Value differential, and if the price remains unchanged, provides the opportunity to achieve greater market share.

The other option is to also raise prices and thus Q and market share will remain unchanged; revenue and profits increase due to the higher price (P).

Resource constraints

If customer demand exceeds output capacity (supply) due to the limitation of a resource, the company has two options: the most immediate is to increase price, and if success and the available resources allow it, then expand production capacity (machinery, equipment, human resources, etc.)

An example of this is a manufacturing company that cannot cope with demand due to a packaging capacity limitation; therefore, a price increase may be the most immediate option; this automatically balances the supply and demand, thereby eliminating the restriction; and if successful, but still cannot meet demand, then it should consider purchasing another packaging machine. (It should be clarified that the price increase should not be excessive, as this may open a breach for the competition).

Again, the key is to balance supply with demand by virtue of price (P) thereby increasing revenue (S = P x Q).

It should be noted that successive price increases can gradually displace sales towards market segments with greater purchasing power.

If the product´s price elasticity is relatively high, particularly in essential goods such as food, such increases may reduce the sales volume (Q) without it being offset by the price (P); this not only reduces the product´s profits, but also opens a gap to the competition in the abandoned segment.

If the price increase does not compensate the loss of volume, the final impact on sales volume can be very unfavorable; the price will have already surpassed its optimal level and successive increases work against sales and profits.

Case 10. Price Decreases

Customers will always be willing to accept price decreases, as long as the product's positioning is not threatened; however, this can be circumvented through the proper use of discounts and promotions.

Price reductions must be supported by a strategy, otherwise the client may feel that he was being previously abused, or that the product has lower quality. For example, more can be offered for the same price; this equates to a reduction in price that the customer perceives as a product improvement.

As in the prior case of price increases, economic circumstances, expectations, competition and output capacity, may also trigger forces that can drive down prices.

Price reductions may also be required for the following reasons:

Product Life Cycle: the decline phase.

When a product is approaching the end of its life cycle, the only way to sustain its Value is through price decreases; at this stage the options for greater benefits will have already been exhausted; this is precisely the reason for its decline.

Examples come not only from products becoming obsolete, but also from products subject to cyclical sales due to fashion or season. At the end of each cycle the slow moving, or dead inventory, must be quickly liquidated to reinvest the funds in other products with more favorable growth prospects; this can be facilitated through the use of discounts and promotions. The sale of winter clothing in spring provides a good example.

Sales velocity

Revenue may be increased by providing higher Value, which translates into offering more benefits and/or setting lower prices; benefits favor products with low price elasticity and lower prices favor those with high elasticity.

Increasing sales velocity is necessary when revenue is not sufficient to absorb fixed costs and obtain an acceptable profit; this may happen at any stage during the product´s life cycle.

Countering penetration strategies.

Responding to competitors´ threats directly aimed at breaching the market with low-priced new products, may require a price reduction response; the challenge is how to go about it without compromising the product´s positioning.

Responding with a direct price reduction may be very costly and risky as it may threaten the firm´s entire market, when in fact threats tend to be more localized. If, however, an extra benefit is offered, instead of the price reduction, the product´s positioning remains firm and customers may thus perceive a powerful incentive to increase their purchasing frequency.

The response can be a promotional strategy that offers "more for the same price"; it can be applied in the specific markets, or locations, where threats appear.

Examples:

- "Buy one, get one free." This sounds more impressive than a 50% discount.
- For the prospective customer "five for the price of four" may be more attractive than offering a 20% discount; after all, math can be a confusing subject!
- Giving away a toothbrush for the purchase of, say, three toothpastes can be a good incentive for a savvy shopper.
- A potential customer may not flinch under a 10% discount offer; if, however, he is offered the opportunity to participate in an attractive sweepstake, he may eagerly proceed to purchase.

Among the strategies suggested to reduce prices, the following may be included:

- Increase the amount delivered without reducing the price of the product. Example: provide a package with a larger quantity for the same price; this way the customer does not notice a price reduction; on the contrary, he perceives a significant improvement (higher Value) in the product.
- Provide a gratuity with the product; again, this is financially equivalent to a decrease in the price, and the customer obtains a great benefit without the risk of compromising the brand´s image.
- Reduce prices gradually and selectively; if done properly, the customers will hardly notice.

Chapter 8

The Value Matrix

8.1 The Value Matrix

The Value Matrix provides a heuristic[42] method for setting and developing pricing strategies. The purpose of the matrix is to obtain a quantitative result for the Value of a product (or business) according to the relationship between benefits and price:

$$\text{Value} = \frac{\sum \text{Benefits}}{\text{Price} + \text{Effort}}$$

The method uses a table to list and quantify benefits for setting the prices of two or more competing (substitute) products; these are indexed on a base of 100 and the Value is obtained by dividing the indexed benefits by the indexed price.

Once the matrix has been developed it may be used for setting prices, or developing different strategies and determine their resulting Value; the one with the highest Value would be the most favorable from a competitive standpoint and the one that determines the best possible price (optimal).

For developing the Matrix the use of a spreadsheet is recommended: this facilitates its understanding and is the most practical way to build and apply it. The Matrix may be completed with information from customer surveys, market research, or with a panel, or group of experts chosen for this purpose.

---

42 Technique for solving problems based upon experience, judgment and criteria.

The group must have a leader who guides it as fairly and objectively as possible. Data is obtained from the average of the subjective opinions of the group. Overall, the group tends to agree, as long as all members are familiar with the market and with the products being analyzed. The larger the group is, the more statistically significant will be the result.

The procedure begins by assigning a score (index) to the price and making a list of all the benefits offered by the products being analyzed. Each benefit is assigned a relative weight, according to its importance and perception by the group. It then proceeds to compare the benefits of the competing products with scores on a scale of 100. A listing of common benefits appears in section "2.10 Benefits".

The scores of all the benefits are added, indexed and divided by the price index; this yields a numerical result for Value that can be used for comparing the products being analyzed. Comparisons are more reliable when the products or businesses analyzed compete within the same market segments.

8.2 Building the Value Matrix

Figure 8.1 Example for two competing *products*

1	2	3	4	5	6	7
VALUE MIX	BENEFIT WEIGHT	% Weight	PRODUCTA		PRODUCT B	
1. PRICE			$10.000		$8.000	
2. PRICE INDEX			100		80	
3. DESIGN	80	27%	60	16	100	27
4. PACKAGE	50	17%	70	12	100	17
5. QUALITY	100	33%	100	33	80	27
6. VARIETY	30	10%	80	8	100	10
7. BRAND, IMAGE	40	13%	100	13	80	11
8. TOTAL	300	100%		82		91
9. **VALUE** =			0,82		1,13	

The development process includes the following steps (refer to Figure 8.1):

1. Set-up the spreadsheet headings as suggested.

2. Row 1: Insert the prices of each product in their respective cells.

3. Row 2: The product with the highest price, product A ($ 10,000), is assigned a score (or index) of 100 (100%). The price index for product B is obtained by dividing the price of B by the price of A ($ 8,000 / $ 10,000) and this yields an index of 80 (80%) for product B. (The percent sign need not be to taken into account). The result in row 2 corresponds to the indexed price.

4. Column 1: This is the *benefits mix*: it is a list of all of the benefits that are considered significant in the sales of each product. This list represents the subjective views expressed by the study group, and contains all those benefits that are considered relevant and are truly valued by the customers.

This list is simply used to develop the example. In a more realistic analysis, it must provide all the elements (benefits) that may be affecting, or promoting the sale of the product.

5. Column 2: Each benefit is assigned a relative weight on a scale from 0 to 100, depending on its order of importance. This weight is the average obtained from the subjective views of the study group. The most important benefit is assigned a weight of 100; thereafter, the weight of each is set with reference to this one. These weights are added together and their sum total is in row 8. (It does not matter how much the weights add up to in this column, as in the next one they are adjusted to a 0 -100 scale).

6. Column 3: This column is built by taking each weight in column 2 and dividing it by their sum total (column 2, row 8). Column 3 is equivalent to column 2 but on a percentage scale, which indicates the relative importance of each benefit. As observed in row 8, the total of all percentages must add to 100%.

7. Columns 4 and 6: Each benefit of products A and B is assigned a comparative score, according to the group's opinion. The product that has the best benefit is assigned a score of 100. The score of the same benefit for the other product is set with reference to this one. For example, if product A has the best quality then it is assigned 100. If the perceived quality of B is somewhat lower, it can be assigned a score of 80 as suggested. Since "variety" is better in B it is assigned 100. In product A "variety" is inferior to B and therefore receives a score of, say, 80, according to the group's perceptions; this process is repeated for each benefit.

8. Columns 5 and 7: These columns are the result of multiplying the percentage weight of each benefit (Column 3) by the score assigned to each benefit in the previous columns 4 and 6. The result of this multiplication is the quantification of each benefit for each product; it indicates not only how important the benefit is, but also how it compares between the two products.

9. Row 8: In this row Columns 5 and 7 are totalized to obtain a score of the benefits of each product. This is the "Σ Benefits" component in the Value formula.

10. Row 9: In this row the Value of each product (A and B) is computed from the total benefits of row 8 (columns 5 and 7) divided by the price

index for each product row 2. This yields the comparative Value for each product analyzed according to the formula:

$$\text{Value} = \frac{\sum\text{Benefits (score)}}{\text{Price (indexed)}}$$

8.3 Pricing and Strategy

The example shown facilitates understanding the concept and mechanics used to quantify Value.

Analysis of Product A

- Must improve the benefits in which it is at disadvantage (DESIGN, PACKAGING and VARIETY) in order to match the Value of B.
- QUALITY is its main strength, since it is the most important benefit.
- By performing various simulations, we conclude that even if A could improve all of its benefits, it would still be at a disadvantage due to its price.
- Consideration should be given to the possibility of reducing its price and, if applicable, its design and/or costs to make it feasible.
- In column 4 of the Matrix changes can be made to the benefits of A to analyze its impact on Value, in order to match B`s Value.
- In row 1 of the matrix, gradual reductions in the price of A can be made to observe how they impact its Value as compared to that of B. In theory, the price could be reduced until the Value of A approaches the Value of B.

Analysis of Product B

- It may easily increase its price and still continue to offer its customers a greater Value than A.
- By improving its QUALITY, its advantage over A will remain firm, even if it increases its price.
- In column 6 of the matrix changes in the benefits of B can be made to analyze its impact on Value, in order to *anticipate* a possible response to A`s strategy.
- In row 1 of the matrix, gradual increases in the price of B can be made, and observe how they impact its Value compared to A. In theory, the price of B could be *increased* until its Value reaches that of A.
- In principle, if all benefits have been sufficiently well analyzed, it is probable that if B raises its price, its sales volume will not fall and therefore its profit will increase.

The result of the example indicates that under the present conditions customers perceive greater value in B than in A. The Value Matrix opens the possibility of analyzing quantitatively the strategies of both competitors. The Matrix may be expanded to analyze more than two competing products; this is particularly useful when it is desired to evaluate several competitors simultaneously.

The model may be adapted to include the effects of promotions and discounts, by making the appropriate substitutions in benefits and/or prices, or in the indexes, as applicable. It should be noted that with the use of this model costs can be linked with prices and sales volume to observe the impact on profits of each decision or strategy. This model is a useful tool for simulating and analyzing competitive situations.

A given Value does not necessarily mean "superior", or "inferior", or "good", or "bad"; it simply responds to the strategy that each company may wish to implement for its products. The real judge is, at the end of the day, the market.

8.4 Business Modeling

The method applied for analyzing *products* can be used for analyzing and comparing *businesses*; the key is to obtain a price index that reflects the price *level* of each business. For example, if is determined that the prices of business Y are 20% lower than those of X, then their price indexes will be 80 and 100 respectively. In these cases only indexes are used, as a single price would not make sense.

The benefits would no longer be applicable to each individual product but rather to each *business*. The Value analysis may be performed in the same fashion.

Figure 5.2 Example for two competing *businesses*

VALUE MIX	BENEFIT WEIGHT	% WEIGHT	BUSINESS X		BUSINESS Y	
PRICE INDEX			100		80	
SERVICE	80	27%	60	16	100	27
QUALITY	100	34%	100	34	80	27
VARIETY	30	10%	80	8	100	10
DECOR	15	5%	90	5	100	5
BRAND	30	10%	100	10	80	8
PROMOTIONS	40	14%	20	3	100	14
TOTAL	295	100%		76		91
VALUE =			0,76		1,14	

Analysis of Business X

- It should improve the benefits that are at a disadvantage to match the Value of Y.
- In particular, it should improve SERVICE, which apart from its price, is its weakest benefit.
- QUALITY is its main strength, so it should take advantage of this with its communication strategy.
- Highlighting this point is recommended in the communication strategy of the business.

- Even if A could improve in all the benefits that are lower than its competitor, it would still be at a disadvantage.
- Business A should consider lowering its price and, if possible, its costs.

Analysis of Business Y

- It can easily increase its prices and still offer its customers a Value greater than X.
- By improving its QUALITY, its advantage over A will remain firm, even if it raises its price.
- It should invest more in advertising its brand.
- Its PROMOTIONS are an important strength and must do everything possible to exploit them further.

The options for each business consist of varying prices across the board, or changing benefits. The aim is to provide a level of Value that is competitive in its relationship of benefits with price. The Value of competing firms can be easily compared.

8.5 Value Matrix Applications

The Value Matrix has several practical applications:

- May be used for diagnosing and benchmarking a product or a company
- Provides a tool for setting prices in freely competitive markets.
- Can be used for setting the prices of new products.
- It is useful for understanding what benefits are truly valued by customers.
- Facilitates detecting "wrong prices".
- Identifies strengths, weaknesses, opportunities and threats ("SWOT").
- Facilitates developing pricing and marketing strategies.
- Can help unveil the strategy of a competitor.

- Contributes towards identifying what can, or should be, the product´s *positioning.*
- Facilitates understanding whether it is necessary to redesign the product to reduce its cost and/or increase its benefits.
- It enables analyzing simultaneously two or more products, companies or strategic business units, with any level of detail (benefits and prices).
- It can be structured with several products simultaneously in order to determine an optimal product mix.
- Quantifies the economic impact of different strategies and business scenarios.
- It is useful for analyzing the competition and understanding its strategy.
- It can be used for increasing product turnover.
- It can be linked to a financial simulation model complete with Income Statement, cash flow, and Balance Sheet items, in order to evaluate the financial impact of different Value (benefit and pricing) strategies.

Chapter 9

Ethics in Marketing and Pricing

The key issue in a sale is the trust that the customer bestows on the product he wants to purchase; but, beyond the product, the customer is relying on the brand and the company supporting it.

A democratic system based on free enterprise requires marketing to facilitate trade; this works successfully as long as there is faith in its institutions. There are mechanisms that govern, regulate and to some extent control, but these mechanisms also rely on good faith.

Pricing depend on good faith and must be free of deception. If a package has misleading information, content, or appearance, the customer may doubt the price and its brand. Once the bond between trust and brand is broken, customer loyalty is lost forever. The same may apply to the quality for which a customer has sacrificed money and effort. This arouses rejection and prompts him to seek other alternatives.

The free play of prices under supply and demand provides society a valuable service for efficient resource allocation. If this system is interfered, obstructed, or used maliciously, it ceases to function properly. Ethics is an integral part of the system and its absence acts as interference.

Ethics protects the foundations of the economic system and maintains confidence in its institutions. Free enterprise enables the free play of supply and demand to allocate resources efficiently, and, therefore, it well deserves defending it against the threats and interferences that can undermine its operation.

Conclusion

Value-based pricing plays a major role in relationship marketing: It is the key to attain customer loyalty. Value is a force that accelerates sales, but it requires removing the resistances that prevent the company from achieving its goals quickly.

Value-based strategies, and their related pricing methods, are developed from the fundamental principles of marketing, economics, accounting and finance; all the marketing effort and management eventually converges on the product´s Value.

If the law of supply and demand is restructured to include Value, it can become a valuable tool for defining product and pricing strategy. The Value-based forces of supply and demand indicate that there is a marketing mix, which optimizes the firm's prices, while maximizing its revenue and profits.

It was observed that is not the same to price in an oligopoly market than in monopolistic competition; it is also necessary to know the type of buyer the product is aimed at, as this affects the strategy required.

Value-based Confrontation strategy increases the Value of the product by increasing benefits and/or reducing prices. It is highly focused on winning market share at the competitors' expense; their reaction can make it a strategy that, if unsuccessful, can quickly deplete the firm´s available resources.

Value-based Complementation strategy maintains Value constant by varying benefits and prices proportionately, and rather than confront the competition, it complements it. This provides it with great "Pareto potential"; in this case the capacity to improve the firm's market position, but without directly affecting that of the competition.

The business strategy and marketing mix (4P) must respond to the customers' needs, providing the benefits that determine prices, costs, quantities, resources and funds required; eventually, all the marketing effort converges on Value. Corporate governance should be focused on delivering Value, not only for the customer, but also for all the other stakeholders (all the parties that hold an interest in the firm).

Value-based pricing leads to understanding that it is not enough to satisfy the customer's needs and to obtain their loyalty: it is necessary to do it in the shortest possible time.

Value is a key determinant of contribution margin and market share. It is the force that increases sales, provides the best strategy for growth, and propels the firm towards rapidly achieving its profitability goal.

Services can be very useful for not only achieving product differentiation and competitive advantage, but also as tools to balance supply with demand, thus achieving an optimum use of limited resources and maximizing profits.

The "Income Statement - Contribution Margin" is a valuable management tool that is useful for analyzing and setting prices. It relies on a clear distinction between fixed and variable costs and facilitates financial modeling and forecasting.

The analysis of sales price, variable and fixed costs, indicates that time is closely related to profits; this leads to the development of a Value-based management model, focused on resource optimization in order to rapidly achieve the financial goals of the firm.

The firm delivers Value to its customers from its entire set of product and services; therefore, maximizing the Value and profitability of the entire product mix, supersedes improving the contribution margin of each individual product. In other words, increasing independently the profit margin of each product leads to suboptimal profits. The growth in inventory profitability directly increases key performance metrics such as ROA and ROE.

Identifying opportunity costs is paramount in Value-based pricing. Seeking an optimum combination of benefits and prices, while keeping track of competitive forces, leads to eliminating opportunity costs: this increases sales and profits.

Prices should remain within the reasonable range required by the product´s positioning. For example, high-end products, such as brand name cosmetics, should not sell at low prices as this will convey a message of low quality that will adversely affect sales.

If all opportunity costs can be eliminated, profits reach a maximum. Value-based pricing seeks to identify and eliminate all opportunity costs by properly balancing benefits and prices while keeping track of competitive forces.

Reducing variable and fixed costs can increase profits, but they have no effect on the optimal price, as it is determined by the product´s Value.

Sales are very price-sensitive; therefore, great caution is required when setting prices. The Value Matrix provides a quantitative method for setting prices based on the product's benefits and its competition; additionally, it facilitates developing business strategies and tactics for planning responses to potential competitive threats.

Appendix 1

Optimization of the Demand Function

Demand can be represented as a simple linear function of the type Q = a • P + b. where "Q" is the quantity demanded; "a" is a constant (slope) that relates changes in the quantity demanded with changes in the price "P"; and "b" is a constant related to the level of demand at any price. (To avoid confusion between different variables, the symbols "•" and "x" are interchanged when necessary to indicate multiplication).

The demand function (orientation model) is given by:

$Q = a \bullet P + b$, where

Q is the quantity demanded in a given period.

P is the selling price of each unit.

"a" is a constant that relates changes in Q with respect to changes in P (the slope of the graph). A high value of "a" makes it "steep"; a low value, relatively "flat".

"b" is a constant that adjusts the level of demand Q at any price P.

The demand function can be represented as follows:

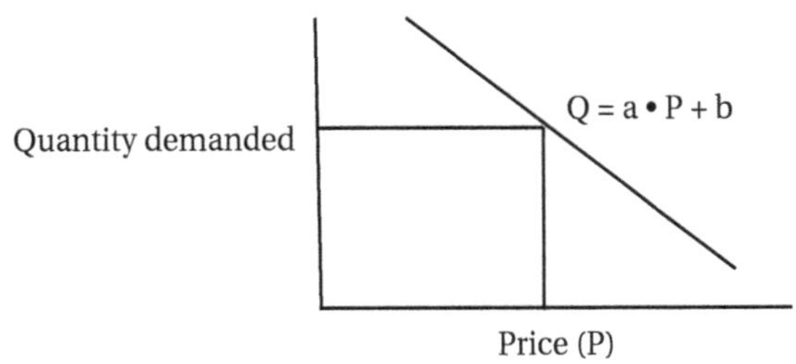

If Q is the quantity demanded and P is the price, then sales (S) is the quantity demanded Q multiplied by price P.

Sales: $S = Q \bullet P$ (in the graph it corresponds to the area of the rectangle)

Replacing $(a \bullet P + b)$ for Q we obtain:

$S = (a \bullet P + b) \bullet P$

$S = a \bullet P^2 + b \bullet P$

Regarding the demand Q, the model indicates how Q would be related to P in the period analyzed, be it year, a month, or day.

Upon a close look at the sales function S, it is evident that the level of sales $(S = Q \bullet P)$ is related to the square of the price: $S = a \bullet P^2 + b \bullet P$.

This suggests that sales (S) may be, one way or another, very sensitive to price. The reason is that a double price effect exists. First, because price plays a key role in demand Q is a function of the price P, and second, because sales in money are obtained by multiplying the quantity sold Q times the price P; therefore P ends up multiplying, not once but twice, and that is why its impact on sales is can be so significant. This indicates that proper pricing is critical because, at the end of the day, price ends up determining the profitability of the firm.

Plotting the sales function S we obtain[43]:

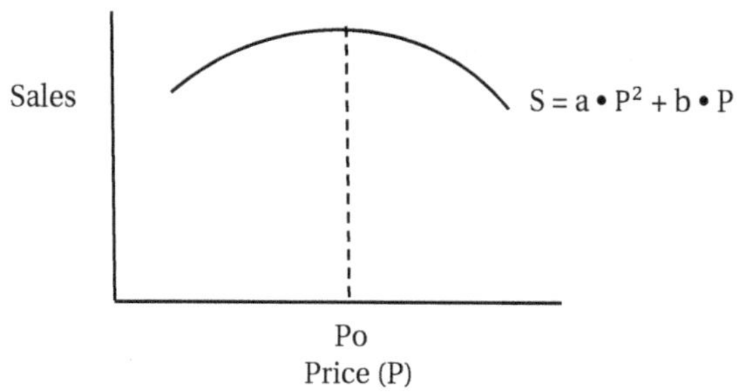

[43] This is a quadratic function that has a maximum which can be determined with differential calculus.

Business experience and intuition suggest that when a price is too low, sales may be very high, but profits will be too low. If prices are excessively high then volume may be too low to generate any profit.

This indicates there is an optimal price (Po) that is the "best"; this price achieves the highest level of sales and profits; any different price, higher or lower, decreases sales and profits. This price, however, is not be obtainable from a mathematical demand function because it is unknown, uncertain or frequently changing.

Products with high elasticity, such as necessities (milk, eggs, flour, etc.), tend to have high sales volume, low differentiation, and intense competition. Their demand curves carry a "steep" slope (high coefficient "a" in absolute value). Products with low elasticity (high-end luxury items) have a comparatively "flat" slope (low coefficient "a" in absolute value); they are less sensitive to price changes.

From differential calculus, the sales maximum (profit optimum) is obtained when dS/dP is set to zero (this is the price Po in which sales reach their maximum level).

$$dS/dP = 2\,a \bullet P + b$$

$$0 = 2\,a \bullet P + b$$

$$P = -b\ /\ 2a$$

This indicates that as elasticity increases (higher "a", "steeper" curve) the optimum price (P) decreases. This means that inventory, or product mix, profitability increases when the prices of products with low-differentiation are comparatively low, and the prices of highly differentiated products are relatively high.

This is an interesting conclusion because it indicates that placing high prices (margins) on a product mix with different degrees of differentiation is sub-optimal. In other words, attempting to place high margins on all products leads to sub-optimal profitability. This is mainly due to the opportunity costs arising from lost sales of products with little differentiation (due to high prices). These may be purchased from competitors, or their purchasing frequency will simply be lower.

This is what Value-based pricing suggests: price according to the product´s benefits while taking into account the competition. Highly differentiated goods should carry high prices (margins), while products with a low degree of differentiation should carry comparatively lower Prices (margins).

Placing high margins (prices) on all products, independently of their Value (benefits to price ratio), leads to sub-optimal profits. This applicable to any business, be it a manufacturing company, supermarket, restaurant, hardware store, etc. Pricing each product in accordance to its Value leads to higher revenue and income. This, of course, should never ignore the product´s brand image, or its positioning, as these are part of the product´s Value.

Prices should remain within the reasonable range required by the product´s positioning. For example, high-end products, such as brand name cosmetics, should not sell at low prices as this will convey a message of low quality that will adversely affect sales.

If all opportunity costs can be eliminated, profits reach a maximum. Value-based pricing seeks to identify and eliminate all opportunity costs by properly balancing benefits and prices while keeping track of competitive forces.

Reducing variable and fixed costs can increase profits, but they have no effect on the optimal price, as it is determined by the product´s Value.

Obtaining a statistically significant correlation between the quantities sold Q and the price P is complex and unreliable for the following reasons:

- Customers do not react instantaneously to a price change.
- Not all customers buy at the same time; they do not purchase constantly, and they react differently to price changes.
- This creates a time lag in and in that span of time many other variables can affect demand: competition, advertising, economics, politics, technology, preferences, cycles, seasons, fashion, etc.
- Isolating non-price related variables can be a very complex statistical task.
- The competition´s response to a price change is unpredictable and may have a significant effect on Q.
- Demand, prices, and elasticity may vary significantly during the product´s life cycle.

Truth be said, the mathematical function that really governs demand based on price is unknown. Since the demand for a product changes as the product progresses through its life cycle, its price and demand function also change constantly; therefore isolating the price variable may not even be necessary, because, as we have seen, demand is governed more by Value than by price.

The main benefit of the orientation model is that while it may not provide the exact mathematical answer, it does contribute towards understanding the underlying principles at work. In this particular case, it does shed some light on why prices have such great impact on sales and profits.

There is no doubt that, whatever the real function is at any point in time, sales are very sensitive not only to price, but also to the benefits offered. This is precisely why the delicate balance between pricing and benefits requires great caution and due analysis.

A linear function was used for demand simply to illustrate a point, and due to its ease of analysis. There are many other possible mathematical functions, but in any case, they must all respond to business experience: given constant benefits, excessively low or high prices lead to low profits.

Appendix 2

Summary of Formulae

Sales S = units sold (Q) x Price (P)

S = Q x P

Total variable cost (TVc) = units sold (Q) x unit variable cost (Vc)

TVc = Q x Vc

Variable cost percentage % = unit variable cost / sale price

Vc% = Vc / P, or

Variable cost percentage % = Total variable cost / sales

Vc% = TVc / S

Unit contribution margin = Price – variable cost

Cm = P - Vc

Contribution margin percentage % = unit contribution margin/ Price

Cm% = Cm / P, also

Contribution margin percentage = total contribution margin/ Sales

Cm% = TCm / S

The total contribution margin using prices and costs of individual products is:

TCm = units sold (Q) x unit contribution margin (Cm)

TCm = Q x (P – Vc)

TCm = Q x Cm

The total contribution margin using sales (S) and percent contribution margin (Cm%) is:

TCm = Contribution margin percentage (Cm%) x Sales (S)

TCm = Cm% x S

Recall: Cm% + Vc% = 100%

Operating profit calculated with units sold and fixed costs (Fc):

Op = Q x (P – Vc) – Fc or Op = Q x Cm – Fc

Operating Profit computed with sales (S), contribution margin percentage (Cm%) and fixed costs (Fc):

Op = S x Cm% – Fc

Appendix 3

Value and Contribution Margin

The analysis of supply and demand based on Value leads to the question: Is there a Value that is optimal for the firm? That is, a Value, which maximizes the total contribution margin, TCm? This Value exists and can be demonstrated by analyzing the equilibrium point with Value.

Recall the graph (Fig. 3.1) used in section "3.2 Supply and Demand with Value":

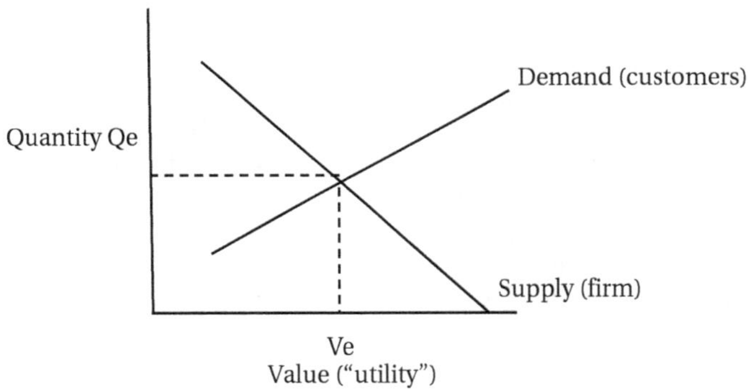

Offering greater Value can be related to a lower contribution margin (Cm) due to the higher cost of added benefits and/or price reductions. This graph can be transformed into an equivalent one, if contribution margin (Cm) substitutes Value on the horizontal scale.

This requires inverting the graphs because the contribution margin (Cm) must *increase* to the right on the horizontal scale.

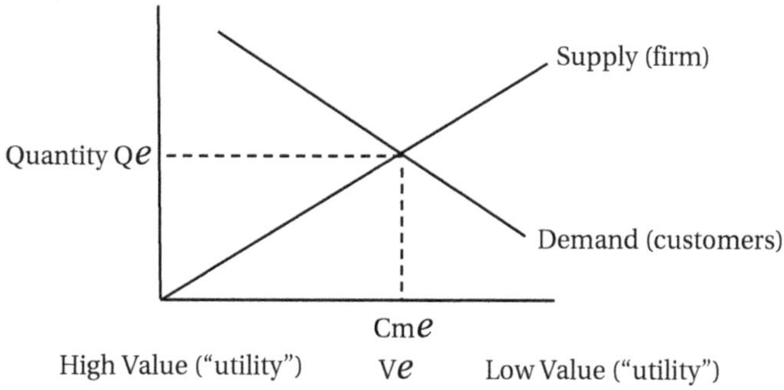

The supply and demand functions based on Value resemble the classical supply and demand functions when replacing Value with contribution margin (Cm) on the horizontal scale. This is consistent with classic supply and demand, as it suggests that with higher Cm (or price), the firm is willing to offer more product Q, and that as Cm increases (or price), customer demand decreases due to the higher prices associated with a higher Cm. If Cm is excessive, then demand would be very low due to the lower benefits and/or higher price.

Recall that low contribution margin Cm reflects high Value; that is, many benefits (high variable and fixed costs) and/or very low price. High contribution margin Cm reflects low Value; that is, few benefits (low variable and fixed costs) and/or a very high price.

Movement along the supply curve indicates how much Q amount the firm is willing to supply depending upon the contribution margin Cm. A very high contribution Cm reflects low Value because it implies the firm will offer few benefits (low costs) at very high prices. The firm would like to sell a lot of this, but customers are not interested in the product; this shows up as slow sales or dead inventory.

The total contribution margin (TCm = Cm x Q) is represented by the area of the rectangle shown in the graph. This is the maximum value of TCm, because that is the maximum Cm that the market accepts by virtue of benefits and price, with the maximum Q that the firm is willing to offer, also due to benefits and price. This takes place with Value V*e*, contribution margin Cm*e* and quantity Q*e*.

Notice that when Cm = 0, the supply Q = 0. This corresponds to delivering such a high Value that the firm makes no longer makes a profit; the variable cost of the product is equal to its price. The total contribution margin is TCm = Q x Cm = 0. At that point, the firm is not willing to produce or sell any output whatsoever; in fact, it incurs a net loss given by Op = 0 – Fc, equivalent to its fixed costs.

At the Value equilibrium point V*e*, the total contribution margin TCm is a maximum. In other words, at the Value level (V*e*), income and profits are at a maximum; any Value lower or higher than V*e* generates lower sales and lower profits. Customers will not accept a lower Value and the firm is not willing to deliver a higher Value.

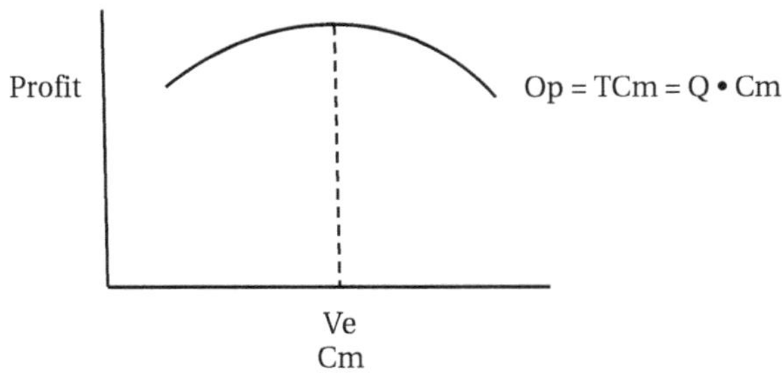

Value-based strategy provides room for Pareto improvements; that is, someone is better off without making anyone else worse off. This model suggests however that Pareto improvements do have a limit: At a Value higher than V*e* the firm is not willing to supply the quantity demanded, and below V*e* the customers are not willing to buy the quantity the firm is willing to deliver; in other words, Value can be added, but too much works against profits.

The combination (V*e*, Q*e*) is therefore the best marketing and pricing strategy; in fact, it is a Pareto optimum: the best for everyone (firm and customers). Beyond this point, the firm is worse off in terms of profits; and below this point, the customer is worse off in terms of the Value received (benefits vs. price).

This leads to conclude that there exists an optimum strategy for the firm that has a combination of benefits and prices, which maximizes its operating profit, and the Value delivered to its customers. The firm will not change its strategy unless its Value needs to be changed in response to the actions of its competitors, given that they can change the customers´ preferences.

Appendix 4

Sales Volume Variance Analysis

An increase in revenue (sales) from one year to the next might be the result of an increase in the number of units sold, or an increase in prices, or a combination of both. Another possibility is that the increase might be the result of an increase in the price, but with a decrease in the number of units sold; there also other possibilities.

The purpose of variance analysis is precisely to decompose the change in sales into its volume (quantity) and price components, in order to track price and quantity effects.

Let us analyze a change in revenue from one year to another.

Revenue (sales) = Quantity sold (Q) x unit Price (P)

Revenue in year 1:

S1 = Q1 x P1

Revenue in year 2:

S2 = Q2 x P2

The change in revenue Δ S from year 1 to year 2 is computed as:

Δ S = S2 – S1

This is the correct order of subtraction because an increase in sales should be seen as a positive number (favorable variance), whereas a decrease should be seen negative (unfavorable variance).

This can be understood better by observing these changes in a graph, as follows:

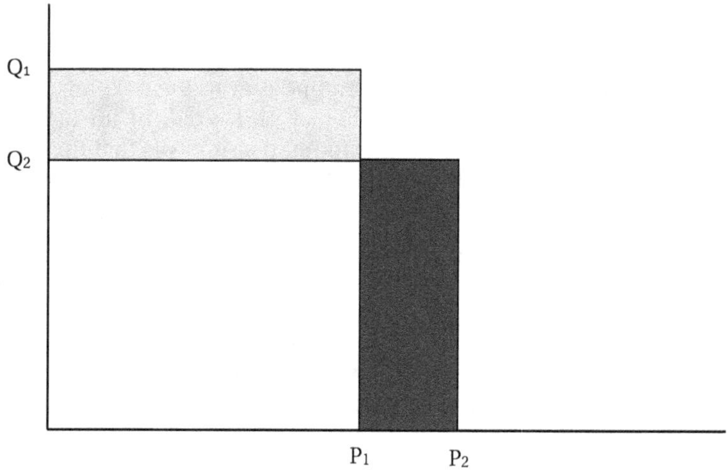

Notice that if there had been no change in price (P) the rectangle given by P1P2 would not exist; this rectangle is the sales variance due to price (Pvar); the area of this rectangle is given by (P2 – P1) Q2. Similarly, notice that if there had been no change in quantity (Q) the rectangle given by Q1Q2 would not exist either; this rectangle is the sales variance due to quantity (Qvar) ; the area of this rectangle is given by (Q2 – Q1) P1.

Proof:

$\Delta S = Qvar + Pvar$

Since

$Qvar = (Q2 - Q1)\ P1$ and

$Pvar = (P2 - P1)\ Q2$, then

$\Delta S = (Q2 - Q1)\ P1 + (P2 - P1)\ Q2$

$\Delta S = Q2P1 - Q1P1 + Q2P2 - Q2P1$ rearranging terms obtain

$\Delta S = Q2P2 - Q1P1 + Q2P1 - Q2P1$,

Given that $+Q2P1 - Q2P1 = 0$, then,

$\Delta S = Q2P2 - Q1P1$

Since

$S2 = Q2P2$ and $S1 = Q1P1$

$\Delta S = S2 - S1$, proven.

Therefore,

$\Delta S = Qvar + Pvar$

<u>Example 1</u>

Year 2:

$P2 = \$\ 17$ $Q2 = 10{,}100$ units.

Revenue

$S2 = Q2P2$

$S2 = 11{,}000 \times 17$

$S2 = \$\ 171{,}700$

Year 1:

$P1 = \$\ 16$ $Q1 = 10{,}000$ units.

Revenue

$S1 = Q1P1$

$S1 = 10{,}000 \times 16$

$S1 = \$\ 160{,}000$

The change in revenue from year 1 to year 2 is:

$\Delta S = Q2P2 - Q1P1$

$\Delta S = \$\ 171{,}700 - \$\ 160{,}000$

$\Delta S = \$\ 11{,}700$

Variance analysis:

Quantity variance:

$Qvar = (Q2 - Q1)\ P1$

$Qvar = (10{,}100 - 10{,}000)\ 16$

$Qvar = 1{,}600$ (favorable)

Price variance:

$$Pvar = (P2 - P1)\ Q2$$

$$Pvar = (17 - 16)\ 10{,}100$$

$$Pvar = 10{,}100 \quad \text{(favorable)}$$

Revenue variance = Quantity variance + Price variance

$$\Delta S = Qvar + Pvar$$

$$\Delta S = 1{,}600 + 10{,}100$$

$$\Delta S = \$\ 11{,}700$$

How can this be explained from a marketing standpoint? It appears that if the price increases, the quantity sold should decrease; but, not necessarily. In this case, both variances are favorable: the price increases and so does the quantity sold; it is very likely that demand for the product far exceeds supply, or that the product is inelastic with respect to price; in fact, given this situation, the price can increase further and still yield higher revenue. A moderate price increase under these circumstances carries little risk.

On the other hand, if volume falls this indicates that the product is elastic with respect to price; if the decrease in volume more than offsets the increase in price then revenue falls; by how much depends upon the product´s elasticity. In this case, price increases do carry a certain level of risk.

Example 2

Sales budget:

Pb = \$ 100 Qb = 1,000, therefore Sb = 1,000 x 100 = \$ 100,000

Market size *budgeted* in units Mb =10,000

Market share *budgeted* MSb= Qb / Mb = 1,000 / 10,000 = 10%

Actual result:

Pa = \$ 120 Qa = 900, therefore Sa = 120 x 900 = \$ 108,000

Market size *actual* in units Ma =15,000

Market share *actual* MSa = Qa / Ma = 900 / 15,000 = 6%

Revenue increase (ΔS = Sa - Sb): Actual revenue vs. Budgeted revenue (this is the correct subtraction order so that a good result appears positive).

Δ S = QaPa – QbPb

Δ S = \$ 108,000 – \$ 100,000

Δ S = \$ 8,000

The change in revenue (ΔS) can be split into two components: a quantity effect (Qvar) and a price effect (Pvar). Let us analyze each variance.

Quantity variance:

Qvar = (Qa – Qb) Pb

Qvar = (900 – 1,000) 100

Qvar = – \$ 10,000 (unfavorable)

Price variance:

Pvar = (Pa – Pb) Qa

Pvar = (120 – 100) 900

Pvar = \$ 18,000 (favorable)

Revenue variance:

Δ S = Qvar + Pvar

Δ S = – $ 10,000 + $ 18,000

Δ S = $ 8,000 (favorable) must be equal to the revenue increase of $ 8,000.

The revenue result is favorable as the actual result exceeds the budget by $ 8,000. The actual price ($ 120) is 20% higher than the budget ($100). However, the quantity sold fell by 100 units from 1,000 to 900, or 10%.

The favorable price variance of $ 18,000 exceeded the unfavorable quantity variance of – $ 10,000. This suggests that the decision to sell at a price higher than that budgeted is wise, because although the quantity falls, it is not sufficient to offset the positive price impact. These decisions require knowledge of the market (customers and competitors) and a reasonable sense of the product´s price elasticity, whether it be high, medium, or low (from a practical standpoint, this is sufficient).

The market size and growth can also be included into this picture. This is significant because the market represents the competition; therefore, if the competition has revenue growth, then the firm´s revenue should also increase; this comparison is important because it indicates sales performance. This performance analysis can be extended from the revenue level to the profit level.

If the market size (quantity) and market share are taken into account, this helps explain the sales quantity variance (above): Qvar = – $ 10,000 (unfavorable).

It seems reasonable to measure the increase in sales quantity, against the size of the market to determine what revenue should be if it increases at the *same* rate as the market. If sales increase at the same rate as the market, then the sales result does not seem to be very impressive (constant market share). This is measured by the market size variance.

However, if sales decrease when the market increases, then the result or performance seems quite poor (decreasing market share). If sales increase in a proportion greater than the market size increase, then performance is judged as good. This is a market share effect and it is measured by the market share variance.

Notice that the market size increases from 10,000 units to 15,000 units.

Market increase: Δ M = Ma – Mb = 5,000 units

If the *budgeted* market share (MSb = 10%) and *budgeted* price (Pb = $100) *do not change,* then actual revenue (S) should increase by: 5,000 x 10% x 100 = $ 50,000. This is the market *size* variance, or the increase in revenue (sales) that would take place simply by virtue of the market´s growth.

Market *size* variance = ΔM x MSb x Pb = 5,000 x 10% x 100 = $ 50,000 (favorable).

In other words, if both *budgeted* market share and price are maintained, a revenue gain of $ 50,000 would be achieved simply by growing in sales volume at the same rate as the market.

However, market share does change, as it *falls* from 10% to 6%; this means a *loss* of 4%.

The quantity amount of this loss can be computed from the *actual* market size (15,000 units): it yields an unfavorable variance of 15,000 x (-4%) = – 600 units. In other words, by not maintaining the 10% market share, and falling to 6%, the firm *loses* 600 units with regard to the new market. If these units are also valued at the *budgeted* price ($100), to be consistent with the market size variance computation, then the market *share* variance is – 600 x $ 100 = – $60,000. This is, of course a *loss* of market share valued in monetary terms.

Market *share* variance = (MSa – MSb) x Ma x Pb

Market *share* variance = (-4%) x 15,000 x 100 = – $60,000 (unfavorable)

This represents how much revenue is sacrificed by virtue of the market share loss.

The quantity variance, Qvar (valued at the budgeted price), can be explained as the sum of the market performance variances: *market size* plus *market share* variances:

Qvar = *market size* variance + *market share* variance

Qvar = $ 50,000 (favorable) + –$60,000 (unfavorable)

Qvar = – $ 10,000 (unfavorable)

In other words, the quantity variance Qvar can be analyzed from a performance perspective: first, simply as the result of a change in market size and, second, as the result of a market share change.

The total revenue variance (ΔS = Sa - Sb) can therefore be broken down into, not two, but three components or effects, as follows:

Revenue variance ΔS:

+ *Market size* variance =	$50,000 (favorable)
+ *Market share* variance =	– $60,000 (unfavorable)
= Quantity variance (Qvar) =	– $10,000 (unfavorable).
+ Price variance Pvar =	$18,000 (favorable)
= Revenue variance (ΔS) =	$ 8,000 (favorable)

If price (P) is substituted by contribution margin (Cm) then the net change in profit (TCm) can be similarly analyzed by taking into account not only prices but also variable costs (Vc), using TCm = Q x Cm instead of S = Q x P. See summary below:

Quantity and price variances					
P and Q	Actual	Budget	Dif	Var	
Market(units)	15.000	10.000	5.000	50.000	Market *size* variance
Market share	6%	10%	-4%	-60.000	Market *share* variance
Q	900	1.000	-100	-10.000	Quantity Variance (Qvar)
P	120	100	20	18.000	Price variance (Pvar)
S	108.000	100.000	8.000	8.000	Revenue variance
Vc	65	70	-5		
TVc	58.500	70.000	-11.500		
TCm	49.500	30.000	19.500		
Cm	55	30	25		

Quantity and contribution margin variances					
Q and Cm	Actual	Budget	Dif	Var	
Market (units)	15.000	10.000	5.000	15.000	Market size variance
Market share	6%	10%	-4%	-18.000	Market share variance
Q	900	1.000	-100	-3.000	Quantity Variance (Qvar)
Cm	55	30	25	22.500	Cm variance (Cmvar)
TCm	49.500	30.000	19.500	19.500	Profit variance

Notice that the change in profit (profit variance) can now be analyzed from what is happening in the market and from quantity, price and variable cost changes.

What stands out from this particular example is that *market share* is *not* the main priority; the key issue is the combination of quantity, price and variable cost. In this particular case, profit *increases* despite a market share and volume loss.

This example, which is perfectly possible in real market conditions, also suggests that the firm may operate at less than full capacity and yet earn a higher profit.

Example 3

The marketing department notices that the total variable cost (TVC) has increased from one period to the next; this would send a warning signal.

TVC2 = $ 108,000 and TVC1 = $ 100,000

Δ TVC = 8,000 extra cost

A closer look reveals the following:

Prior period:

Vc1 = $ 100 Q1 = 1,000

Present period:

Vc2 = $ 90 Q2 = 1,200

Let us analyze each variance.

Quantity variance:

Qvar = (Q2 – Q1) Vc1

Qvar = (1,200 – 1,000) 100

Qvar = $ 20,000

Variable cost variance:

Vcvar = (Vc2 – Vc1) Q2

Vcvar = (90 – 100) 1,200

Vcvar = – 12,000 (curiously, *more positive cost* variance would be "bad", but *more negative cost* variance is "good", as it represents savings).

Total variable cost variance:

Δ TVc = Qvar + Vcvar

Δ TVc = $ 20,000 + (– 12,000)

Δ TVc = $ 8,000

Explanation? There really is no problem at all: it seems the buying team did a great job as they managed to save a good $ 12,000 in costs. Of course, this was more than offset by an increase in sales volume (also "good") that made total variable cost seem "bad".

If the buying team had not done their homework properly, the variable cost variance would have been very different, as follows:

Total variable cost without the cost savings would be = $ 100 x 1,200 = $ 120,000

Prior total variable cost = $ 100 x 1,000 = $ 100,000

Total increase = $ 20,000 instead of $ 8,000.

The buying department therefore "earned their keep"! They managed to save $ 12,000.

These examples illustrate the analytical potential that variance analysis carries, especially in marketing and sales.

Appendix 5

Discounts

Discounts are usually short term incentives that temporarily add Value to product because they decrease the amount paid by the customer, although its benefits may remain unchanged. The increased Value increases sales velocity; more is sold in less time.

It must be clear to the customer that the product's *original* price is maintained and so is its positioning; the discount is temporary; any message to the contrary may send confusing signals.

Extending a discount without any reciprocal concession on the part of the customer should be avoided, as it can make him leery. He may conclude that somehow the product lacks quality; its price could be abusive; or perhaps he could have even received a larger discount if he had insisted; contrary to expectations, this will very likely lead to a loss of his confidence and loyalty; in fact, it may create cognitive dissonance in him.

A discount can be seen as rebate given to the customer, in exchange for providing the firm added liquidity due to a payment made in advance, or by purchasing a larger quantity. It is equivalent to receiving the full amount and simultaneously giving a refund.

This is the reason why a discount, from a marketing standpoint, can be considered a variable cost: the customer is being paid for his concession. There are very many types of discounts depending upon sales terms, type of customer, product, etc. However, they are basically different forms of prompt payment, quantity, or liquidation discounts.

Discounts may have several objectives[44]:

- Induce different behaviors in customers.
- Provide traders an incentive to purchase a product and resell it.
- Increase sales and market share.
- Improve inventory turnover, particularly of perishable, cyclical or slow-moving products.
- Liquidate dead inventory.
- Entice customers to try a new product or to switch to another brand.
- Reward customer loyalty.
- Increase purchasing frequency.
- Negotiate different concessions from customers (additional purchases, or paying forward).

Prompt payment discount

Discounts are Pareto improvements: one party does not benefit at the other's expense; they both benefit: the firm obtains funds promptly, and the customer in turn receives a reduction of the amount to be paid for each unit purchased.

An interesting question is how to compute discounts, or how to measure their implications. Let us assume, for the sake of simplicity, that money can be invested at, say, 1% per month. If a customer offers to pay $ 1,000 thirty days in advance, this would imply that the firm has the possibility to invest these funds, and earn $ 10 per month. However, if the customer is offered this same discount, he will very likely reject it, as he can just as well make this investment on his own; he must be offered more.

---

[44] Carlos R. Sánchez S, "*Administración del Precio en Mercadotecnia*", Thomson, 2003, p. 34

Suppose firm has $ 100,000 in assets and that it makes an average annual profit of $30,000, equivalent to a 30% rate of return on its assets. Therefore, if the firm receives an extra $1,000 (an asset), its best option is to invest it within the firm, and by doing so it is very likely that after one year the firm will earn $ 300 from these funds, which averages $ 25 per month, or 2.5% of $ 1,000. If the firm earns $ 25 and pays out $ 10 (discount), it obtains a profit of $ 15.

From a negotiation standpoint, it would not be very wise to offer the customer the 2.5% discount, as it is entirely possible that he may be willing to pay in advance for a discount higher 1% and yet lower than 2.5%. This, of course, depends on each particular situation, the market´s interest rates, and other financial considerations.

Quantity discounts.

A quantity discount rewards the customer for purchasing more. Again, this is another Pareto improvement, as it benefits both parties: the customer pays less for each unit and the seller, in turn, sells a larger quantity. Selling more in one transaction may save selling and transportation expenses.

Let us analyze an example with discounts. Suppose the customer is willing to purchase 1,000 units (Q) at a price (P) of $100. Revenue would therefore be: S = 1,000 x 100 = $ 100,000.

The customer requests a discount of 5% ($5.00) for increasing his purchase by 10% (100 additional units). Revenue would be S = 1,100 x 95 = $ 104,500.

Assume the product has a variable cost (Vc) of $ 70; therefore, the contribution margin is Cm = 100 –70 = $30 per unit. If the negotiation is carried forward, then the Vc = 70 + 5 = $ 75, when considering the discount as part of the variable cost.

It really makes no difference to deduct the $ 5.00 from the price, or to add it into the variable cost: the contribution margin is still the same. The point is that from a marketing positioning perspective, a discount should not change the product's price; it merely offers a temporary purchasing incentive; the math should be in line with this concept.

The financial picture looks as follows:

a) No quantity discount.

TCm = Q x (P – Vc)

TCm = 1,000 x (100 – 70) = $ 30,000

b) Quantity discount.

Q = 1,000 + 100 = 1,100

Cm = 100 – 75 = 25

TCm = (1,100) x (25)

TCm = $ 27,500

The deal is still profitable as the firm will make $ 27,500. But, the question lingers: is this a good negotiation? The truth of the matter is that the customer indeed wants a discount, and if the firm wants to sell more units, it has to come up with a counter proposal that will be acceptable to him.

If no quantity discount is extended, then the negotiation´s profit is $ 30,000. However, if the firm wants to maintain the $ 30,000 gain, then it must propose the customer to increase his purchase, as follows:

$ 30,000 = Q x 25

Q = 30,000 / 25 = 1,200 units (this is 20% over the original amount of 1,000).

If the customer purchases these units, he obtains a clear benefit, which is a cost reduction of $5.00, from $100 to $95; the firm, on the other hand, obtains an increase of 200 units instead of 100. Therefore, this would be a more reasonable proposal; but, the customer may not be willing; he may not be able to stock this quantity, or perhaps may not have the funds required.

However, the negotiation can take an interesting twist: accept the customer´s proposed discount, but *against the additional volume.* This is how the picture would look:

S = 1,000 x 100 + 100 x 95

S = 100,000 + 9,500 = 109,500.

The customer´s original proposal is S = 1,100 x 95 = $ 104,500.

The new proposal brings in a little more revenue than the customer´s: it accepts his proposed discount, but applied against the extra volume he is willing to purchase.

If we take a closer look at the customer´s original proposal, we are in for an unexpected surprise:

Customer proposal: S = 1,100 x 95 = $ 104,500.

Initial deal: S = 1,000 x 100 = $ 100,000.

This translates into 100 additional units with added revenue of $ 4,500. If we compute the average price of each additional unit, it comes to:

P = 4,500 / 100 = $ 45!

This effectively comes to a whopping (100 – 45) /100 = 65% discount!

Should the firm be willing to sell at $45 a product whose variable cost is $70? Certainly not. Of course, there are many arguments on each side´s favor, but during a sales call, when things may get "complicated", the sale can be easily lost. Moreover, if the customer´s proposal is accepted, and he turns out to be an astute negotiator, it is possible that in a future purchase he may request the 65% discount supposedly awarded in his prior purchase: a seller´s nightmare!

Let us apply variance analysis to compare the proposals:

Quantity variance: Qvar = (Q2 – Q1) x P1

Price variance: Pvar = (P2 – P1) x Q2

Initial proposal:	S = 100,000	Q1 = 1,000	P1 = 100
Customer proposal:	S = 104,500	P2 = 95	Q2 = 1,100

Qvar = (1,100 – 1,000) x 100 = \$ 10,000

Pvar = (95 – 100) x 1,100 = – \$ 5,500

Δ S = \$ 10,000 – \$ 5,500 = \$ 4,500

The gain in sales quantity (Qvar) of \$ 10,000 is offset by the loss in price (Pvar) of – \$ 5,500

Let us compare the initial proposal with the new proposal, which applies the discount only to the additional quantity.

Qvar = (Q2 – Q1) x P1 Pvar = (P2 – P1) x Q2

Initial proposal: S = 100,000 P1 = 100 Q1 = 1,000

New proposal:

S = 1,000 x 100 + 100 x 95 = \$109,500

P2 = 109,500 / 1,100 = \$ 99.55

Q2 = 1,100

Qvar = (1,100 – 1,000) x 100 = \$ 10,000

Pvar = (99.55 – 100) x 1,100 = – \$ 500 (rounded)

Δ S = \$ 10,000 – \$ 500 = \$ 9,500

In this case the effect of the quantity increase on revenue is \$ 10,000, but the price loss effect is only – \$ 500. This is certainly a better deal as the negative impact on price is minimal.

Liquidation discounts

These are aimed at exchanging inventory for cash in a short period of time. A product's Value is increased temporarily by way of a price reduction. These discounts are quite common and are used as a tool for increasing inventory turnover in slow-moving products. Good examples are toys discounted after Christmas, or out of season clothing.

Once inventory has been quickly exchanged for cash, it can be reinvested in products with a higher turnover; this increases average total inventory turnover, and leads to higher short term revenue.

This practice is also a useful tool for eliminating inventory of obsolete goods: there comes a point in which a product may no longer be desired, as it may be replaced by a more profitable substitute. At this point the firm can only entice buyers to purchase if the price is sufficiently low; this gives the product its last breath in the market before it finally disappears.

Appendix 6

Solved Problems in Pricing

This appendix provides solved problems in marketing, sales and pricing for readers who wish to learn more about the use of prices and costs. (For ease of learning, the level of complexity gradually increases.)

1. A retailer purchases a shirt for $ 10.00 with the purpose of reselling it with a $ 5.00 profit. The selling price is therefore $ 15.00.

What is **P**, **Vc**, **Cm**, **Vc%**, **Cm%**?

P = 15.00   Vc = 10.00

Cm = P - Vc

Cm = 15.00 – 10.00

Cm = 5.00

Vc% = 10.00 / 15.00

Vc% = 67%

Cm% = 100% - 67% = 33%, or

Cm% = 5.00 / 15.00 = 33%

2. A retailer purchases a lamp for \$ 15.00 with the purpose of reselling it.

a) If the goal is to obtain a contribution margin (Cm%) of 25%, at what price should it he sell it?

Computation using Cm:

Cm% = Cm / P

Cm% = (P - Vc) / P

25% = (P - 15) / P

25% P = P - 15

15 = P - 25% P

15 = 75% P

P = 15 / 75%

P = 20

Therefore, if a lamp has a variable cost of \$ 15.00 and the desired contribution margin is 25%, it should be sold for \$ 20.00.

Computation using Vc:

Recall that Cm% + Vc% = 100%, therefore if Cm% = 25%

Then

Vc% = 100% - 25% = 75%.

This indicates that Vc of \$ 15.00 is 75% of the selling price.

Vc% = Vc / P, such that 75% = 15.00 / P.

Solving for P,

P = 15.00 / 75%

P = 15.00 / 0.75

P = \$ 20.00

b) If 2,000 lamps are sold, what would be the sales level (S) and what would be the total contribution margin (TCm) obtained?

Q = 2,000

P = 20,000

Vc = 15,000

Recall that sales S = Q x P, therefore

S = 2.000 x 20.00

S = $ 40,000

Cm = P - Vc

Cm = 20.00 - 15.00

Cm = 5.00

TCm = Q x Cm

TCm = 2,000 x 5.00

TCm = $ 10,000

3. In a hardware store, a hand drill has a retail price of $ 50.00. The cost at which the retailer purchases it is $ 30.00. The store sells 100 drills per month.

a) What is P, Vc, Cm, S, Q, TVc, TCm?

P = 50.00, Vc = 30.00 Q = 100

Cm = P - Vc = 50.00 - 30.00

Cm = 20.00

S = Q x P, therefore

S = 100 x 50.00

S = 5,000

TVc = Q x Vc, therefore

TVc = 100 x 30.00

TVc = 3,000

TCm = Q x Cm, therefore

TCm = 100 x 20.00

TCm = 2,000, or equivalently

TCm = S - TVc

TCm = 5.000 - 3.000

TCm = 2.000

b) To boost sales a discount of 10% is proposed. By how much should sales increase so that the discount can be justified?

TCm = Q x Cm

The *current* contribution margin is: TCm= 100 x 20 = 2,000

The discount is worth 50 x 10% = 5.00 per unit.

The discount-adjusted contribution margin per unit is:

Cm = 20.00 - 5.00

Cm = 15.00

TCm = Q x Cm

TCm = 2,000

2,000 = Q x 15.00

Solve for Q

Q = 2,000 / 15.00

Q = 133 units (drills) required to maintain the same TCm.

This indicates that to justify the 10% discount the number of drills sold should be at least 133 units. This represents an increase of

(133 – 100) / 100 = 0.33 or 33%.

From a marketing standpoint, it makes sense to offer a discount, if more turnover is desired, but without reducing the current profit level. If fewer than 133 units are sold then the profit would be lower, and offering the discount would not be a wise decision, unless the purpose is to liquidate the inventory.

Also, it must be realized that it is unlikely that with a discount of 10% sales will increase by 33%, unless the products have high elasticity.

4. In a clothing store monthly sales are \$ 100,000. The cost of goods purchased from suppliers costs \$ 40,000. Sales commissions amount to 5% of sales.

The store has the following monthly fixed operating expenses:

Rent \$ 10,000,

Payroll \$ 20,000

Utilities \$ 5,000

Note that in this example there is no unit price, no unit variable cost and no sales units.

a) What is S, TVc, Vc%, TCm, Cm%, Fc?

S = \$ 100,000

Sales commissions (5%) are a variable cost and must be added to the total variable cost (cost of goods) of \$ 40,000. Thus, 5% of \$ 100,000 = 0.05 x 100,000 = \$ 5,000 in commissions. Therefore, the total variable cost including sales commissions is:

TVc = 40.000 + 5.000

TVc = 45.000

Vc% = TVc / S

Vc% = 45,000 / 100,000

Vc% = 0.45 = 45%

TCm = S - Vc

TCm = 100.000 - 45.000

TCm = \$ 55,000

Cm% = TCm / S

Cm% = 55,000 / 100,000

Cm% = 55%

Alternatively,

Cm% = 100% - Vc%

Cm% = 100% - 45%

Cm% = 55%

Fc = 10,000 + 20,000 + 5,000

Fc = $ 35,000

Using Vc%:

Op = S - Vc% x S - Fc

Op = S - 45% x S - Fc

Op = 120,000 - 45% x 120,000 - 35,000

Op = 120,000 - 54,000 - 35,000

Op = 66,000 – 35,000

Op = $ 31,000

b) What is the store´s operating profit?

Operating profit, Op = Sales (S) – Total variable costs (TVc) - Fixed costs (Fc)

Op = 100,000 – 45,000 – 35,000

Op = $ 20,000

Alternatively, using the contribution margin Cm%:

Op = S x Cm% - Fc

Op = 100,000 x 55% - 35.000

Op = 55.000 - 35.000

Op = $ 20,000

c) If the store´s monthly sales were to increase to $ 120,000, what would be the *expected* profit?

Apply the formula Op = S x Cm% - Fc,

From point a) Cm% = 55%

Op = 120,000 x 55% - 35.000

Op = 66.000 - 35.000

Op = $ 31,000

d) What is the store´s breakeven point?

Breakeven is sales level at which all costs are absorbed but there is no profit,

Op = 0 …at the breakeven level.

0 = S x Cm% - Fc

Solving for S

Fc = S x Cm%

S = Fc/ Cm%

S = 35,000 / 0.55

S = $ 63.636 ...breakeven level of monthly sales required to absorb all variable and fixed costs without any profit.

5. The accounting ledger of a supermarket has the following data:

Monthly sales: $ 30,000

Beginning Inventory value: $ 40,000 (first day of the month)

Monthly purchases: $ 10,000

Ending Inventory value: $ 30,000 (last day of the month)

Rent: $ 2,000

Payroll: $ 3,000

a) What is the percentage contribution margin (Cm%)?

Compute Cost of Goods Sold (or TVc) sold for the month.

TVc = Beginning Inventory + Purchases – Ending Inventory

TVc = 40,000 + 10,000 – 30,000

TVc = 20,000

Total contribution margin: TCm = S – TVc

TCm = 30.000 – 20.000

TCm = 10.000

Cm% = TCm / S

Cm% = 10,000 / 30,000

Cm% = 33%

b) What is the store´s income for the month?

Data: S = 30,000 TVc = 20,000 Fc = 5,000

Op = Sales (S) – Total variable cost (TVc) – Fixed costs (Fc)

Op = 30,000 – 20,000 – 5,000

Op = $ 5,000 ...this is the month´s income.

c) If the store were to sell $ 40,000 instead of 30,000, what would be the *expected* profit?

Data: S = $ 30,000 TVc = $ 20,000 Cm% = 33% Fc = $ 5.000

It should be *assumed* that the percent variable cost (Vc%) is maintained constant at any level of sales (S), otherwise, by definition, it would not be a variable cost; this also applies to the Cm%, given that Cm% + Vc% = 100%. This assumption is an acceptable approximation when product mix and variable costs are stable; this is very likely in a well-established business; in fact, there is no other solution, or better approximation. Moreover, if the Vc% has a significant change, the change should still be investigated, as this is an important business control variable. (See Section "6.5 Variable Cost Percentage").

Op = S x Cm% – Fc

Op = 40,000 x 33% – 5,000

Op = 13.200 – 5.000

Op = $ 8.200 ....*expected* profit on sales of $ 40,000

d) The store´s owner is planning on refurbishing the store with a budget of $ 20,000. How much is required in sales to generate enough cash for paying the renovation?

The amount to be absorbed is the refurbishing cost for $ 20,000. This value is handled like a "fixed cost". It aims to absorb the $ 20,000 with no profit (Op = 0)

Fc = $ 20,000

Apply the formula Op = S x Cm% – Fc, then

Op = 0 = S x 33% – 20,000

Solve for S

S = 20,000 / 0.33

S = $ 60.606

This is the sales level needed to yield enough cash (profit) or sufficient contribution margin in order to pay for the renovation cost of $ 20,000.

Proof:

Op = 60.606 x 33% – 20,000

0 = 20.000 – 20.000

0 = 0

e) What is the store´s breakeven sales level?

The breakeven is that level of sales needed to be able to absorb the fixed costs without any profit.

Fixed costs Fc = $ 5,000

Cm% = 33%

At breakeven Op = 0

0 = S x Cm% – Fc

0 = S x 33% – 5,000

Solve for S

S = 5,000 / 0.33

S = $ 15.152 ...is the sales level needed to absorb the fixed cost of $ 5,000 without any profit.

f) If the store hires a salesperson for $ 2,000 / month, how much does he need to sell in order to pay for his salary?

Recall that Cm% = 33%

In this case, the sales level needed will be just sufficient to absorb the "fixed cost", which is the salesperson´s salary and with no profit (Op = 0).

Fc = $ 2,000

Op = S x Cm% – Fc

Again, if Op = 0 then

S = Fc / Cm%

S = 2,000 / 0.33

S = $ 6.061

This is the minimum sales the salesperson needs to make in order to “earn his keep”. Note that if Cm% were lower, the sales level required would be much higher. This method can be very handy when it comes to setting sales quotas, in order to determine their profits.

g) If the store hires the same salesperson for $ 2,000 / month, but with a commission of 5%, then how much would he need to sell just to pay for his own salary and commission?

Recall that Cm% = 33% without taking into account the commission cost.

The Cm% is the percentage that remains after absorbing the variable costs. The commission is a variable cost that must be added to the variable cost, or subtracted from the contribution margin; the end result is the same.

Subtracting from the contribution margin:

Cm% = 33% - 5%

Cm% = 28%

S = Fc / Cm%

S = 2.000 / 0.28

S = $ 7.143 ...sales required to absorb his salary plus commission.

h) If the store hires the same salesperson, under the same terms, but aiming for a profit target of $ 5,000 a month, how much does he need to achieve in sales?

Apply Op = S x Cm% - Fc with the previous values but with Op = 5,000

5,000 = S x 0.28 - 2,000

Solving for S

S = (5.000 + 2.000) / 0.28

S = $ 25.000 ....needed in sales to achieve the profit target.

i) The same as the previous example, but in this case the profit desired needs to be the firm´s target percentage operating profit on sales: 10% on sales.

Substitute for Op the target 10% x S

0.10 x S = S x 0.28 - 2,000

Rearranging terms,

2,000 = 0.28 S - 0.10 S

2,000 = S (0.28 - 0.10)

2,000 = 0.18 S

Solving for S

S = 2,000 / 0.18

S = $ 11.111 ... needed in sales to achieve the profit target of 10% sales.

Proof:

Op = 10% of $11.111 = 1.111

1.111 = $ 11.111 x 0.28 - 2.000

$ 1.111 = $ 3.111 - 2.000

$ 1.111 = $ 1.111 (proved)

j) The store´s manager decides to place a performance goal for the salesperson and he sets a sales quota of $ 20,000 per month. How much will this quota yield in profit for the store?

Apply Op = S x Cm% - Fc, therefore

Op = 20,000 x 0.28 – 2,000

Op = 5,600 – 2,000

Op = $ 3,600 .... in monthly profit provided by the salesperson if his sales quota is met.

6) A company has a product with the following price and cost structure:

Price (P): $ 10,000 per unit.

Variable cost (Vc): 4,000 (raw material).

Sales commission: 10% of sales, or 10% of the retail price (P); this is an additional variable cost.

If the Company wants to obtain a contribution margin (Cm%) of 60%, what should be the Sales Price?

Vc = $ 4,000 + commissions

Vc = $ 4,000 + 10% P

Recall: 100% = Vc% + Cm%

If Cm% = 60%, therefore

Vc% = 100% - 60% = 40%

Vc% = Vc / P, therefore

P = Vc / Vc%

P = (4,000 + 10% P) / 40%

Solving for P

40% P = 4,000 + 10% P

40% P – 10% P = 4,000

P (40% - 10%) = 4.000

P (30%) = 4.000

P = 4,000 / 30%

P = 4.000 / 0.3

P = $ 13.333

It is important to highlight the following (another method): The 60% is Cm% *net*, this means *after* the 10% commission has been deducted.

For Cm% to be 60% *after* the 10% commission has been deducted requires *adding* the 10% commission:

Cm% = (60% +10%) = 70%

100% = Cm% + Vc%

Vc% = 100% - 70%

Vc% = 30%

Vc% = Vc / P,

Therefore

P = Vc / Vc%

Since Vc = 4,000,

Therefore,

P = 4,000 / 30%

P = $ 13.333 (same as above)

7) A supermarket sells the following products (for simplicity), with the following data:

Product	P	Vc	Quantity
Poultry	10,00	7,00	1.000
Beef	12,00	8,00	1.300
Fish	15,00	11,00	1.200

The business has the following expenses:

Rent: $ 1,000 / month

Payroll: $ 5,000 / month

It is estimated that the direct selling expenses (transportation, stationery, etc.) are variable and amount to 10% of sales.

- How much are the average monthly sales, S?
- What is the unit variable cost, Vc?
- What is the variable cost percentage, Vc%?
- Contribution margin, Cm?
- Contribution margin percentage Cm%?
- Total variable cost, TVc?
- Total contribution margin, TCm?
- Monthly Fixed cost, Fc?
- Monthly operating income, Op?
- What is the product mix % in sales (% share of each product)?

Solution:

Product	**P**	**Vc**	**10%P**	**Vc+**	**Q**	**Sales**	**TVc**	**TCm**
Poultry	10,00	7,00	1,00	8,00	1.000	10.000	8.000	2.000
Beef	12,00	8,00	1,20	9,20	1.300	15.600	11.960	3.640
Fish	15,00	11,00	1,50	12,50	1.200	18.000	15.000	3.000
Total	**12,46**			**9.99**	**3,500**	**43.600**	**34.960**	**8.640**
							80,18%	19,82%
Fixed Costs:								
Rent								1.000
Payroll								5.000
Total								**6.000**
Operating Income								**2.640**

- If sales increase to \$ 50,000, how much would be the expected operating income, as long as there is no change in fixed costs and product mix remains the same?

S = \$ 50,000 Cm = 19.82% Fc = 6.000

Op = 50.000 x 19.82% - 6.000

Op = 9,910 – 6,000

Op = \$ 3.910 ....is the expected profit when S = \$ 50,000

- If a salesperson is hired with a salary of \$ 1,500 and a commission of 5%, how much should be the minimum sales that he must achieve in order to pay for his salary plus commission?

Cm% = 19.82% Fc= \$ 1,500

If the salesperson is paid 5% of his sales, then the adjusted contribution margin is:

Cm% = 19.82% - 5%

Cm% = 14.82%

Given that no profit is expected, then Op = 0

Op = S x Cm% - Fc

S = Fc / Cm%

S = 1,500 / 14.82%

S = $ 10,121 ...minimum sales to be achieved.

- What is the supermarket´s breakeven point?

Fc = 6,000   Cm% = 19.82% (no discount assumed)

S = Fc / Cm%

S = 6,000 / 19.82%

S= $ 30,272

This is the sales level that only absorbs fixed costs and leaves no profit.

Bibliography

Thomas Corbett, "*Throughput Accounting*", The North River Press, 1998

Eliyahu M. Goldratt, J. Cox, "*The Goal: A Process of Ongoing Improvement*", North River Press, 1992

Eliyahu M. Goldratt "*The Haystack Syndrome*", The North River Press, 1990

Edward Chamberlin, "*The Theory of Monopolistic Competition*".

K. Douglas Hoffman, John E.G. Bateson, "*Essentials of Services Marketing*", Harcourt College Publishers, 2nd, 2002.

M.W. Johnston, G. Marshall, "*Relationship Selling*", McGraw-Hill/Irwin, 2005

N. Braidot, *Neuro Marketing*, Ediciones Gestión 2000, 2009

Martin Lindstrom, *Buyology*, Doubleday, 2008

C. Morin, *Neuromarketing*, Thomas Nelson, 2007

Inés Kuster, Sergio Román, "*Venta Personal y Dirección de Ventas*", Thomson, 2006

Donald R. Lehmann, R.S. Winer, "*Product Management*", McGraw-Hill, 2007

Thomas Nagle, Reed K. Holden, "*The Strategy and Tactics of Pricing*", Pearson, Prentice Hall, 2002

Carlos R. Sánchez S, "Administración del Precio en Mercadotecnia", Thomson, 2003

Rosann L. Spiro, W.J. Stanton, G.A. Rich "*Management of Sales Force*", McGraw-Hill

Irwin, 2003

W.J. Stanton, M.J. Etzel, B.J. Walker, "*Marketing 13th edition*", McGraw-Hill, 2004

"*El Mundo del Envase*", Editorial Gustavo Gili, S.A., Barcelona, 1995

Index

I

J

L

M

N

O

P

Q

R

S

T

U

V

www.ingramcontent.com/pod-product-compliance
Lightning Source LLC
LaVergne TN
LVHW010722210926
848485LV00007B/1415/J

* 9 7 8 1 6 2 2 7 3 0 2 0 9 *